Brexit Gr...
Halevor, C.

REBELLION

IN GALWAY

EASTER RISING 1916

KEVIN JORDAN

Published by Kevin Jordan

Copyright © Kevin Jordan 2016.

First published in 2016.

No part of this book may be reproduced in any form without the permission of the copyright owner.

ISBN: 978-1-5262-0085-3

While every effort has been made to ensure that the details in this book are accurate the author and printers accept no liability for errors.

Printed by Turner's Printing Company, Earl Street, Longford, Co, Longford, Ireland.

Rebellion in Galway

*In memory of those involved in the activities of 1916, on
all sides;
history has a lot of lessons we can learn, if only we would
listen.*

*I gcuimhne na ndaoine go léir a ghlac páirt in eachtraí
1916, ar gach taobh;*

*Is imoaí rud a fhoghlaimímid ó stair, ach caithfimid
éisteacht léi.*

Contents.

Rebellion in Galway

Introduction.

As far back as I can remember I was interested in History. I first recall hearing about the 1916 Rising in 1966, the 50th anniversary. Apart from the excitement generated locally and nationally in celebrating what was seen as the start of our drive for independence there was the additional matter of Stephen Jordan. He was my paternal grandfather and a leading figure in the Galway 1916 Rising. To me, without knowing the details, it was important that there was action in Galway, where I was from. It wasn't until years later I realised that few outside of the county ever heard of it as for them it was a Dublin based event only.

Stephen was a Fianna Fail T.D. for ten years, a local councillor, a noted All Ireland referee, an inter-county footballer (holding three Connaught titles), owner of a public house and secretary of the Athenry Agricultural Show. However, to me, as a young child, he fought the British and survived. I am reputed to have commented 'he must have found a great hiding place.' Though, I doubt if he was too taken by that. To me this was real action, Cu Chulainn, Battle of Clontarf, Hugh O'Neill and 1798 stuff and it was part of our family history. He was a man I knew as Granddad and met every week.

I can still visualise the army and F.C.A. military parade on the 50th anniversary of Easter Sunday. The parade was to the mass in the old Sack Factory, in Athenry as the new church was being built. My father Willie was a Lieutenant in the F.C.A. (Reserve Army Force) and as an eight year old I was so excited by the whole day. At the time R.T.E. ran a mini series called 'Insurrection' which ran nightly for eight nights and we watched it each night as a family.

In later life when studying History I came to realise that things were really not all that simple. There were always two and in most historical cases many more sides. Indeed, there are those who were on no side at all and just caught up in events.

Rebellion in Galway

In the lead up to 1916 Galway was a very troubled county. There were the landlords trying to hold on to their estates that were in the family for generations. There were the tenants who were hoping for land division from these estates and were willing to go into some form of land purchase scheme if they could get the landlords to sell. There were a number of organisations like the Fenians (I.R.B.), the Town Tenants' League and the United Irish League vying for the right to be the most legitimate organisation to represent the tenants in their struggle for land reform. On the other hand there was the R.I.C. trying to keep law and order in all disputes between tenants and these organisations. Murders, other violent incidents and boycotting resulted with the R.I.C. generally caught in the middle. This was complicated by the fact that most of them were Irishmen and sons of farmers from neighbouring counties.

In the early 1900's things got more complicated as there was a resurgence of nationalism due to the arrival on the scene of the G.A.A., the Gaelic League and the Literary Revival movement. These refocused people's attention on nationalism and a desire for independence. There was the great work of the Irish Parliamentary Party in the British parliament which finally seemed to have got the British government to deliver on Home Rule for Ireland in 1914. However, the advent of World War 1 meant this was now postponed until after the war. Disappointed nationalists, like the I.R.B., felt this was yet another excuse not to grant it. The Irish Volunteers, an armed force had been set up to help ensure that the promised Home Rule would be delivered, while the Ulster Volunteer Force was set up in the north to help ensure it would not become law. Events were at boiling point and maybe the outbreak of World War 1 spared us from a Civil War between north and south over Home Rule.

Then the ever popular Irish split occurred as the Irish Volunteers divided between those who felt it was best to support Britain in the war and hopefully get Home Rule as a reward and those who would under no circumstances fight for Britain. The I.R.B now saw their chance to work towards a rebellion on the theory,

'That England's difficulty was Ireland's opportunity.'

They infiltrated the Irish Volunteers who did not support joining the British army and worked towards using this readymade army as their troops for a rebellion.

In Galway they had a ready audience. A huge number of young men and women who felt aggrieved due to land and other issues flocked to join the Irish Volunteers and Cumann na mBan (the Volunteer's sister organisation). The number of men training and drilling within the county grew steadily. The authorities became increasingly alarmed but they hoped that as World War 1 continued these would willingly join the British army in Flanders or be conscripted, should it be introduced.

However, many men living in rural areas refused to join the war effort and joined the Irish Volunteers instead. The vast majority of these were committed nationalists and republicans who were long since waiting for an opportunity to fight for Irish independence. They were not duped by the I.R.B. element within the Volunteers who had them thinking the action on Easter Sunday 1916 was just a routine route march. They clearly knew by Monday afternoon in Galway that this was a rebellion and if you mobilised you were likely going to see action against the authorities, the R.I.C and the British army.

Since the early 1900's the active nationalist organisations and figures such as Tom Kenny, Larry Lardner and Stephen Jordan had helped to build a strong sense of active republicanism in Galway. This started as an overwhelming desire for land redistribution but grew into a hope for independence. This was recognised by the inner circles of the I.R.B. in Dublin who were planning for a rebellion. They sent Liam Mellows to Galway to tap into this rebel spirit in the hopes that the county would rise in tandem with any revolt in other areas. Despite some local tensions in relation to Mellows's role he was extremely successful in motivating local men and women to fight for Irish independence.

This is the story of all these sections in Galway at that time and their efforts to do what they felt was right. The rebellion lasted a week in April 1916 and saw the British send warships to Galway Bay in an effort to quell it.

So with the Galway businessmen, the R.I.C., the I.R.B., Cumann na mBan, the Irish Volunteers, the National Volunteers, the Ulster Volunteer Force, the Irish Parliamentary Party, the Home Rulers, the M.P.'s, the British army (with both British and Irish men in it), the army wives, the United Irish League, the tenants, the landlords, the Town Tenants' League, the G.A.A, the Gaelic League, the Literary Revivalists and the clergy for and against the rising, how many sides was that?

That is what makes history so intriguing.

Towns and villages in County Galway

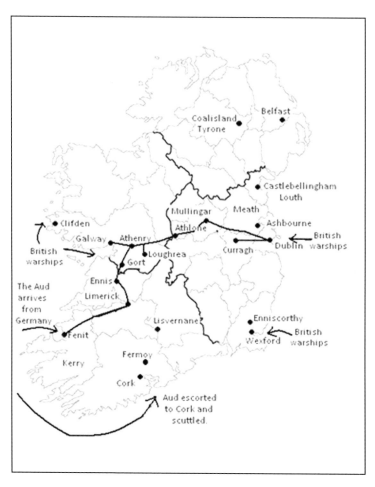

A map of Ireland showing the main areas where there was activity during the 1916 Rising. Also, the rail network on which guns from the Aud were to be delivered to the West and on which British troops were moved to Dublin from the Curragh and to the West towards Loughrea. Also shown are warships in place around the coast.

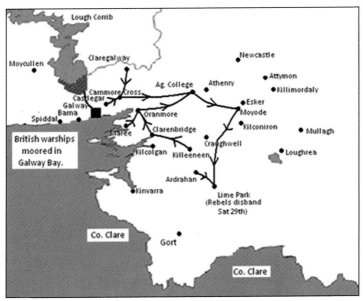

The Irish rebel movements during Easter week 1916 are shown above starting in Killeeneen, Clarenbridge, Maree, Oranmore, Castlegar, Claregalway, Ardrahan and Athenry on Monday/Tuesday April 24th/25th and ending in Lime Park House on Saturday 29th at 3 a.m. when they disbanded and returned home or went on the run.

Rail Network in County Galway

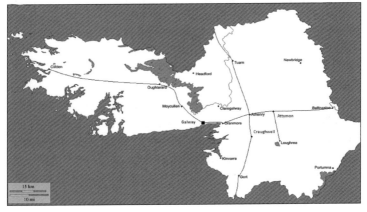

10

Terms and Abbreviations used in the book.

Boycotting.
This was where neighbours would have nothing to do with a person against whom they had any objection.

British Army.
This was the official army force in the country. Many Irishmen joined as a career particularly following the outbreak of World War I. In Galway the Connaught Rangers were the main regiment.

Clann na nGael
This was an American organisation that grew out of the Fenians after 1867 following the failed I.R.B. Rising in Ireland of that year. It drew huge support from the large Irish emigrant community in New York and Boston after the Famine.

Defence of the Realm Act 1914
This was passed by the British Parliament on August 8th 1914 a few days after World War 1 was declared. Under it a range of things were forbidden such as discussing military activities in public, feeding wild animals and birds, buying binoculars, etc. The act gave special powers to the government so as to control the war effort. One of the things forbidden in Ireland under the act was promoting anti-recruiting activities.

The Fenians.
This was a secret society set up in 1858 in America by John O'Mahony to fight for Irish independence. They believed in the use of physical force as the most suitable way to achieve it. It was a companion force of the I.R.B. in Ireland.

Rebellion in Galway

Home Rule
This was an idea started by Isaac Butt in the 1870's hoping to set up a parliament in Ireland to control Irish affairs but it would still be subservient to the British Parliament.

Irish Volunteers.
This was an organisation set up in 1913 to have armed support to help the movement for Home Rule in Ireland. It was a reaction to the Ulster Volunteers set up in Northern Ireland in 1912 to oppose Home Rule by armed rebellion if necessary. In September 1914 it split into the National Volunteers and the Irish Volunteers.

Irish Republican Army (I.R.A.)
During the War of Independence 1919-1921 the I.R.B. became known as the I.R.A.

Irish Republican Brotherhood (I.R.B.)
The I.R.B. was founded in Ireland in 1858 by James Stephens to fight for Irish independence (Also known as the Fenians).

Irish Parliamentary Party (I.P.P.)
This referred to the Irish M.P.'s who organised into a party controlled by Charles Stewart Parnell after 1881 for the purpose of winning Home Rule for Ireland. It was also referred to as the Home Rule Party.

Land-grabbers.
These were farmers who took over a farm from which a previous tenant was evicted. Generally they were hated locally and often they were subjected to 'boycotting'.

The Gaelic Athletic Association (G.A.A.)
The Gaelic Athletic Association was founded in Thurles in 1884 by Michael Cusack. Its aim was to organise hurling and

football as Ireland's national games. Cusack wished to see the standardisation of rules and the formulation of competitions to popularise these pastimes. Originally Cusack approached the Bishop of Clonfert Patrick Duggan with the idea of holding the inaugural meeting in Loughrea. This shows the strength of these pastimes in the Galway area particularly east Galway at this time.

The Land League.

This was an organisation founded in 1879 by Michael Davitt to look for greater rights for tenant farmers. Charles Stewart Parnell was its President.

The Land War.

This referred to the period between 1879 and 1881 when there was an outbreak of violence associated with the struggle for tenants' rights. Davitt and Parnell distance themselves from this which was mainly orchestrated by the Fenian/I.R.B. elements in the country. However, the violence did focus minds in Westminster to come up with plans to solve the land problems in Ireland.

Member of Parliament (M.P.)

A member of the British Parliament. Ireland generally had about 105 seats in the British Parliament since the Act of Union in 1801.

Proscription

This was when there were special laws in an area to give the police the right to arrest people they thought were a danger to law and order. In the early 1900's Galway was a proscribed county. As a result there was a curfew in place and people had to be in their houses by a certain time at night.

> 'Then they said there was a curfew and I would have to go to the station.'[1]

1   O'Regan's Athenry – Athenry History Archive Margaret Browne – Courier Holy Week 1916

Rebellion in Galway

Royal Irish Constabulary (R.I.C.)
Royal Irish Constabulary was an armed police force set up in 1836 by Thomas Drummond. The title 'Royal' was given in 1867 following their successful suppression of the Fenian Rising.

Teachta Dála (T.D.)
A Teachta Dála was a member of the Irish Parliament or Dáil Eireann from the time it was set up by Sinn Fein in 1919.

Town Tenants' League (TTL)
This was set up in the Athenry area to get land for townspeople when landed estates were being sold and divided up in the early 1900's. They engaged in agitation to press their case like cattle driving and wall knocking. Members of the I.R.B. were involved.

United Irish League (U.I.L)
The United Irish League This was an organisation founded by William O'Brien M.P. in 1898 hoping to get rights for tenants. It was set up after the Land League was defunct as there was a very serious situation re tenant farmers in Ireland at the time. By 1901 it had 100,000 members most in the west of Ireland.

Ulster Volunteers Force(U.V.F.)
This was a force set up in Ulster in January 1913 with the aim of preventing Home Rule from being passed. The two most important leaders were Edward Carson and William Craig. There were up to 100,000 members and they drilled openly. They secured arms and ammunition through the Larne gun-running when 25,000 guns and 5 million rounds of ammunition were imported from Germany. Many members fought in World War 1 on the side of the British army hoping their efforts would be rewarded by Home Rule being suspended.

Timeline.

Significant dates in recent Irish history.

(Ones relating specifically to Co. Galway are in bold type).

1798	United Irishmen Rebellion, 1,000's of Irish were killed and deported in a bitter revolt.
1801	The Act of Union came into effect joining the Irish and British parliaments.
1803	Robert Emmet's Rebellion in Dublin was a catastrophic failure.
1824	Free trade between Britain and Ireland allowed British goods tax free into Ireland and seriously affected local Irish industries.
1828	Daniel O'Connell was elected M.P. for Co Clare.
1829	Catholic Emancipation Act allowed Catholics to sit in parliament.
1831	National School's Act saw the start of universal primary school education for all children in Ireland.
1831 – 1836	The Tithe War, Catholics embarked on a period of protest and periodic violence against paying tithes, money to the Anglican clergy (the established or official church).
1834	The first railway was opened in Ireland from Dublin to Dun Laoghaire.
1837	**The foundation of the Tuam Herald newspaper by Richard Kelly to serve County Galway.**
1838	The Poor Law Act saw a system of workhouses set up to provide relief for the poor.
1839	The G.P.O. was opened to the public in Dublin.
1839	The Night of the Big Wind caused huge damage across Ireland.
1843	Daniel O'Connell's monster meeting at Clontarf was banned and the Repeal of the Act of Union movement failed.
1845 - 1848	The potato Famine saw one million die and one million emigrate

Rebellion in Galway

1848	The Young Irelanders' Rebellion, mainly in Tipperary, was easily defeated.
1848	The tricolour was adopted as the Irish flag. It was first flown in Waterford on March 7th by the Young Irelander Thomas Francis Meagher.
1851	The railway-line from Dublin to Galway was completed.
1858	Foundation of the Irish Republican Brotherhood (The Fenians) by James Stephens.
1858	The Irish Times became a daily newspaper.
1864	**Birth of Mary Kate Walsh N.T. Killeeneen N.S. in whose house Liam Mellows spent a lot of time.**
1866	Paul Cullen was appointed Ireland's first cardinal.
1867	The Fenian Rebellion saw revolts in Dublin, Cork, Limerick and Tipperary easily defeated.
1869	The Irish Church Act. This disestablished the Anglican Church as the official church and thus Catholics no longer had to pay tithes to the Anglican clergy.
1869	**The attempted shooting of landlord Captain Thomas Eyre Lambert of Castle Lambert.**
1870	The Home Government Association was founded by Isaac Butt to look for Home Rule for Ireland.
1870	Gladstone's First Land Act had little effect on the tenant landlord relationship but it was a marker that the Liberal government intended to support tenants.
1872	The Secret Ballot Act freed tenants from interference from landlords when voting.
1874	Isaac Butt's Home Rule motion in the House of Commons was defeated.
1875	Charles Stewart Parnell was elected to the British Parliament as M.P. for Meath.
1878	**Birth of Tom Kenny in Ardrahan.**
1879	**Birth of Padraig Fahy in Gort.**
1879	The Land League was founded in Mayo by Michael

Davitt to help tenant farmers.

1879 – 1882 The Land War in Ireland. There were eight murders in Galway associated with the disturbances at this time.

1880   Parnell was elected leader of the Home Rule Party.

1881   Gladstone's Second Land Act effectively gave the 3F's (Fair Rent, Fixity of Tenure and Free Sale) to Irish tenants.

1881   Birth of Fr. John William O'Meehan in Clarenbridge.

1882   Gladstone's Land Amendment Act meant 1,000's more tenants were included in the 1881 Act.

1882   The Home Rule Party changed its name to the Irish Parliamentary Party with Home Rule rather than land reform as its main aim.

1882   Birth of Constable Patrick Whelan in Kilkenny. He was shot in the 1916 rebellion in Galway.

1883   Birth of Larry Lardner in Athenry.

1884   The G.A.A. was founded in Thurles in Tipperary.

1886   The Unionist Party was founded in Belfast by Edward Saunderson.

1886   The First Home Rule Act failed to pass in the House of Commons.

1886   Anti Home Rule riots in Belfast lasted for three months.

1887   Birth of Stephen Jordan in Athenry.

1888   Birth of Fr. Tom Fahy in Esker, Kiltullagh.

1888   The first All–Ireland hurling final. Meelick (Galway) lost to Thurles (Tipperary).

1885   Ashbourne Land Purchase Act made £5 million available for tenant land purchase. Under it 25,000 tenants purchased their holdings.

1889   Birth of Bridget Walsh in Killeeneen Craughwell, later Bridget Malone.

1889   Birth of Fr. Henry Feeney in Castlegar.

1889   **Birth of Alf Monahan in Belfast.**

1890   The Irish Parliamentary Party split, 28 pro-Parnell and 45 anti-Parnell led by Justin Mc Carthy.

1891   Balfour Land Purchase Act advanced £33 million from the British government for land purchase. 47,000 tenants purchased their farms under the scheme.

1891   Under the Wyndham Land Purchase Act the Congested Districts Act was set up. This identified counties along the west coast which were congested with large numbers of people living in poverty and money was made available for schemes to provide relief for these people. Galway was one of these counties.

1891   Death of Charles Stewart Parnell in Brighton in October. He was buried in Glasnevin.

1892   **Birth of Liam Mellows in Ashton-Under-Lime, England.**

1892   **Birth of Julia Morrissey, who founded Cumman na mBan in Athenry.**

1893   The Second Home Rule Act was passed in the House of Commons but was defeated in the House of Lords

1893   The foundation of the Gaelic League by Eoin McNeill and Doughlas Hyde to encourage the revival of the Irish language and culture.

1898   The United Irish League founded by William O'Brien to agitate for major land reform as the Irish Parliamentary Party seemed more interested in Home Rule.

1898   **Birth of Bridget Ruane (nee Morrissey) Galway Cumann na mBan.**

1898   **Birth of May Higgins Galway Cumann na mBan.**

1898   The Local Government (Ireland) Act gave limited local powers based on counties. It lessened the power and influence of landlords through the abolition of the Grand Jury system.

1900   John Redmond united the Irish Parliamentary

Party which had split in 1890 over Parnell's leadership.

1903   Wyndham Land Purchase Act, £100 million was made available by the British government for land purchase by tenant farmers. 270,396 farms were purchased under the scheme.

1904   The Abbey Theatre opened.

1905   The first edition of the Irish Independent.

1905   Sinn Féin was founded by Arthur Griffith.

1908   The Irish Transport and General Workers Union was founded by James Larkin.

1909   The Old Age Pension was first paid on January 1st to people over 70 years.

1909   Bulmer Hobson and Countess Markiveicz started Na Fianna Eireann, a boy scouts movement promoting the Irish language and an interest in independence. Many members later join the I.R.B.

1909   **Constable Martin Mc Goldrick was shot in Craughwell.**

1909   **The foundation of the Connaught Tribune newspaper serving Galway City and county.**

1912   The Labour Party was founded in Clonmel by James Connolly and James Larkin.

1911   The Parliament Act limited the powers of the House of Lords thus clearing the way for the passing of Home Rule for Ireland.

1912   The Third Home Rule Bill was passed in the British House of Commons but was rejected in the Lords. However, due to the Parliament Act 1911 it must become law within two years.

1912   The Ulster Volunteers were founded declaring they would fight Home Rule being granted to Ireland.

1913   The foundation of the Irish Volunteers in Dublin to ensure the passage of Home Rule.

1913   **The Irish Volunteers were established in Galway City at a meeting in December.**

Rebellion in Galway

1913 – 1914   The Dublin Lockout when 29,000 workers led by James Larkin and James Connolly were in dispute with up to 300 employers led by William Martin Murphy.

1913   Irish Citizen Army was founded by James Connolly to protect workers.

1914   Cumman na mBan was founded to help support the Irish Volunteers.

1914   57 British army officers, in the Curragh, threatened to resign if they were sent to disarm the Ulster Volunteer Force.

1914   The Larne gunrunning when the Ulster Volunteers landed 24,600 guns and 5 million rounds of ammunition.

1914   John Redmond took control of the Irish Volunteers.

1914   The Howth gun running, when 900 rifles and 29,000 rounds of ammunition were landed by the Irish Volunteers.

1914   Outbreak of World War 1 in August.

1914   Home Rule was passed by the British Parliament but deferred until World War 1 was over.

1914   John Redmond's speech at Woodenbridge saw a split in the Irish Volunteers. Some 170,000 now called the National Volunteers backed Redmond in joining the British war effort while some 11,000 led by Eoin McNeill decided not to join the war effort. They retained the name the Irish Volunteers and retained most of the arms brought ashore at Howth in 1914.

1914   An intensive recruitment campaign to the British army throughout Ireland as about 10% of men of military age join (206,000). Conscription was not extended to Ireland though emigration from Ireland was banned.

1915   The I.R.B. reorganised their Supreme Council with men in favour of a rebellion put in place. These hoped to use the Irish Volunteers, loyal to Eoin McNeill, as troops for a rebellion. As many of the Volunteers were also in the I.R.B. they felt this would easily work. They set up the Military Council, a secret committee within a secret organisation, for this purpose.

1915   Pádraig Pearse gave the oration at the funeral of Jeremiah O'Donovan Rossa in Glasnevin.

1916   The Supreme Council of the I.R.B. brought James Connolly into their confidence about the secret plans for an Easter rebellion as he was already planning one with the Citizen Army.

1916   **Easter Rising Monday April 24th – Saturday April 29th. Rebellion took place mainly in Dublin with engagements also in Cork, Galway, Louth, Meath, and Wexford.**

1916   Execution of the leaders of the Rising May 3rd to May 12th.

1916   The executions and whole-scale arrests saw the sympathies of the majority of the people turn in favour of the rebels and this expressed itself in support for the Sinn Fein party.

1916   By December most of those interned were released and immediately rallied to Sinn Féin.

1917   Sinn Féin won by-elections in North Roscommon, South Longford and East Clare.

1918   World War 1 ended on November 11th.

1918   The British general election on December 14th returned 73 Sinn Féin M.P.'s for Ireland out of 105 seats. The Unionists won 26 seats and the Home Rule Party 6.

1919 – 1921   The War of Independence between Ireland and Britain.

1921   Talks between Ireland and Britain led to the signing of the Anglo Irish Treaty on December 6th. This set up the Irish Free State comprising of 26 counties while 6 counties in Ulster remained with Britain.

Reasons for the 1916 Rebellion in Galway

1. Land issues were central to the disquiet within the county by the early 1900's.

2. The extreme poverty of County Galway.

3. There were many successful nationalist organisations within the county promoting everything from culture to revolution.

4. The advent of World War 1 had the effect of militarising the county as a whole.

5. When the Irish Volunteers split in 1914 the majority in Galway remained with the Irish Volunteers as opposed to the National Volunteers.

6. Liam Mellows was sent to the county in January 1915 as a local organiser for the Irish Volunteers.

7. The tension between republicans and police due to the large numbers of R.I.C. stationed in Galway.

Outside of the main rebellion in Dublin there was relatively little activity throughout the country except for some minor activities in Cork, Louth and Tyrone, while Wexford saw action later in the week for three or four days. There was the serious engagement with the R.I.C. in Ashbourne and aside from these the only other area of rebellion was in Co. Galway. Why was there such activity in the Galway area when so little action occurred elsewhere? When examining this it becomes obvious that there were a number of local as well as national issues which led to Galway being an area of intense military and republican activity at this time.

The national issues like the failure to deliver Home Rule, the formation of the Irish Volunteers, the upsurge of interest in nationalism and republicanism, the rise in the number of cultural and political organisations and the importation of arms are well known but the issues pertaining particularly to Galway need some additional discussion and elaboration. While there are many and varied reasons for Galway being more disposed towards rebellion than other counties the above reasons can be seen as the most significant.

While all the these reasons were prevalent in other areas and counties to varying degrees they all came together at the one time in Galway and this accentuated the situation within the county leading to the rebellion.

1. Land issues were central to the disquiet within the county by the early 1900's.

In the early 1900's there was considerable disquiet in County Galway in relation to land issues. Though there had been a number of government sponsored acts to help tenants purchase their farms from their landlords it did not always happen in Galway. In 1870 and 1881 Liberal British Prime Minister William Gladstone had passed Land Acts which favoured tenants and set them on the road towards land purchase. This was followed by the Conservative government who introduced actual land purchase acts. These were the Ashbourne Land Act 1885, the Balfour Land Act 1891 and the Wyndham Land Act 1903. These loaned money to tenants to buy their farms from their landlord. However, if the landlord refused to sell there was little the tenant could do to force them and so tension was high. In addition landlords found that stocking their estate with large numbers of cattle made a lot more money selling to the buoyant British market then coping with the difficulties of having large numbers of tenant farmers. These grazing farms were the envy of many local farmers who felt that if the landlords were removed the land could be divided among locals and support many families.

During the 1880's when Parnell and Davitt were campaigning

for tenants' rights some of the more extreme elements in the country fought what was known as the Land War. This occurred from 1879 to 1882 and saw violence throughout the country in an effort to bring pressure on the British authorities to solve all land issues. The Land War was particularly violent in Galway and there were a number of high profile murders in the county. There were also land related murders and attempted murders in the early 1900's all of which served to heighten tension between the rural community and the authorities. The R.I.C. were central to attempting to maintain law and order in the county and as such there was often serious division in the community. These murders and attempted murders are outlined in the chapter on Serious Agrarian Outrages in Galway 1881 – 1910. The effect was that murder was seen by some as a means of attempting to solve problems like getting rid of troublesome or unpopular landlords and or their agents.

Resulting from this agitation Galway had by far the highest number of unlet grazing farms in the country between 1905 and 1910. Obviously some landlords found it difficult to let farms for grazing and tenants were slow to rent or in many cases gave up leases rather than face intimidation and boycotting. In 1905 of 96 unlet grazing farms nationwide 45 were in east Galway and 4 in west. The next highest county was Tipperary with a total of 14. In 1906 Galway had a total of 36 in east and 4 in west of 67 in the country. In 1908 of 284 unlet farms nationwide 114 were in Galway.[2] This shows the depth of feeling in relation to the idea of land redistribution within the county in the lead up to 1916. Grazing farms took up much of the acreage in Galway and figures from 1907 give a picture of the situation. Galway had 145,055 acres devoted to grazing farms and 320,464 acres of untenanted land.[3]

2   Fergus Campbell, 'Land and Revolution Nationalist Politics in the West of Ireland 1891 – 1921.' Oxford p101.

3   Fergus Campbell, 'Land and Revolution Nationalist Politics in the West of Ireland 1891 – 1921.' Oxford p15

Reasons for the 1916 Rebellion in Galway

There were many notorious landlords within the county who had very large estates and often treated their tenants poorly. Of these, Lord Clanricarde had the worst reputation. Hubert de Burgh (Burke) 1832 – 1916 the second Marquis of Clanricarde was an absentee landlord living in London. His estate of 52,000 acres in south east Galway yielded £20,000 a year from some 2,000 holdings. The population of the estate had declined from 22,000 to under 10,000 in post famine times as deaths and evictions saw farms cleared for cattle grazing. He insisted on the full payment of high rents despite hard times and his reputation was such that he was even an embarrassment to the British government. His land agent John Blake and his servant Thady Ruane were murdered in 1882 but not even that changed his attitude. The Congested Districts Board tried to get him to sell to his tenants but to no avail. Unmarried, he died in 1916 and the estate was then sold to tenants.[4] It was cases like this that set the scene for extreme tension in Galway. This and nationalist ideals among many sections of the community ensured that thoughts of rebellion were never far from the minds of many young men and women.

The importance of the land issue can be clearly seen from the number of United Irish League members within the county. In 1901 there were 79 branches with 9,733 members. This had risen from 13 branches in 1898 with 1,065 members and 64 branches in 1899 with 8,112 members.[5]

2.   **The extreme poverty of the county.**

By 1911 Galway was one of the poorest counties in Ireland. It was one of the counties in Congested Districts Board area. As such there were various schemes afoot to try to improve

---

4   www.advertiser.ie/galway/article/25789/woodford-stood-up-to-the- power-of-lord-clanricarde

5   Fergus Campbell, *'Land and Revolution Nationalist Politics in the West of Ireland 1891 – 1921.'* Oxford p30

the lot of the people. There included agricultural and fishery incentives as well as road building and land redistribution. Yet there were over 3,000 people on Poorhouse relief either residential or outdoor. Child mortality was high with three and four children dying in many families. Birth rates and marriages were considerably below the national average.[6]   Farms were small and incomes were low. Details can be seen in the chapter The Economy and Society in Galway 1901 - 1911. Many in the county were of the opinion that an Irish government running an independent country would be better placed to improve the economy of the country and the standard of living of the people. Most of the rebels in Galway were young and from a farming background and felt that land was the key to solving the problems and poverty levels. From a sample of 211 of the 1916 rebels in Galway 60% were farmers or farmers' sons while a further 31% were labourers or artisans. [7]

While most of those involved in subversive movements were farmers' sons and tradesmen there was a wide variety of professions involved. Many commentators believed that they were uneducated but that would be just in relation to achieving an education other than primary school. However, it must be remembered that there was universal primary education since 1831 and these would be among a third generation since then. All would have been to primary school with most in those days staying on until the age of 14 or 15.

It was only the very rich that could afford to send their children to second level school. Second level schools were not available in most towns in the west of Ireland until the beginning of the twentieth century. It was only in the1920's that the Presentation nuns set one up in Athenry. For most the only

---

6   http://www.census.nationalarchives.ie/exhibition/galway/main.html

7   Fergus Campbell, 'Land and Revolution Nationalist Politics in the West of Ireland 1891 – 1921.' Oxford
     p186

way to get a second level education was to gain a scholarship through an exam or to join a religious order and be educated as a brother, priest or nun. Thus, it would be disingenuous to state that the greater number of these were uneducated just because they did not attend second level school.

It would have been neigh impossible to organise local and national movements such as the Land League, the United Irish League, the G.A.A., Cumman na mBan, the Irish Volunteers or the I.R.B. without a raft of super intelligent people. These movements also attracted a number of local priests to their ranks who had the organisational skills needed to aid the movements. It can be seen from the amount of those associated with the 1916 Rising who went on to hold high office following the foundation of the state in 1922 that the standard of intelligence among them was very high. Liam Mellows, George Nicholls, Frank Fahy, Seán Broderick, Eamonn Corbett, Pádraig O Máille, Martin Neilan and Stephen Jordan all went on to be T.D.'s. while many more were local County Councillors. Larry Lardiner, Stephen Jordan, Tom Kenny and many more were top class G.A.A. officials and the list goes on.

3. **There were many successful nationalist organisations within the county promoting everything from culture to revolution.**

The G.A.A. the Gaelic League, the United Irish League, the Towns Tenants' League, the Gaelic Revival, the National Volunteers, the Irish Volunteers and the I.R.B. were among the successful organisations in the county in the lead up to the 1916 Rising. Each had a part to play in reviving a combination of nationalist and republican ideals among the people at the time.

During the era of the Penal Laws in the 1600 and 1700's there were a whole series of laws against Catholics. During this time it was the intention of successive British governments to make the Irish people as British as possible in every way from culture to religion, education to pastimes. However, with Catholic Emancipation in 1829 and the introduction of free primary education in 1831 Catholics began to become more Irish again. This reached new heights in the late 1880's with organisations like the G.A.A. Also, by this stage a third generation of literate Irish were more confident in their nationality and expressive of their culture. As a result organisations reflecting Irish interests and ideals flourished. What started as sporting, linguistic and literary independence was soon translated to political independence. There were very few parishes in Galway that did not have a G.A.A. club and most had a Gaelic League organisation where it was possible to learn the Irish language at evening classes. Padraig Fahy from Gort, a member of the I.R.B. and the Irish Volunteers, was a travelling Irish teacher working for the Gaelic League teaching Irish at evening classes around the county. Generally speaking many men within the county were members of the G.A.A., the I.R.B. and the Irish Volunteers. Thus, it was possible to amalgamate the work of all three organisations more effectively as you constantly met the same people. As the G.A.A. and the Irish Volunteers were legal they provided a perfect cover for I.R.B. activities throughout the county. Men such as Larry Lardner, Stephen Jordan and Tom Kenny were able to go around Galway and up to Dublin in their capacity as top G.A.A. officials. Whilst on these journeys they held meetings with others to arrange I.R.B. business. They were constantly able to meet with Pearse, Mac Diarmada, Clarke and others.

The G.A.A. was hugely successful at the time and both hurling and football were popular games within the county. Hurling was particularly strong in the mid and south of the county with football more confined to the north and west, very much as it is today. Peterswell, Gort, Ardrahan, Mullagh, Derrydonnell, Craughwell and Kilconiron had all won county hurling titles by 1913 and all of these were active in the Rising. The local G.A.A. club was often a recruiting ground for young men to join the I.R.B. or least the Irish Volunteers. There was less interest in joining the British army in rural areas and recruiting was much more successful in Galway City and towns such as Loughrea and Tuam. Thus, the activities of the G.A.A., Gaelic League and the Irish Volunteers were intermingled in the county.

Other organisations such as the Town Tenants' League in Athenry saw anti-authoritarian agitation grow in the early 1900's. As local farmers looked for the division of estates so as to gain access to more land the townspeople of Athenry also sought their share of any land being divided out. Wall knocking, driving off cattle and intimidation of landlords and agents formed the backbone of their activities. Such actions showed their determination to stand up to authority and they paid little regard for the R.I.C. who were charged with keeping the peace. This was to be a precursor to Easter week within the county.

In this regard, the people of Galway seemed to have a new found confidence and a belief in their capabilities and a determination to pursue their goals in the face of British authority. While few had education beyond National School virtually all were literate and had been at school up to the age of 14 or 15. This in itself was a new phenomenon for rebellions in Ireland. The Young Irelanders in 1848 and the Fenians in 1867 would have had far less well educated adherents. Judging by the set up for the 1916 Rising the increase in general education played a role ensuring a more organised preparation took place. The fact that some of this broke down when the rebellion broke out says more about the distances involved than anything else. When word did get to areas such as Moycullen, Barna and Spiddal they didn't rise more due to lack of arms than lack of information. Other areas that didn't seem to get word to rise such as Portumna and Woodford are over thirty miles from Athenry while areas like Tuam and Loughrea had large police presence from the beginning of Easter week.

4. **The advent of World War 1 had the effect of militarising the county as a whole.**

There was now a general call to arms. Huge numbers joined the military in Ireland on a voluntary basis as there was no conscription. The National Volunteers, as the followers of John Redmond were now known, were encouraged to answer the call to arms and join the British forces to bring a speedy end to the war. There were up to 160,000 of them nationwide though over half did not join up. Figures for those who joined the forces, for Galway alone, were staggering. On the outbreak of war 621 men of the Connaught Rangers, based in Renmore barracks, were sent to Aldershot, on August 7th 1914 to reinforce their regiment there. 1,623 recruits joined at Renmore Barracks between August and October 1914. By January 1915 there were over 700 men from Galway City alone serving in the armed forces. This was out of a city population of around 13,000.[8] The Claddagh in particular saw huge numbers join the armed forces especially the navy as it was an important fishing village. By April 1915 there were over 250 signed up from the Claddagh.[9]

The willingness to join the armed forces was as much to do with economic conditions as anything else. At that time conditions were financially difficult for many in the county particularly around the city.

Many areas of the county also contributed to the armed forces and supported the war effort. Loughrea saw many young men join the army,

> 'The town population was almost 100% anti-national. During World War 1, large numbers of young men of the town, encouraged by the local M.P., the late Mr. William Duffy, and others imbued with the same ideas, joined the army'.[10]

---

8   William Henry, *'Galway and The Great War.'* Mercier Press p33

9   William Henry, *'Galway and The Great War.'* Mercier Press p33

10   W/S 1,202 Martin O'Regan

Reasons for the 1916 Rebellion in Galway

There were huge recruitment rallies all around the county through 1914, 1915 and on into 1916. In June 1915 there was a recruiting campaign visiting Tuam, Headword, Cliften, Oughterard, Maam Cross, Loughrea, Athenry and Galway City.[11] In July the Irish Central Recruiting Council came to the city and held three meetings and then travelled around the county to places such as Moylough, Mountbellew, Ballygar, Ballinasloe, Eyrecourt, Laurencetown and on to Portumna.[12]   On February 2nd 1916 there was a 'Great Recruiting Conference' in Galway.[13] Many prominent figures arrived in the city including John Redmond and Lord Wimborne, the Lord Lieutenant, many M.P.'s and local businessmen and clergy. These recruiting drives were always accompanied by bands and often by soldiers in uniform to inspire the local youth to join the forces. Stephen Gwynn M.P., who joined the Connaught Rangers during the war, was one of those to the fore in encouraging men to join up.

Most of the clergy around the county actively encouraged the men of the Galway to join the war effort. Bishop Patrick Kilmartin of Clonfert spoke of our right 'to defend our rights within the laws of God.'[14]   Bishop Thomas O'Dea of Galway urged Irishmen and Irish Catholics to join the Allied cause.[15] Thus, between the British army, the R.I.C., the new recruits, the National Volunteers, the Irish Volunteers and the secret society the I.R.B., all of whom were armed, there was a militarisation of society in general at this time. In addition, it was now accepted that military action could be seen as the solution to issues and problems. The authorities went to any lengths to recruit men for the armed forces. The recruiting tours going all over the county to encourage young men to take up arms offered various reasons to do so. Among the reasons were, to defend Belgium, to help

---

11   William Henry *Galway and The Great War* Mercier Press p51

12   William Henry *Galway and The Great War* Mercier Press p49

13   William Henry *Galway and The Great War* Mercier Press p55

14   William Henry *Galway and The Great War* Mercier Press p58

15   William Henry *Galway and The Great War* Mercier Press p58

Rebellion in Galway

Britain defeat Germany, to help Ireland gain self-government should we help Britain in her hour of need, to defeat the pagan Germans who were committing atrocities against the Catholic people of Europe, to ensure that the war would not spread to Ireland and so threaten our homes and people, to ensure the war would be short and so not threaten our economy or lead to higher taxes to cover its cost. So the whole effort of the country was turning to war and the glorification of defending your ideals, property and people by taking up arms.

Young men were encouraged by politicians, bishops, priests and community leaders to fight. All local newspapers such as the Connaught Tribune and The Galway Express were filled with advertisements calling for army and navy recruits. Men joined up for various reasons be they economic, idealistic, looking for adventure etc. but it did have the effect of seeing military action as a solution to problems.

Those opposed to recruiting and joining the army were just as likely to see their efforts to arm in defence of their beliefs as equally important. Thus, the I.R.B. men in Galway who now controlled most of the Irish Volunteer companies in the county were doing all in their power to secure arms and train for what they saw as their opportunity to take action against Britain.

This atmosphere of military activity meant that drilling openly with arms went on all over the county. Many Irish Volunteer companies paraded with their arms and held mock battles with the R.I.C. in attendance. The police did not interfere or attempt to confiscate the arms.

When marking the Manchester Martyrs' anniversary in Athenry in 1915 the Irish Volunteers paraded and fired a number of rounds.

> '...and we marched round the town past the
> barrack to the place appointed. We fired three
> volleys and needless to say it was like a terrific
> explosion in the silent streets. We waited some
> time to see if the peelers would come but there

was no sign of them.' [16]

No doubt, the R.I.C. and the British authorities felt that men trained in military discipline may end up as recruits for the war. In 1914 and 1915 there was no inclination that a rising was planned and though at the heart of the community the police had no inclination of what was to come. They were aware of an I.R.B. presence in the county and later of the Irish Volunteers opposition to recruiting but as of yet it did not stretch to a planned rebellion.

5. **When the Irish Volunteers split in 1914 the majority in Galway remained with the Irish Volunteers as opposed to the National Volunteers.**

Following John Redmond's speech at Woodenbridge, Co. Wicklow on September 20th 1914 there was a serious split in the ranks of the Irish Volunteers. Redmond encouraged the members of the Volunteers to join the British army and fight with Britain in World War 1. He hoped that this show of loyalty would encourage the British authorities to deliver on the promise of Home Rule for Ireland following the ending of the war. He also felt that it was the right course of action in defending nations against the aggressions of the German Empire. However, many Volunteers disagreed with him and refused to consider joining up. They felt that the Volunteer movement was to promote Irish interests and help secure Home Rule for Ireland rather than help what they now saw as aiding and abetting the British Empire. Thus, the movement split with Eoin Mc Neill, one of the founders of the movement leading the opposition to joining the British army. Redmond now renamed his group the National Volunteers. Of the estimated 180,000 members 11,000 remained with Mc Neill with some 169,000 siding with Redmond.

---

16   W/S 446 Frank Hynes

Rebellion in Galway

When the split occurred, the majority of the Volunteers in Galway sided with Eoin Mc Neill's Irish Volunteers. It was mainly in Galway City and Loughrea that the National Volunteers dominated. Here you had Stephen Gwynn M.P. in Galway and William Duffy M.P. in Loughrea. Following the split, the Irish Volunteers in Galway dramatically increased their numbers while the National Volunteers dwindled significantly.

'By April 1916, there were 1,791 Irish Volunteers in the county, signifying an increase of 141 per cent since the spring of 1915. Moreover, the Mc Neillite Volunteers were the most active political organisation in Galway.' [17]

At the same time the National Volunteers saw a drop in their numbers within the county.

'Between August 1914 and January 1916, the Galway National Volunteers' membership had dropped by 4,961 (50 per cent), leaving 56 companies with 5,008 members most of which were described by police as 'inactive'.'[18]

It seems that this unwillingness of the National Volunteers to be active was that many felt that activity might lead to them being recruited to the army, should conscription be introduced. Thus, while they agreed with Redmond's sentiments many were unwilling to put these into action by joining the army. Many of the Irish Volunteer companies were in areas of the county where, due to land issues, secret societies traditionally held sway. Therefore, their members were far less likely to be supporters of Redmond's call to join the British army.

17 Fergus Campbell, 'Land and Revolution Nationalist Politics in the West of Ireland 1891 – 1921.' Oxford University Press p199.

18 Fergus Campbell, 'Land and Revolution Nationalist Politics in the West of Ireland 1891 – 1921.' Oxford University Press p198.

Reasons for the 1916 Rebellion in Galway

The differences between the Irish and National Volunteer organisations in relation to the increase in numbers and activity were particularly noticeable in Galway and were significant reasons for the intense revolutionary activity there during Easter week. It is clear that of those who sided with Mc Neill almost 2,000 of them out of 11,000 were in Galway. Even if the figure of 1,791 is an over exaggeration it does demonstrate that Galway was seriously behind Mc Neill and that if there was to be a county likely to rise in rebellion Galway was it.

Some companies did follow Redmond like those in Galway City and Loughrea where recruiting to the British army was strongly encouraged by local M.P.'s Stephen Gwynn and William Duffy respectively. Also, many in Craughwell sided with Redmond as Tom Kenny, the leading I.R.B. man in the area had fallen out with some locals over land issues and those opposed to him followed Redmond as he sided with Mc Neill. In places such as Ballycahalan and Mullagh where some remained squarely behind Redmond their companies faded in significance while the Irish Volunteer companies though small were very active. Commenting on the split in the Ardrahan Company and the demise of the National Volunteer company there Peter Howley said,

> 'He (John Naughton the instructor) then said that any Volunteer who was not satisfied to guard the shores of Ireland for England against the invasion was at liberty to leave the company....
> .....Out of the eighty or so men on parade only five left the ranks. They were Volunteer John Coen, my three brothers, Patrick, William and Michael and myself. The five of us never afterwards attended any parade of the company, which disintegrated shortly afterwards.' [19]

19   W/S 379 Peter Howley.

6. Liam Mellows was sent to the county in January 1915 as a local organiser for the Irish Volunteers.

From the moment he arrived he made an immediate impression on the local nationalists.[20] He linked up with the already strong Fenian activity and tradition in the area and soon he became very well respected. Immediately Mellows proved to be a very capable military advisor. One of the first things he did when he arrived in the area was he organised the county on a brigade basis. There was a county brigade and four battalions.[21] He saw to it that local leaders were appointed in charge of these and regular meetings were held for planning.

He reorganised drilling in the area and put it on a very disciplined footing. He gave lectures on military activity and held manoeuvres, route marches and mock battles. Within a short period of time the general level of fitness and military awareness of the Irish Volunteers especially in the mid and south county improved. In addition, he succeeded in motivating several key personnel to work hard at drilling and training companies other than their own so as to spread the enthusiasm into surrounding areas. Thus, men like Stephen Jordan would travel to other companies than his own in Athenry to help with training and indeed indoctrination.

Mellows gained the confidence of the local people. Staying with a local republican families, the Brodericks and the Hynes, was the kind of thing that ensured he was welcomed into the community quickly. He arrived at a time when the ex-British soldiers who had initially trained the Irish Volunteers were recalled to help with British military duties and the locals who took over the training did so with limited and varying degrees of success. Thus, his reorganisation and improvement of training

---

20 W/S 343 James Barrett.

21 W/S 344 John Broderick.

structures was very much needed, popular and well respected.

He operated out of Athenry which was in the middle of the county and the area he wished to control. This meant he had relative ease of communicating with groups in the area. Also as Athenry was a mainline rail station on the Galway - Dublin line communication with leaders in Dublin was a lot easier. The majority of the surrounding companies were all within ten to fifteen miles of the town. Therefore, in a radius of fifteen miles there were active companies in Athenry, Craughwell, Rockfield, Coldwood, Kiltullagh, Clostoken, Monivea, Galway City, Barna, Clarinbridge, Oranmore, Claregalway, Castlegar, Maree, Loughrea, to name some of the more active groups. In addition, some farther afield were Gort, Mullagh, Mountbellew, Kinvarra, Peterswell to name but a few.

However, his arrival as a 24 year old to take over as organiser sowed some rifts within the county. Tom Kenny, the blacksmith from Craughwell, who for many was the acknowledged leader of republicanism in Galway was pushed out as Mellows took over training. Kenny was the leading I.R.B. figure in the area, acting as Co. Galway 'centre' and a member of the Connaught I.R.B. Council.[22] He was against a rising at this time as,

'... he believed the time was not ripe.' [23]

The position of Larry Lardner was also a difficult one, he was appointed Galway Brigade O/C by Mellows but as to who was in ultimate charge was often hard to know. Mellows organised lectures, manoeuvres, mock battles and was seen as the man in charge during the week of the rebellion but he did hand over command briefly to Lardner in Moyode and again in Lime Park when he (Mellows) refused to disband the men.

---

22 W/S 874 Gilbert Morrissey.

23 W/S 874 Gilbert Morrissey.

7. **The tension between republicans and police due to the large numbers of R.I.C. stationed in Galway.**

Galway had the highest number of R.I.C. constables per head of population of any county in Ireland. At the time of the 1911 census there were 93 R.I.C. barracks distributed throughout the county. Over 1,000 constables were stationed in the county in addition to military personal stationed at Renmore barracks in Galway City. However, it was the day to day activities of the R.I.C. that most angered many local people. The police were doing their duty in being vigilant and sending reports to headquarters in Dublin. However, in the process tensions in Galway rose to high levels as Irish Volunteers and I.R.B. members found that there was constant surveillance of their activities. There was continual attrition between the groups as each tried to out-manoeuvre the other. Volunteers would parade openly with guns pushing the limits and the R.I.C. would retaliate by arresting men they thought were a danger to law and order. When it came to shotguns you could have a single barrel shotgun without a licence but you needed a licence for a double barrelled one. This would explain the large number of shotguns available to the Irish Volunteers during the Rising.

In Athenry the local I.R.B. were always planning activities to infuriate the R.I.C. There was constant attrition between them as the area was a hotbed of agrarian action. The Town Tenants' League succeeded in getting some land division in the area to the benefit of townspeople and local tenants. However, this was only after prolonged agitation. Even low level incidents like taking the R.I.C. transport horse for three weeks, taking the crown from over the barracks door and hanging it on a telegraph wire and flying a tricolour from the chimney were causes of disputes between the opposing sides.

'...credit for these and other similar incidents was
due to that energetic worker, the late T.V. Cleary,
who was mainly responsible for the planning and
execution of all these incidents.' [24]

The R.I.C. of course hit back, when failing to get information
that might lead to arrests and they often,

'... framed charges against men of disorderly
conduct, drunkenness , etc.' [25]

In September 1914 when the Volunteers split the
members in rural Galway stood squarely behind Mc Neill as
most were staunchly nationalist, republican and anti-British.
Scenes like that in Athenry were repeated throughout the mid
and south of the county.

'...a special meeting of the Company was held
to decide which side the Volunteers would take.
The position was explained by Captain L. (Lawrence)
Lardner who said that anyone who did not stand behind
Mc Neill was free to leave; no one left.' [26]

When Liam Mellows arrived in Athenry things were
only going to get worse and the tension increased.

'Liam played many tricks on the peelers.'[27]

---

24   W/S 346 Stephen Jordan.

25   W/S 346 Stephen Jordan.

26   W/S 343 James Barrett.

27   W/S 446 Frank Hynes.

Rebellion in Galway

As a result of these on-going incidents mid and south Galway was always going to be more disposed towards rebellion and there was an expectation that people did not co-operate with the authorities. Liam Mellows was able to exploit and harness this attitude and use it to garner support in building up the profile of the Irish Volunteers over the National Volunteers in the lead up to the rising.

> 'As a result of all these activities the I.R.B.
> became numerically very strong and remained so
> up the year 1913 when the Volunteer organisation
> was founded. The national spirit was so strong
> at this particular time owing to the activities I have
> already mentioned, that the foundation of a
> sound Volunteer organisation was a foregone
> conclusion.' [28]

---

28 W/S 346 Stephen Jordan.

The Plans for the Easter Rising.

Once World War 1 broke out sections of the Fenians (Irish Republican Brotherhood) in Ireland came to the conclusion that 'England's difficulty was Ireland's opportunity'. Thus, they began to think along lines of an armed rebellion. As there were so many Irishmen parading openly with arms and the supply of these had improved since the Howth and Kilcoole gun-running they felt that it was now or never. The split in the Irish Volunteers was a great boost to their plans as there was now a significant number of Volunteers who decided not to make themselves available to fight for the British cause, as in supporting the army in World War 1, whatever was their reason for doing so.

When World War 1 broke out the leadership of the I.R.B. were split as to the question of organising a rising. People such as Sean Mac Diarmada, Padraig Pearse and Thomas Clarke saw it as a suitable opportunity for a rebellion. However, this ideal was not shared by Bulmer Hobson (I.R.B. Supreme Council member) who felt the time was not right as most Irish people were not in favour of a rising and there was a lack of arms for such a venture.

Hobson was removed from the Supreme Council and the more military minded pressed ahead with plans for a rising. In 1915 Thomas Clarke decided to move and set up a Military Council that would plan a rising. This was to be a secret committee within a secret organisation. In addition to Pearse, Mac Diarmada and Clarke, Joseph Plunkett, Thomas Mc Donagh and Eamonn Ceannt were added to the planning committee. They hoped to use the Irish Volunteers as soldiers for the rising unbeknownst to them if necessary. In many cases members of the Volunteers were also in the I.R.B. and they would be actively hoping for an opportunity to fight for independence. It was hoped that those not in the I.R.B. could be persuaded to partake by the time the rebellion was organised. Guns were to be imported from Germany to augment those already in the possession of the Volunteers. With this in mind Roger Casement was sent to Germany to secure help on two fronts. Firstly to send arms and ammunition to Ireland and secondly to send German troops and Irishmen who were prisoners of war captured in the war since 1914. Casement only succeeded in obtaining arms and ammunition but no troops of any kind. These were sent to Ireland in April 1916 in a ship called the Aud.

At the last minute he felt this was not enough for a successful rebellion and he set out from Germany after the Aud had sailed to try to get to Ireland and stop the rebellion. He managed to get the Germans to send him by submarine to Kerry where the shipment of arms was to be landed.

Like Hobson, Eoin Mc Neill who was the leader of the Irish Volunteers, following the split in August 1914, was not in favour of a rebellion. He believed that such action should only take place should the leading Irish Volunteers be arrested, conscription for World War be forced on Ireland, the Irish Volunteers be disarmed by the authorities or the promise of Home Rule be overturned. He felt that a rising was not sought by the majority of Irish people and to do so at this time was unwarranted and most unlikely to succeed.

Most of the Irish Volunteers were staunch followers of Mc Neill and would await his word and follow his leadership. However, unknown to Mc Neill many of the leadership in key positions were also I.R.B. men as were a considerable number of members around the country, as in Galway.

In Dublin James Connolly, who had founded the Irish Citizen Army in November 1913, during the Lock-Out, was also planning a workers rebellion in his own right. He was close to the Irish Volunteer movement and the I.R.B. element in it but grew impatient with their lack of progress in organising and holding a rebellion. He pushed ahead with his own plans for one even though there were just about 200 in his Citizen Army. When the I.R.B. Military Council became aware of this they feared that if he went alone ahead of them it would seriously disrupt their plans. Thus, they took him on board and shared their plans with him. He decided to join with them and the rising was now set for Sunday April 23rd 1916.

It was hoped to have the German arms by this time and being a holiday weekend it was a good time to catch the British authorities off guard.

By Wednesday April 19th the I.R.B. were all set for the rising. They knew the arms were on their way from Germany and now all they needed was to persuade Eoin Mc Neill to give the order for a rising. This would ensure that all Irish Volunteers, especially those not in the I.R.B., would follow the instructions and partake in the rising. A document on paper from Dublin Castle was published in the newspapers on Wednesday. It contained the names of people that the British authorities were about to arrest. On this list were leading members of the Irish Volunteers. This became known as the 'Castle Document.' It persuaded Mc Neill to issue instructions for a rebellion on Easter Sunday to all Irish Volunteers. This was in line with his stated belief that a rising was justified if the British attempted such arrests.

On Thursday Mc Neill found that the 'Castle Document' was forged by Pearse and his co-conspirators to trick him into calling a rebellion. He and Hobson confronted Pearse and then cancelled his orders for a rebellion.

The next day, Friday April 21st, Pearse, Mc Donagh and Mac Diarmada convinced Mc Neill to reissue the order for the rising. They informed him that a ship load of arms was about to land in Kerry from Germany. In light of the arms delivery and knowing that when the authorities would arrest all the leading Volunteers as soon as they found out about it he reissued orders to rise on Sunday. Now the plans had the backing of Mc Neill and a full turnout could be expected.

By Saturday morning April 22nd rumours abounded in Dublin that the Aud was captured and scuttled and all the arms were lost. Now facing a situation of a serious lack of arms for the rebels, particularly in the west, Mc Neill again changed his orders. He dispatched messages to all areas that all Irish Volunteer manoeuvres for Sunday were called off. He also published a notice in the Sunday newspapers to that effect.

The Military Council of the I.R.B. and Connolly of the Citizen Army decided to go ahead with the rising on Monday April 24th as it was their only chance of ever having a rising as they were likely to be arrested shortly. So the rising was on again.

Thus, the rising was on, on Wednesday, off on Thursday, on, on Friday, off again on Saturday and on again on Monday. One can only imagine the utter confusion relating to the plans for the rising.

The British authorities met on Sunday, in Dublin Castle, and decided to take no immediate action as they now believed the danger to be over. The guns were at the bottom of Cork harbour where the Aud had been sunk. In addition Roger Casement, the presumed leader, was captured off Banna Strand in Kerry when he came ashore from the submarine. They also noted that Mc Neill had issued orders that all Irish Volunteer activities were cancelled for Sunday. It was a holiday weekend and they felt the situation was under control. Thus, they did not issue orders for a general round-up of other known leaders either Irish Volunteers or I.R.B. men.

The Plans for County Galway.

The 11.000 or so who retained the name of the Irish Volunteers, under the leadership of Eoin Mc Neill decided they would not support the war effort. Many of those in these ranks were already I.R.B. members who had joined the Irish Volunteers when they formed in late 1913 and early 1914. This was particularly true of Galway where the I.R.B. was strong. Many of the local young men fired by their feelings that there were grave injustices in the county pertaining to land distribution were members for up to five or more years. Following the foundation of the Irish Volunteers many companies were formed in Galway. These sprang up in places such as, Athenry, Craughwell, Cussane, Rockfield, Belclare, Newcastle, Mullagh, Loughrea, Gort, Ballycahalan, etc. There were over thirty companies within six months of the launch date in the Town Hall in Galway City in December 1913.

The first plan of the I.R.B. was that their members should be the leading lights of this new and armed organisation. Thus, they succeeded in making sure that their men were the company captains, lieutenants, quartermasters, etc. This was clearly shown when Morgan Healy was elected as captain when the Rockfield Company was formed near Athenry in 1914. He was not in the I.R.B. and this did not sit well with Tom Kenny of Craughwell one of the foremost Fenians in Galway and a former I.R.B 'centre' for the county. He thus arranged that Healy be removed and Gilbert Morrissey, an I.R.B. man, be installed. [29]

Michael Kelly, a member of the I.R.B. from 1913 and the Irish Volunteers from 1914 also states,

'It was also the general policy of the I.R.B. to fill officer- ships in the Irish Volunteers by members of the I.R.B.' [30]

In early 1915 Padraig Pearse visited Athenry where he met with Larry Lardner and Dick Murphy two prominent Irish Volunteers men in the town. However, they were essentially I.R.B. men and it was in this capacity Pearse met them. He wanted them to hold a line along the Suck at Ballinasloe and on to the Shannon. This was to ensure that there was a barrier between Dublin and the west. This would hopefully tie down a significant number of troops in the west and give the rebels in Dublin a greater chance to gain a stronghold in the city and

29   W/S 874 Gilbert Morrissey.

30   W/S 1,564 Michael Kelly.

hopefully a better chance of an overall success. There was also a notion recorded in Laurence Garvey's witness statement that the Irish Volunteers in the east Galway region were to blow up the bridge at Banagher, if instructed. This would cut off the crossing between counties Offaly and Galway. He claimed that the Mullagh Company were charged with this plan. [31]

The next plan for the Galway region was to supply them with arms in advance of the rising. This was to be done with the arms and ammunition that were scheduled to be landed at Banna Strand in Kerry in mid-April. The west had received very few of the arms landed in Howth, Athenry got twelve rifles. Therefore the area was poorly armed relying mainly on shotguns that farmers had. It was necessary to hold a licence for a double barrelled shotgun but not for a single barrelled. These arms and the accompanying ammunition were to be brought from Kerry north to Galway by train from Tralee and supply Irish Volunteers in Limerick, Clare and Galway. As Galway was the most organised area, with Liam Mellows having operated in the area since January 1915, men there were expected to receive the bulk of the delivery. The railway line ran through Ennis and on to Gort and Craughwell before reaching Athenry on the Dublin to Galway line. If this plan had worked a lot of guns would have been distributed to a wide area of Galway in a short space of time. However, as we now know the Aud was captured at sea before the arms and ammunition could be landed.

Each company in the Galway region was to attack the local R.I.C. barracks in their area and get arms and ammunition from the barracks. They were also to take the constables as prisoners and hold them as prisoners-of-war. They were then to meet in the vicinity of Oranmore and take the rebellion to the next stage. This may have meant attacking Galway depending on how things were progressing. [32]

Locally members of the Irish Volunteers were to gather as many guns as was possible. Houses that were known to have

31 W/S 1,062 Laurence Garvey.

32 W/S 572 Thomas 'Sweeney' Newell.

guns were to be raided and collections were to be made where people friendly to the cause would be asked for the guns they had in their homes.

> 'Fr. O'Meehan then gave us General Absolution and told us to collect all the arms and ammunition we could in the town of Kinvarra and neighbourhood.....
> .....Most of the owners gave them up willingly.' [33]

These plans were known only to a few of the most senior leaders in the Galway area. The rank and file members certainly did not know of the details of the plans. Most members of the Irish Volunteers in Galway were I.R.B members and were fully behind a rebellion. They knew that a rebellion was in the offing and they were training and drilling for this event. However, they did not know exactly when it would happen. Anyone not interested in revolution would have been fully aware that being in the Irish Volunteers was not the place to be if you did not wish to rebel against the authorities at some stage in the future.

In Galway City, there were specific plans to take over the main post office in Eglinton Street. This would control telegraph and other communications and was a major building in the city. They were also planning to capture some of the most prominent men in Galway,

> 'It was our intention to take a few prominent men
> - Martin McDonagh (Máirtín Mór), Joe Young, etc.,
> and occupy the Post Office. This was George
> Nicolls' plan.' [34]

These plans had to be radically altered following the outbreak of the rebellion in Galway on Monday April 24th. At this stage the R.I.C. were aware of the rebellion in Dublin

33 W/S 1,173 Michael Hynes.

34 W/S 714 Thomas Hynes.

and took immediate precautions on Monday morning. Once they were aware of the rebellion in Dublin they anticipated trouble in County Galway. On Monday before the Galway Irish Volunteers had time to mobilise they withdrew all constables from outlying barracks and huts and moved them to larger barracks in the towns. They brought all their arms and ammunition with them so it could not be captured from the smaller units. It also reinforced the larger barracks and made it harder to attack them. Thus, constables from Newford and the Agricultural College huts went to Athenry, Kinvarra constables went to Gort barracks and New Inn barracks went to Loughrea. This pattern was repeated around the county.

The fact that the plans had to be altered at the outbreak of the rising had a detrimental effect on its success in the county. Mellows continued with the attack on barracks in Clarenbridge and Oranmore as the constables were not withdrawn from them and there was a reasonable chance of success in capturing them. However, the constables barricaded themselves inside the barracks in both locations and the rebels found that their limited fire power of a few rifles and shotguns were not sufficient to capture the barracks. They withdrew from Clarenbridge after it became apparent they could not capture the barracks. Likewise, the original effort to capture Oranmore failed and when Mellows and the Craughwell and Clarenbridge men joined the Oranmore and Maree companies they too failed to capture it. They were then forced to retreat in the face of reinforcements from Galway.

Mellows was also led to believe that other counties around Galway would rise at the same time. The guns that were to come from the ship landing in Kerry were to supply companies in Limerick and Clare and then these counties too would rebel. However, the capture of the Aud put an end to this and no action took place in either Limerick or Clare.

Westmeath was also to have contributed to the rebellion. There had been a top level training camp held in Coosan just outside the town in 1915. It was organised by local leader

Peadar Melinn and many leaders from around the country such as Larry Lardner (Galway). Terence Mc Swiney (Cork), 'Ginger' O'Connell (Sligo), John Brennan (Roscommon), Dick Fitzgerald (Kerry) and Mick Allis (Limerick) attended. If Athlone barracks was taken it would have meant a huge supply of guns and ammunition to help the rebels. However, the organisation and determination in Westmeath was far short of what it was believed to be. The only action in the area saw,

> 'Sean Mitchell had taken a boat-load of arms
> from Athlone to Banagher, but finding nobody
> mobilised there had returned disappointed in
> torrential rain.' [35]

In fact, so confident were the authorities that there was no danger in the midlands that Athlone sent military aid to Dublin during the week. Also, by Friday a train load of soldiers from Dublin and Athlone headed for Loughrea to attack Mellows and his fellow rebels in the Athenry area.

Following these setbacks Mellows had little option but to abandon the original plans. He now could do little but avoid being attacked and hope that by being in the field his forces would attract the attention of the R.I.C and military and keep the pressure off Dublin. During the week they moved first to the Agricultural College outside Athenry on Tuesday, Moyode Castle on Wednesday and Thursday and finally to Lime Park near Ardrahan on Friday evening. They then dispersed early on Saturday morning and went on the run or returned to their homes.

Tom Kenny, the leading republican in the lead up to the rising and a major figurehead in the I.R.B. would have felt vindicated in the wake of the failure to achieve any meaningful success. From the start he was against the rising taking place at this time as he felt preparations were not in place. Having returned from Dublin, _____

35   C Desmond Greaves, *'Liam Mellows and the Irish Revolution.'* An Ghlór Gafa p 90.

'...late on Easter Monday night he visited us at our
place of mobilisation and told us the rebellion was
called off......He also told us that he expected that a
certain section of Dublin men would strike. I asked
him if he was in favour of a rising and he said he
was against it; that he believed the time was not ripe.'[36]

It is likely that Kenny returned on Sunday night with this
information as he was at a G.A.A. convention that day in Dublin
and would have heard rumours of the Rising going ahead on
Monday. He was close to the Dublin I.R.B. being in constant
contact with Pearse, Clarke and Mac Diarmada. He must have
visited the Volunteers as they mobilised in Killeeneen on
Monday evening. However, it does shed further light on the
difficulties caused by the tensions between Mellows and Kenny,
the confusion due to the countermanding orders from Mc Neill
and the need to alter the plans in the wake of the Rising being
rescheduled for Monday that made the success of the rebellion
in the county highly unlikely.

---

36   W/S 874 Gilbert Morrissey.

Timeline for the 1916 Rising in Ireland.

January 1916

The I.R.B. planned a rebellion for Easter of that year. In the early months of the year many of the I.R.B. leaders visited places around the country urging the local leaders to step up their readiness for a rebellion. Padraig Pearse visited Athenry where he met with Larry Lardner and Dick Murphy letting them know that there was going to be a rebellion early in the year. Mobilisation orders for Sunday 23rd April were kept secret from most outside of a select group so as to minimise any possibility of the British authorities finding out the plans.

Sunday April 9th

The Aud left Lubeck in Germany, disguised as a Norwegian ship, under the command of Captain Karl Spindler with a crew of twenty one. It carried 20,000 rifles, 10 machine guns and ammunition to be landed in Kerry for the Irish Volunteers. The rifles were mainly Mosin-Nagant (1891), a 5 round magazine fed rifle. They were captured from the Russians during the early stages of World War 1 and would deliver reasonably rapid fire. It was planned to distribute these around Ireland to ensure the Volunteers were suitable armed for the rebellion. As there was a reasonable supply of arms and ammunition as a result of the landings at Howth and Kilcoole it was intended that these arms were to supply the Irish Volunteers in the west of Ireland in particular.

Wednesday April 19th
Dublin

A document was published in the newspapers written on Dublin Castle headed paper with a list of names including leading Irish Volunteers whom it claimed the British Authorities were set to arrest. Eoin Mc Neill thought it was a genuine leaked document and as he had publicly stated if this were to happen he was prepared to order a rebellion. So he agreed to proceed with plans for a rebellion. It was likely this document, known as the 'Castle Document' was forged by the I.R.B elements within the Volunteers (Pearse, Mac Diarmada and Plunkett) to get Mc Neill to agree to a rebellion.

Galway

Liam Mellows stayed in Garbally College Ballinasloe, the Clonfert Diocesan College, with Fr. Connolly on his way back to Galway for the rising. He had returned from deportation to England and returned to Ireland through Glasgow. Earlier in the week he was in Dublin to meet Padraig Pearse to finalise the plans for the rebellion in Galway.

Thursday April 20th
Dublin

Eoin Mc Neill discovered the 'Castle Document' was a forgery and decided to abandon plans for a rising with the Irish Volunteers.

Galway

Word came from Dublin to various places in Galway that the rising was set for Sunday. Margaret Browne delivered a dispatch to Sean Broderick at Athenry station. Brian Molloy arrived in Oranmore with the message from Dublin that the rising would take place on Sunday at 7p.m. Bridget Walsh, from Killeeneen in Craughwell, went to Dublin by train met Tom Clarke and brought back a uniform for Liam Mellows.

Friday April 21st
Dublin

Early in the morning Pearse, Mac Diarmada and Mc Donagh went to see Mc Neill and told him that they had arranged a shipment of arms from Germany and that they were arriving to help arm the Volunteers for a rebellion. Mc Neill realised that when these arrived the leaders of the Irish Volunteers would be arrested on foot of the delivery and they had a better chance of resisting arrest if they used the arms in a rebellion. Again he changed his mind and ordered all Volunteers to proceed with the rebellion.

Galway

Liam Mellows stayed in Loughrea with a sympathetic old Fenian Joseph O'Flaherty. Mrs. Martin Conroy delivered the orders for the rebellion to Michael Thornton in Spiddal. There was no sign of the arms that some expected to be landed in Galway Bay from a German ship.

Antrim/Tyrone

The Irish Volunteers in Belfast had decided they would go to Coalisland, Tyrone to take part in the rebellion there. They sent their arms, in the region of 42 rifles, on ahead in cars that came up from Coalisland on Good Friday. The Ulster Volunteers were numerous and well armed in the north and would be a formidable force to take on. Thus the Irish Volunteers were to assemble in Tyrone and march to Connaught and support Liam Mellows efforts there. This was the plan agreed to by Denis McCullough in Belfast and Pat Mc Cartan of Tyrone. Hugh Rogers, Seamus Tomney, Tommy Mc Guigan and William John Kelly were in the two cars that arrived to collect the arms.

Kerry

In the morning three Irish Volunteers were drowned at Ballykissane Pier on their way to capture radio equipment in Cahersiveen to use to contact the Aud. One of those drowned was Alf Monahan's brother Charlie. Little did they know that the Aud didn't even have a radio. These were the first casualties of the 1916 Rising. Roger Casement was captured on Banna Strand, Kerry having been dropped off there from a German submarine. The Aud, with arms and ammunition for the Rising, was captured by a British ship, the Bluebell, off Banna Strand and escorted to Cork Harbour. Austin Stack and Con Collins were arrested in a severe blow to the local efforts at rebellion.

Saturday April 22nd
Dublin

Word filtered through to Dublin of the capture of the Aud and its cargo of guns for the rising. Mc Neill now realised a rebellion without these arms would be futile and countermanded Friday's orders and published a notice to this effect in the Sunday Independent for April 23rd. Dispatches are also sent out around the country to this effect. Thus, the rising was now cancelled again. These on, off, on, off instructions caused general confusion in Dublin and around the country.

Galway

Liam Mellows arrived in Walsh's in Killeeneen near Craughwell in advance of the rising taking place and had a meeting with many of the local leaders. John Hosty was sent from Galway City to Dublin to find out what was the state of affairs as regards the rising as there were rumours that it had been cancelled. Meanwhile word was circulated in Galway that the rising was on and to mobilise for 7 p.m. on Sunday evening.

Cork

The Aud was scuttled in Cork Harbour by its captain and crew. They boarded a lifeboat before it sank. All those who had been aboard the Aud were arrested and imprisoned.

Louth/Meath

Word was circulated in Dundalk to meet for a route march on Sunday morning at 9 a.m. Irish Volunteers were to bring all their gear, arms, ammunition and rations. While many volunteers were not told that they were going to be part of a rebellion people such as Thomas Hamill, in his Witness Statement 232, was in no doubt that it was a very likely scenario.

Tyrone

The Belfast Volunteers collected off the Falls Road and went to Coalisland by train in three different groups so as not to arouse too much suspicion. When they arrived there they journeyed to Dungannon, some three miles away to the south west, where they were billeted by locals in sheds and barns. In all about 132 men arrived from Belfast. Up to 200 local men gathered to join the Belfast men in the vicinity of Coalisland and Dungannon hoping to form a group from the North to go to Connaught to assist Irish Volunteers there in the rebellion rather than stage a northern one. They were to help Mellows to tie down crown forces west of the Shannon and hold a line along it to stop military reinforcements getting to Dublin. Nora Connolly (James's daughter) arrived in Dungannon with dispatches and she was impressed with the numbers of armed men she saw.

Wexford

In the absence of any concrete word and amid confusing rumours Paul Galligan went to Dublin to seek out the leaders to find out what was happening.

Sunday April 23rd
Dublin

A meeting of the I.R.B. leaders and James Connolly of the Irish Citizen Army was held in Liberty Hall and they decided to go ahead with the mobilisation plans for noon on Monday morning as they feared if they waited they may soon be arrested and their chance of a rebellion would be gone. The likelihood of any success was now seriously curtailed but a token rising would be better than none. A meeting of the British authorities in Dublin Castle decided the danger seemed to have passed, the guns and ammunition were captured as was Roger Casement and so rounding up of any suspects was not immediately necessary. They thought it was unlikely anything serious would happen over the weekend as instructions had been issued cancelling all Irish Volunteer activities and had been published in the national newspapers.

Galway

Irish Volunteers assembled after mass in numerous places around the county to carry out activities. In the morning and early afternoon there are assemblies in Athenry, Kinvara, Killeeneen and Carnmore Cross and word was circulated to other areas to mobilise as soon as possible. However, by late afternoon there was word that all activities were cancelled and companies were stood down. However, all company leaders told their men to stand by as they may be needed in the near future.

Cork

Tomás Mac Curtain led over 1,000 Irish Volunteers who mobilised in various centres throughout Cork City. Many were on their way from Cork City to Macroom but with contradictory orders circulating it caused serious confusion in the county. All Volunteers were disbanded that evening as there were no orders to proceed with the rising. Up to 1,000 Volunteers mobilised in west Cork but with no orders forthcoming disbanded that evening.

Louth/Meath

The Irish Volunteers began their march from Dundalk and went south through Collon and on towards Slane. A car met them on the way with 40 Lee Enfield rifles which were distributed among the men. A dispatch reached them that the rising was called off. The leaders decided to go on towards Slane but 12 were allowed fall out and return to Dundalk. Two R.I.C. men Sergeants Wymes and Connolly followed them in a car all the way.

Tyrone

The men from Belfast and local areas of Tyrone were ready and armed and willing to fight for Ireland. However, local priests Fr. Daly and Fr. Coyne seem to have advised Mc Cullough and Mc Guigan that to attempt to march to Connaught would be folly and discussions on how to proceed were held. In the end it was decided to abandon the efforts at the rising and the men were stood down. The local men dispersed and the Belfast men returned home. Local priests Fr. Daly and Fr. Coyle's persuasion, rather than the countermanding orders from Eoin Mc Neill, seem to be the reason for the Volunteers disbanding rather than marching to Connaught.

Wexford

Paul Galligan was in Dublin and read in the papers that the rising was cancelled. Back in Wexford, in the absence of any word, there was no action.

Monday April 24th
Dublin

At noon the G.P.O was occupied by a force of Irish Volunteers led by Padraig Pearse and the Irish Citizen Army led by James Connolly. More Irish Volunteers and Citizen Army are deployed in various buildings and strategic areas around Dublin. The I.R.B. forces of 1,558 were led by Pearse and the Citizen's Army forces of 219 by James Connolly. Pearse read the Irish Proclamation from the steps of the G.P.O. The 1st Battalion led by Edward Daly took over the Four Courts, Jameson's Distillery and North King Street. The 2nd Battalion led by Thomas Mc Donagh took over Jacob's Factory. Eamon de Valera was in charge of the 3rd Battalion at Boland's Mills, Westland Row, Mount Street Bridge and Landsdowne Road Station. Eamon Ceannt led the 4th Battalion at the South Dublin Union, James's Street Hospital, Roe's Distillery and Cork Street. The Citizen Army fought in two areas, St. Stephen's Green and the Royal

Rebellion in Galway

College of Surgeons under Michael Mallin and City Hall led by Sean Connolly. Up to 2,500 British armed forces arrive from the Curragh to engage the rebels. A rebel attack on Haddington Road barracks failed. The British forces attacked the South Dublin Union.

Galway

Word arrived in Athenry at noon that Dublin had risen and that they were to remobilise for the rebellion. A dispatch was brought to Athenry by train from Dublin by Margaret Browne who was later to marry Sean Mc Entee. Liam Mellows, still in Craughwell, was notified at once. Stephen Jordan went to notify Galway City. Pat 'The Hare' Callanan and Joe Fleming travelled around Galway to spread the word to mobilise. Other men are sent around the county to mobilise all units as soon as possible. Word was also sent to all R.I.C. barracks that there was a rebellion in Dublin. They decided to withdraw all constables from outlying barracks and huts and fortify the main barracks in the county. Padraig Fahy, one of the leading Irish Volunteers in the county, was arrested in Kinvarra.

Ashbourne/South Meath

Commandant Thomas Ashe was in charge of the Fingal Battalion in Dublin and he mobilised his battalion which amounted to about 60 men. He was ordered to send some to Dublin to help there. He sent 20 men under Captain Dick Coleman to the city.

Cork

When Tomás Mac Curtain heard of the rising in Dublin he mobilised a group of men and set up headquarters in the Volunteer Hall in Sheares Street. The rebels' headquarters was surrounded by the R.I.C and British forces. However, there was no exchange of fire.

Louth/Meath

The rebels returned from Slane towards Dundalk through Dunleer and Castlebellingham, as they thought there was no rising. John Mc Entee met with them near Castlebellingham and assured them there was a rising in Dublin. In Castlebellingham they stopped and commandeered a number of cars. These were full of people returning from Fairyhouse, it being a bank holiday. They wished to use these to go to Dublin for the rising. The Volunteers captured Constable Charles Mc Gee (23) of Giblinstown R.I.C. barracks but during the commotion and he was shot and killed. Also wounded was Lieutenant Robert Dunville of the Grenadier Guards. Some of the men then tried to make their way to Dublin. They used the cars they commandeered to transport the volunteers. However, one of the cars crashed into a ditch blocking the road and it couldn't be removed.

Tyrone

The Volunteers had dispersed as there seemed no hope of a rising locally and going to Connaught was never a serious likelihood. Nora Connolly returned to the area hoping to persuade some men to travel to Dublin to help the effort there but none travelled. Cathal O'Shannon form Antrim was the only man from the north to make it to Dublin to take part in the rising there.

Wexford

While in Dublin Paul Galligan heard the rising had started at noon. He went to the G.P.O. to meet the leaders. He met Pearse and Connolly there and got orders for Wexford. He was to capture the rail line and stop trains from going to Dublin. Having a rising there would tie down some British forces in the county and the south east in general. They were not to waste ammunition by attacking R.I.C. barracks.

Rebellion in Galway

Tuesday April 25th
Dublin
More British reinforcements arrived from Belfast and Templemore and artillery was sent from Athlone. General W.H.M. Lowe took over command of the British forces in Dublin. A cordon was secured by the British around the city. Attacks on the rebels continued in a number of areas around the city particularly on St. Stephen's Green.

Galway
Word of the rising quickly spread as dispatches were sent all around the county. Irish Volunteers from Rockfield and Clarenbridge mobilised early in the morning in Killeeneen under Liam Mellows and moved from there towards Clarenbridge. There they attacked the R.I.C. barracks but failed to capture it and they moved on to Oranmore. Around mid-day the Maree and Oranmore volunteers attacked the Oranmore R.I.C. barracks but fail to capture it. Constable Joseph Ginty was wounded during the attack on the barracks. Later in the day when the Craughwell and Clarenbridge Volunteers arrived in Oranmore under Liam Mellows it was decided to again attack the R.I.C. barracks. However, when they approached it they came under attack from the constables in the barracks. In addition, troops and R.I.C. arrived by train from Galway and their arrival ensured that all the Volunteers retreated towards Athenry. The rebels moved on to the Agricultural College near Athenry where they joined up with the Athenry Volunteers and remained there for the night. The Castlegar and Claregalway Volunteers were mobilised and marched towards Oranmore hoping to link up with Mellows' group but on hearing they had already gone towards Athenry they waited in the vicinity of Carnmore for the night. During the day most of the leading republicans in Galway City had been arrested by the R.I.C. and put on board a ship in Galway Bay.

Timeline for the 1916 Rising in Ireland

Ashbourne/South Meath

Commandant Thomas Ashe and his First Lieutenant Richard Mulcahy began to organise their troops and see what they could do to help disrupt the British forces and R.I.C. in the area. They cut telegraph wires in the area to disrupt communications.

Cork

There was no action in Cork as the Irish Volunteers continued to hold the Volunteer Hall. There were manoeuvres in Millstreet, but with no orders coming through to the area the men were stood down.

Louth/Meath

The men who had continued south towards Dublin used back roads to avoid attention. They arrived at Tyrrellstown House near Mulhuddard.

Tipperary

Two R.I.C. men were shot and fatally wounded as they attempted to arrest Michael O'Callaghan, of the Irish Volunteers at his home in Lisvernane on the Limerick-Tipperary border. Constable John Hurley, aged 23, from Castletownbere died on April 26th and Sergeant Thomas Rourke, aged 42, also from Cork, died on April 27th.

Tyrone

There was no action as the men were disbanded and sent home.

Wexford

Galligan set out from the G.P.O. at about 2p.m. to cycle to Enniscorthy and deliver the news from Dublin. Sean Doyle was still waiting in Enniscorthy for news of what to do.

Rebellion in Galway

Wednesday April 26th
Dublin

The Helga, a British gun-ship, sailed up the Liffey and fired on Liberty Hall. Two battalions of troops arrived from England one landing at Skerries and the other at Dun Laoghaire. The Volunteers halted the British troops from Dun Laoghaire at the Battle of Mount Street Bridge and inflicted huge casualties on them, over 234 men killed or wounded for the loss of eight Volunteers. The rebels burned the Linenhall Barracks and the garrison surrendered. The attack on the South Dublin Union continued. The British forces now had a cordon around the whole of Dublin City.

Galway

A large group of soldiers and R.I.C. and military moved out of Galway to survey the area east of the city for rebel movement. At about 5.00 a.m. their motorised group of about 60 men encountered a group of Irish Volunteers from Castlegar and Claregalway at Carnmore Cross. Following an exchange of fire lasting for up to half an hour Constable Patrick Whelan was shot dead and Constable Hugh Hamilton was wounded. These Volunteers then proceed to Athenry. There was a force of about 600 to 700 rebels at the Agricultural College at this stage. There was a brief exchange of fire with a small group of R.I.C. men from Athenry barracks hoping to estimate the strength of the rebels. There were no casualties on either side. That day the Irish Volunteers decided that the College was too vulnerable a position to defend and they decided to move to Moyode Castle about five miles away to the south east. Shells were fired inland from the British ship the Laburnum moored in Galway Bay but did no damage.

Ashbourne/South Meath

The Battalion commanded by Thomas Ashe attacked and defeated R.I.C. garrisons at barracks in Swords and Donabate.

This added to their stash of weapons. They now had up to 20 rifles, 12 Mausers, 20 Martini carbines a number of revolvers and a large amount of ammunition. In addition to these they had some home-made grenades. They also destroyed rail tracks at Donabate and telegraph lines at Swords. This would stop any reinforcements coming to Dublin from the north. They then intended to attack Garristown R.I.C. barracks but it had been abandoned. They moved to Baldwinstown, two miles away, for the night.

Cork
The stand off at the Volunteer Hall continued though there was no exchange of fire.

Louth/Meath
According to Frank Necy in his Witness Statement 239 an attempt to take a motor boat to Dublin with a load of volunteers fell through when too few showed up to make it worth the effort. The group in Tyrrellstown House waited here as it was impossible to get to Dublin due to military activity. They disbanded the following Monday and returned home.

Wexford
Paul Galligan arrived back in Enniscorthy late in the evening. A meeting of local leaders was called to decide how best to proceed with the plans from Pearse and Connolly.

Thursday April 27th
Dublin
Communications between the various Volunteer out-posts had been cut and the British closed in on the rebels. The G.P.O. and the Four Courts were shelled. The British attacked the North King Street area and Boland's Mills but retreated form the South Dublin Union area. Many buildings in the city centre were now on fire. Many civilians were also killed or wounded.

Rebellion in Galway

Galway

The Volunteers settled into Moyode and sent scouting parties out to get food and to ascertain the presence of any British or R.I.C. forces in the area. There was an engagement with an R.I.C. patrol from Athenry but again there were no casualties on either side. There were rumours of advancing British troops circulating among the men. Over 200 troops came by boat from Cobh and were landed in Galway City. This ensured that there was no threat to Galway City from the rebels. That evening up to 200 men, mainly unarmed, departed from the Moyode camp but many returned early on Friday morning.

Ashbourne/South Meath

Thomas Ashe and Richard Mulcahy reorganised their battalion. They sent home those they thought too old or too young for action and split their forces into four companies for action on Friday. They also procured food for their force which was now in the region of 50 men.

Cork

Negotiations were ongoing between both the Irish rebels and the British military. The Lord Mayor of Cork Thomas Butterfield and Bishop Daniel Coholan intervened to seek a solution.

Wexford

A group of up to 600 Irish Volunteers assembled under the leadership of Robert Brennan and in a surprise attack took over the town of Enniscorthy. Paul Galligan, Seamus Doyle and Sean Etchingham were other leading members. The rebels had 10 to 20 rifles some shotguns and pikes and 2,000 rounds of ammunition and flew the tricolour. The rebels made an unsuccessful attempt to capture the town's R.I.C. barracks and had to settle for blockading it. Roads were blocked at the entrance to the town and the railway line dismantled. There was a short exchange of fire between the rebels and the R.I.C.

in which two civilians and an R.I.C. man were injured. The men were blessed by local priests Fr. Patrick Murphy and Fr. Coad. This shows there was some local clerical support for the men.

Friday April 28th
Dublin
General Sir John Maxwell took over the British command. The G.P.O. was abandoned and the rebels advanced to Moore Street by 8p.m. The O'Rahilly was killed escaping from the G.P.O.

Galway
Amid further rumours of British advances on Moyode it was decided to move farther south towards Clare and the rebels marched about twelve miles to Lime Park near Ardrahan. There were still about 500 men and women in the group.

Ashbourne/South Meath
Ashe sent some of his men to attack Ashbourne R.I.C. barracks and others were to destroy local railway lines. The Irish Volunteers were preparing to attack Ashbourne R.I.C. barracks when word came through that R.I.C. reinforcements were arriving from Slane, numbering over sixty. This was almost double the number Ashe had in the Ashbourne area at that time. Following a fire fight lasting over some five hours seven R.I.C. men were killed with an eighth dying a week later. Fifteen were wounded. Two civilian drivers and two passers-by were also killed. This was the only major engagement outside of Dublin during the Easter rebellion and the only victory won by the rebels. One Irish Volunteer, John Crennigan, was killed in the engagement and another Thomas Rafferty died of his wounds later. In total up to 90 prisoners were captured by the rebel forces. This included the R.I.C. convoy who surrendered and the R.I.C. men in Ashbourne barracks who also surrendered. The R.I.C. dead included District Inspector Harry Smyth, who was the leader of the convoy, and County Inspector Alexander

Grey. The battalion then spent the night in the Kilsallaghan area a few miles south of Ashbourne.

Cork
The stand-off between the military and the rebels, led by Tomás Mac Curtain, continued at the Volunteer Hall in Sheares Street.

Wexford
British forces were sent towards Enniscorthy under the command of G.A. French. He was a retired British army Lieutenant-Colonel in Wexford and he was ordered to take command of the British forces in the area. The Volunteers marched in uniform through the town but did little else. The remainder of the rebels still failed to take the R.I.C. barracks. Many more men arrived in from Ferns and Gorey, seven and sixteen miles away respectively. Cumann na mBan arranged food for all the men and were a great support to the efforts of the rebels.

Saturday April 29th
Dublin
Padraig Pearse realised the situation was hopeless and hoping to avoid further casualties signed an unconditional surrender. At 3.45 p.m. he signed an order for all other out-posts to surrender. Nurse Elizabeth O'Farrell accompanied Pearse at the surrender to General Lowe. The rebels were defeated and the tricolour was taken down from the G.P.O. Most of the buildings in the centre of Dublin were destroyed as a result of the fighting.

Galway
The Volunteers reached Lime Park near Gort about 1 a.m. on Saturday morning. Rumours abounded as to the movements of British troops. By now they knew that the rising in Dublin was over. Fr. Tom Fahy had left the camp, on Friday morning,

to go to Galway to ascertain the situation. He had returned at about midnight and knew that Dublin was about to surrender. Following an all-night meeting it was decided to demobilise the Volunteers. The men were instructed to return to their homes and hide their arms. Most of the leaders went on the run hoping to avoid arrest. Liam Mellows, Alf Monahan and Frank Hynes headed south towards Clare and found safety in a number of safe houses over the next few weeks. Eventually they all escaped out of the country.

South Meath/North Dublin

Thomas Ashe was waiting for further orders from Dublin to arrive but when the order arrived it was to surrender. Richard Mulcahy went to Dublin to verity the command and when he returned they reluctantly did so. All the members of the 5th Battalion, Dublin Brigade were arrested and imprisoned. Ashe was later sentenced to death for his role but it was commuted to penal servitude for life.

Wexford.

Arrangements were afoot to send the British garrison from Arklow south to attack Enniscorthy. British troops were landed, from Cobh, in Wexford town and they were also ready to attack the town, which was fifteen miles away. The British had an armed warship in Wexford harbour that had the capability of firing shells as far as Enniscorthy. News of the Dublin surrender filtered through to the volunteers but they didn't believe it. They were called on to surrender by Lieutenant-Colonel French and the British troops but they refused.

Sunday April 30th
Dublin

64 rebels were killed during the week with 103 British troops killed and 357 wounded. In all up to 20,000 British troops were involved in suppressing the Rising. Martial Law was proclaimed

in Dublin and throughout the country, by the military, and 1,000's were arrested. The centre of the city and much of the suburbs were destroyed.

Galway
The rank and file volunteers returned to their homes and hid their arms. The leaders went on the run hoping to avoid capture.

Wexford
Lieutenant-Colonel G. A. French, leader of the British troops, gave safe passage to Sean Etchingham and Seamus Doyle to go to Kilmainham prison to see Padraig Pearse and get confirmation of the Dublin surrender. Having got this confirmation they returned to Enniscorthy.

Monday May 1st
Dublin
Arrests continued around Dublin with the military authorities in charge of the city.

Galway
Huge numbers of police and military scoured the county arresting people suspected of being part of the rising or of being sympathetic towards it or of helping it in any way. Many of these were R.I.C. constables down from the north to help. Many hundreds were arrested and brought to R.I.C. barracks around the county, to Galway Military Barracks in Renmore or Galway jail.

Cork
The Irish Volunteers eventually agree to hand over their weapons to Lord Mayor Butterfield on the understanding that they would be returned at a later date.[37]

37 www.cork city.ie/services/corporateandexternalaffairs/museum/museumexhibitionsarchives/
    1916exhibition

Wexford

Doyle and Etchingham returned from Dublin with news of the surrender and so the rebels surrender unconditionally and 100's of arrests followed. They were the last group of rebels to surrender.

Tuesday May 2nd
Dublin

Arrests and Courts-Marshall continued and the main leaders are identified and sentenced to death.

Cork

The R.I.C. surrounded the Kent home in Fermoy, Co. Cork hoping to arrest four brothers (Thomas, Richard, William and David) who were active in the Volunteers in the area. They had hoped to take part in the rebellion but little had happened in Cork and they had failed to make their way to Dublin. There was an exchange of fire lasting almost four hours. In this exchange the R.I.C Head Constable for Co. Cork William Nelson Rowe was killed. Richard Kent was also killed and all members of the family were arrested.

Louth/Meath

Four men were captured and sentenced for the shooting of Constable Mc Gee in Castlebellingham. Later these were sentenced and three had death sentences commuted to prison sentences and the fourth got 10 years commuted to five.

Wexford

Many participants in the rising were arrested. The numbers rose to 270 in the week after the rising.

Wednesday May 3rd to Friday May 12th
Dublin

14 leaders of the Rising are executed in Kilmainham Jail and

buried in Arbour Hill.

May 3rd Padraig Pearse, Thomas Clarke and Thomas Mc Donagh.

May 4th Joseph Plunkett, Edward Daly, Michael O'Hanrahan and Willie Pearse.

May 5th John Mc Bride.

May 8th Eamonn Ceannt, Michael Mallin, Sean Heuston and Con Colbert.

May 12th Sean Mac Diarmada and James Connolly.

Monday May 9th.

Cork

Thomas Kent was executed in Cork Detention Barracks.

August 3rd.

London

Sir Roger Casement was hanged in Pentonville Prison, London.

Information on the above from,

Ashbourne

The 1916 Rising Personalities and Perspectives PDF Version Ashbourne Co.Meath and www.1916rising.com/plc_battleashbourne.html

Cork

www.corkcity.ie/services/corporateandexternalaffairs/museum/museumexhibitionsarchives/1916exhibition

Dublin

D.J. Hickey and J.E. Doherty A Dictionary of Irish History 1800 – 1980 Gill and Macmillan pp 143-146

Galway

The 1916 Rising Personalities and Perspectives PDF Version Co. Galway

Louth/Meath

www.mcresearch.com/County_Louth/Descriptions/1916.htm

Tipperary

www.irishmedals.org/the-rising-in-other-areas.html

Timeline for the 1916 Rising in Ireland

Tyrone
http://www.freewebs.com/rsfeasttyrone/easttyronehistory.htm
Wexford
The 1916 Rising Personalities and Perspectives PDF Version Enniscorthy, Co. Wexford

The aftermath

During the rebellion over 1,000 civilians were injured and 230 were killed whereas 132 British military and police were killed and just 64 rebels.

The security forces of army and police arrested 3,430 men and 79 women of these 1,841 were interned in England. About 2,700 were released by August. Of those arrested 190 men and Countess Markievicz put on trial for organising the rising and 90 were sentenced to death. Of those sentenced 16 were eventually executed.[38]

In over-reacting and hastily executing 15 by May 9th the British authorities turned the majority of Irish people in favour of the rebels and their cause. Originally many were against the rising following the deaths and destruction but the summary executions had the effect of making the leaders martyrs and their popularity steadily grew. General Sir John Maxwell had arrived in Dublin on Friday April 28th and was appointed 'military governor.' Under martial law he was in complete control of the city and the trials of the rebels. Eventually the British government, under Prime Minister Asquith, became alarmed at the reaction to the executions and put a stop to the remainder of them. They realised that the tide of sympathy was turning to favour the rebels and they wanted to stop the executions before things got worse. However, it was already too late and the leaders became iconic figures to many.

In Galway the R.I.C. and the military forces swept the county for rebels and others who were sympathetic to the

38 www.bbc.co.uk/history/british/easterrising/aftermath/af01.shtml

rising or indeed anyone they felt was a dangerous subversive of any kind. R.I.C. from the Belfast area and the Royal Munster Fusiliers helped the local R.I.C. in this work. They arrested 270 men and captured 7 rifles, 86 shotguns and 7 revolvers.[39] However, another article claims that over 400 were arrested and detained in Galway Jail and later in Richmond Barracks in Dublin. Of these 328 were eventually deported to Frongoch prison camp in north Wales.[40]

---

39 www.irishmedals.ogr/the-rising-in-other-areas.html

40 www.historyireland.com/20thcentury-contemporary-history/the-most- shoneen-town-in-irelandgalway-in-1916/

The Economy and Society in Galway in the early 1900's (Gleaning information from the 1901 and 1911 census).[41]

In the lead up to the 1916 Rising Galway was one of the poorest counties in Ireland. It was one of the counties included in the Congested Districts Board area. This was a board set up in 1891 to bring relief to the western seaboard counties that were congested with large populations of poor people. Other counties included Donegal, Mayo, Sligo, Leitrim, Clare, Limerick and Kerry. Originally it had a role in building harbours, developing fishing and cottage industries and modernising farming methods. Following the Wyndham Land Act (1903) it got increased funding and it was authorised to purchase landlords' estates and redistribute the lands among small farmers. In time, it purchased over 1,000 estates and re-divided up to 2 million acres.[42]

However, all this work could not make Galway a wealthy economy and at the turn of the century the people were so poor that many were unable to emigrate. Looking at the 1901 and the 1911 census for the county a picture can be drawn of the conditions within the county at the time.

At the time of the 1911 census there were 2,614 getting workhouse relief, of these 1,301 were residents while 1,313 were getting outdoor relief while still living in their own houses. There were poorhouses (workhouses) in Clifden, Oughterard, Gort, Mountbellew, Galway, Glenamaddy, Loughrea, Portumna, Tuam and Ballinasloe. These poor unfortunate people are only recorded in the census by initials rather than by name.

The population of the county was in serious decline since the Famine reflecting the poverty of the area. Pre Famine the population was in the region of 423,000 but was now down to

---

41 http://www.census.nationalarchives.ie/exhibition/galway/main.html

42 D.J. Hickey and J.E. Doherty, 'A Dictionary of Irish History 1800 – 1980.' Gill and Macmillan p 87.

182,224. There was sustained emigration with 24,464 leaving between 1901 and 1911. Indeed, this was an improvement as over 50,000 left between 1891 and 1901 though it may also reflect an inability to pay for the cost of emigration. Between the two census Stephen Jordan, my grandfather, was to see four of his sisters emigrate to New York. This was a familiar story throughout the county. When World War 1 broke out there was an embargo on emigration, as it was hoped that young men would join the armed forces but in Galway it meant that many of those who were forced to stay were recruited into the I.R.B. rather than the British army. Thus, we see a number of sets of brothers involved in the Rising, Barretts (Athenry), Morrisseys (Rockfield), Cloonans (Maree), Newells and Molloys (Castlegar) and Grealishs and Concannons Claregalway. If emigration were allowed many of these would likely have emigrated and lessened the strength of the Volunteers and the I.R.B.

The county saw a reduction in population between 1901 and 1911 of 5% leaving it at 182,224. Only Ballinasloe recorded an increase in the ten year period as all other areas witnessed a decline in numbers. Galway City experienced a decline from 13,426 to 13,225. This reflected a decline in economic activity in the city. The Persse family distillery closed in 1908, the fishing industry in the Claddagh was in decline with larger trawlers affecting the catch, the proposed development of the docks into an Atlantic stop-over did not materialise and the rail developments only meant the importation of foreign goods which undercut local industry. This decline in the economy led to serious poverty.

Prior to the Great War farmers fared little better. The county was rife with land holding problems as large landlords held on to their estates rather than sell out under the Land Purchase Acts like Wyndham and Ashbourne. There were many who evicted tenants and grazed the land with cattle and sheep.

The Economy and Society in Galway

By 1911 Galway was still a proscribed county with over 1,000 R.I.C. constables stationed in it. Over 30% of all 'boycotting' incidents in the country happened in Galway. These facts led to tensions that resulted in wall knocking, cattle drives and often attempted murder and indeed murder. The poverty of the people was a serious matter and there was near famine as late as 1904. Thus there were many in the county willing to join secret societies such as the I.R.B. and plan rebellion, against what they saw as the tyrannical authorities, in the hope of a better future. The R.I.C. on the other hand had a job to do in keeping law and order for the betterment of society as they saw it. In most cases the R.I.C. were the sons of farmers from neighbouring counties, second, third or fourth sons that did not inherit the farm and had to make a living somehow. Farming prices did improve with the outbreak of war as food supplies were required to feed the army and supplement the food supply to Britain.

Jobs could be got joining the R.I.C. and the British army. The main regiment in the county were the Connaught Rangers. However, there were significant numbers who were more inspired by ideals of Irish freedom and joined the ranks of the I.R.B. hoping for an opportunity to fight for land as much as independence.

For women, the main jobs were as domestic servants, dressmakers and seamstresses. Over 30% of women working outside the home were in service as domestic servants. Stephen Jordan's sister Mary was a housekeeper for Canon Canton, the Parish Priest, in the 1901 census. In many ways the landlord's house was an important place of employment and this can be seen in Moyode House, in the 1901 census, where 22 servants and their families were living in the environs of the mansion. In 1911, 41 people resided on Portumna Demesne, the estate of the absentee landlord the Earl of Clanricarde. However, there was still a lot of poverty as not all could secure such employment.

Another indicator of poverty was the high infant mortality rate. Some indication of this can be got from the 1911 census. Parents were asked how many children, if any, were born to them and how many were living. There is hardly a family that had not a child who died at a young age. From a family of 11 children three of Stephen Jordan's brothers died as infants and a fourth Michael, of T.B., aged 23. Michael and Mary Barrett of 9 Court Lane Athenry were married 30 years with nine of twelve children living. John and Lizzie Broderick of Church St. Athenry had ten children born but three had died young. John and Bridget Morrissey of Knockatoor fared better as just one of their ten children died. Thus, poverty and disease were rampant at the time. It was no different from many other areas of the west of Ireland but many within the farming classes felt that if they had their own farms things would improve. Thus, when the opportunity arose for rebellion many were ready to take part as they thought success would improve their lot.

Galway Landlords

In the late 1800's as the era of landlordism was coming to an end there were many large landlord holdings in Co. Galway. Access to land was one of the major problems for the Irish. Tenant farmers were farming unviable holdings and were often in dire poverty. There were up to 200 landlords in the county at the time with the largest properties as follows;

- Lord Ashtown from the Woodford area in east Galway owned 23,000 acres.

- Lord Berridge around Ballynahinch in Connemara owned 171,000 acres.

- Lord Clanricarde in south east Galway owned 52,000 acres.

- Lord Clonbrock in Ahascragh in east Galway owned 28,000 acres.

- Earl of Clancarty, near Ballinasloe owned 24,000 acres.

- Allan Pollock near Ballnasloe owned 29,000 acres.

- Sir Henry Burke, Marble Hill, Loughrea owned 25,000 acres.

- Henry Hodgson on the west of Lough Corrib owned 18,000 acres.

- Sir Authur Guinness owned 20,000 acres at Ashford Castle, Cong.

- The Earl of Leitrim owned 18,000 acres near Loughrea.

- Walter Blake owned 10,000 acres at Ballyglunin near Tuam.

- The St. George family owned 7,500 acres in Headford.

Rebellion in Galway

- Martin Mc Donnell owned 10,000 at Dunmore.

- Daniel Lafiff in Gort owned 11,000 acres.

- The Daly family, Athenry owned 15,000 acres.

- The Earl of Westmeath owned 14,000 acres.

- Robert Ffrench in Monivea owned 10,000 acres.

- In Clarenbridge Christopher St. George owned 15,000 acres.

- Lord Dunsandle in the Loughrea area owned 37,000 acres.

- Presse Family Moyode, Athenry owned 12,000 acres.[43]

Given that there was a population of 192,549 in Galway in 1901 it was difficult to believe that these twenty families owned a total of half a million acres of land between them. It explains why issues relating to landholding and tenant right were very much to the fore at the turn of the century.

Following the famine many landlords cleared their estates of tenants and turned to cattle grazing as a greater source of profit. Additionally, it had fewer problems associated with rent collection. As long as prices for beef stayed high in Britain, with its growing urban population, cattle grazing was far more profitable and trouble free than dealing with tenants and associated problems often involving middlemen and land agents collecting the rent for you.

So access to land became the single most important issue in Galway in the late 1800's and into the early 1900's. Many of the large landlords were reluctant to sell their estates even following the Land Purchase Acts. These land purchase acts advanced money with which tenants could purchase their farms from a landlord and repay the loans in what were termed

---

43 eprints.maynoothuniversity.ie/5077/1/Tom_Tonge_20140620152731.pdf p 16

'land annuities' over a set number of years ranging from forty nine to sixty eight and a half years. However, this depended on the landlord being willing to sell and many wished to hold onto their family estates. This created tensions in the area as many of the local population hoped to benefit from land redistribution and purchase. However, their expectations were denied in many cases.

Tenants paid rent to a landlord and holdings were termed large if over thirty acres, though the vast majority were under this size. Landlords usually employed Land-agents to collect this rent, which was taken up twice a year. Land-agents were often corrupt and set a rent higher than the landlord requested keeping the inflated portion for themselves which was known as 'rackrenting'. Tenants held land on 'lease' or 'at will'. Leases gave security so long as you could pay the rent but tenants 'at will' held the farm from year to year. Leases in Ireland, in the 1880's, were considered to be up to 20% dearer than for comparable land in England. There were 391,528 families renting farms of below twenty five acres and most of these were in Connaught, Clare, Kerry and Donegal. So a considerable number of these were in Galway. This would have accounted for up to three million people. Average farm valuation in Leinster was £39 while it was only £12 in Connaught. While conditions in the 1860's and early 1870's were reasonable the poor harvests of 1877, 1878 and 1879 saw the return of near-famine conditions to many areas of the west. When all this is considered it shows that most farmers in Galway were living at a subsistence level whether they owned or rented their farms. Real fear of another major famine returned particularly in the west and people feared for their lives. Many of these people believed they would be better off if they owned their own farms and had more control of their destiny.

The Land League, working from 1879 to 1882, under the

leadership of Michael Davitt and Charles Stewart Parnell had done considerable work for the benefit of tenants. Many in Galway had succeeded in purchasing land but those unable to afford purchase or on estates where the landlord refused to sell were still likely to be paying high rents and were at the mercy of their landlord.

Landlords were Irish as well as British, Catholic as well as Protestant but to the tenant it was the fairness rather than the religion or the nationality that mattered most. However, given that most were Protestant with a British heritage much of the anti-landlord focus was also pro-nationalist with an emphasis on independence which locals were convinced would see them prosper once the dreaded foreign landlord was gone.

Organisations such as the United Irish League, which operated from 1898 to 1919 were active in the county and were to the forefront of seeking land redistribution. As a result of their activities Galway was one of the counties where most agrarian troubles took place. This in turn saw a huge presence of R.I.C. personal based in the county and it grew steadily between 1900 and 1916. This can be clearly seen in the census returns for R.I.C. in both 1901 and 1911.

During the so called Land War of 1879 – 1881 violence erupted in many areas of Ireland. This occurred when many Fenian elements throughout the country, impatient with Davitt and Parnell's progress on land reform, felt that a more militant effort was needed. Such secret societies took the law into their own hands and wide ranging violent attacks took place. The Fenian's (The Irish Republican Brotherhood) had a failed national rebellion in 1867 and were still a force to be reckoned with on all national matters. They were committed to a rebellion to free Ireland from Britain whenever the opportunity arose.

These elements were to the forefront of many violent activities in the late 1870's and early 1880's mainly threatening and killing landlords, land-agents and land-grabbers. Land-grabbers were tenants who took over farms of evicted tenants and they were particularly despised in many areas. Killing and maiming animals, burning sheds, boycotting and such like activities were common place at this time and took considerable R.I.C. efforts to combat. The Fenians had huge support in America among the Irish emigrants and vast amounts of money raised there made its way to Ireland to support the parliamentarian activities of Parnell and Davitt and the more violent activities of the Fenian element. Clann na nGael was the main Irish American group that supported Irish activities and they did a lot of fund-raising to send money to Ireland for various uses. Most of this money was used by constitutional politicians like Parnell and Davitt to promote and support their activities. However, some of it got waylaid to support more subversive activities run by diehard Fenians.

The level of violence mirrored the level of evictions in Ireland as can be seen from the following table. [44]

Year	Agrarian outrages	Evictions [45]
1877	236	463
1878	301	980
1879	863	1238
1880	2585	2110
1881	4439	3415

44 *'Kiltullagh/Killimordaly As The Centuries Passed.'* Edited by Kieran Jordan Kiltillagh/Killimordaly Historical Society p99.

45 *Kiltullagh/Killimordaly As the Centuries Passed, The Land Wars in Kiltullagh 1879 – 1882.'* Edited by Kieran Jordan, Kiltillagh/Killimordaly Historical Society. p 99

Rebellion in Galway

To combat the spiralling violence agrarian reforms, like Land Purchase Acts were introduced. However, Coercion Acts were also introduced. Under these people could be arrested on suspicion, curfews were imposed and Land League meetings were banned.

It must be viewed, therefore, that all was not normal in Galway, which was one of the most volatile counties in Ireland at the time. There was a special Galway correspondent for the Irish Times at the time and their reports appeared in the paper at regular intervals. During this time there were eight murders in County Galway all related to agrarian activities. Thus, by the turn of the century all these issues were still fresh in the minds of most people in the county. Most of the participants of the 1916 Rising were born in or around this time, their parents born around the time of the Fenian (I.R.B.) rebellion and their grandparents the time of the Famine. Much of a person's childhood at this time was spent listening to stories and songs about the past and no doubt they would have been entertained by listening to the songs and stories of their parents and grandparents, neighbours, friends and school teachers relating to these troubled times. It is no wonder that many were influenced to seek a path to independence. However, whether it was to choose rebellion over peaceful means was still open to decision.

Into the early 1900's there were still a considerable number of large landlords with estates that had not been sold to tenants. Therefore, there was agitation on an ongoing basis particularly in the Athenry and Craughwell areas where tenants still hoped to benefit from landlords selling their estates. The knocking of walls and the driving off of cattle belonging to landlords and land grabbers was one way in which local subversive groups protested at the situation. The Lambert estate at Castle Ellen to the north of the town of Athenry was an untenanted demesne of 370 acres. This was the kind of estate that many local farmers felt should be sold and the lands made available for local farmers who were trying to survive on small holdings at a subsistence level. Even in 1922 at the foundation of the state about 100,000 holdings amounting to some 3,000,000 acres remained to be dealt with.

It is easy to see how locals in Galway, many on holdings less than fifty acres, felt that land redistribution was one way in which their lot could be improved. Their expectation was that this was more likely to be done a lot quicker by an Irish government than that of the British crown. Thus, access to land was a major issue in Galway and one which saw many in the community support the idea of a rebellion as a solution.

There was a Town Tenants' League in Athenry from 1908 and they succeeded in getting some landlords' land sold to local farmers to give them additional farmland. However, this heightened the sense of injustice that farmers who did not get additional land felt. This meant that movements like the I.R.B. had many local youths willing to join their organisation in the hope of forcing through violent means, if necessary, a change in the situation.

Serious Agrarian Outrages in Galway 1881 – 1910.

The eight murders related to agrarian issues that took place in Galway between 1881 and 1882 are worth mentioning as they indicate that violence was seen as a method, at least by some elements, of hoping to gain concessions from the government or to run landlords out of the area and secure their land under some form of land division.[46]

May 12th 1881, James Connors, Killariff, Kiltullagh, Galway.

He was a bog ranger and tenant farmer on the estate of Lord Dunsandle. He was shot on his way home from a funeral. Three local members of the Land League were arrested on suspicion of the murder but no one was ever convicted.

May 29th 1881, Peter Dempsey, Hollypark, Loughrea, Galway.

He had taken over a farm vacated by Murty Hynes. Hynes had come under pressure to do so as he had taken it over from the evicted Martin Birmingham. Dempsey was thus seen as a land-grabber. He was shot in front of his two daughters on his way to mass. No one was ever convicted of his murder. [47]

July 24th 1881, R.I.C. Constable James Linton, Loughrea, Galway.

A native of Co. Down he was stationed in Loughrea for over 20 years and was considered a very diligent member of the force. Many of his observations were considered to have led to arrests of Land Leaguers. He was murdered in Church Lane at 10 a.m. Regardless of the reasons for his murder and despite the fact that the street was crowded at the time no one was

---

46 'Kiltullagh/Killimordaly as the Centuries Passed, The Land Wars in Kiltullagh 1879-1882 pp97-104.' Kevin Jordan. Edited by Kieran Jordan, Kiltullagh/Killimordaly Historical Society.

47 'Kiltullagh/Killimordaly as the Centuries Passed, The Land Wars in Kiltullagh 1879-1882 pp97-104' Kevin Jordan. Edited by Kieran Jordan, Kiltullagh/Killimordaly Historical Society.

convicted of his killing.[48]

November 8th 1881, Peter Doherty, Carrigan, Craughwell, Galway.

He had taken over a farm and was seen by many as a land-grabber and boycotted. He heard noise in the yard and went out to investigate with his sister. He was shot dead. 33 were arrested for this incident. Two were sent for trial and convicted. They were Pat Finnegan and R.I.C Constable Michael Muldowney. They were originally sentenced to hanging but this was commuted to life in jail. They served twenty years even though the evidence against them was very dubious and it seemed more important to gain a conviction then to convict the real murderers. [49]

June 8th 1882, Walter Burke, Rahassane Park, Gort, Galway.

He was a landlord owning land in Mayo and a 2,000 acre estate near Gort. As a result of evicting many tenants he was not a popular landlord. He and his bodyguard were shot near his house by a gang of up to five men and killed instantly. There was no conviction for the murder despite a reward of £2,000 being offered.[50]

June 8th 1882, Corporal Robert Wallace, Rahassane, Gort, Galway.

Corporal Wallace was a member of the Royal Dragoons and was working with Walter Burke as his bodyguard. He was shot while accompanying his employer near his residence in Rahassane, Gort. No one was ever convicted of his killing. [51]

---

48 *'Kiltullagh/Killimordaly as the Centuries Passed, The Land Wars in Kiltullagh 1879-1882'* pp 97-104 Kevin Jordan. Edited by Kieran Jordan, Kiltullagh/Killimordaly Historical Society.

49 Pat Finnegan, *'Pat Finnegan The case of the Craughwell Prisoners'* Four Courts PressLtd.

50 www.advertiser.ie/galway/article/52516/the-case-of-the-craughwell-prisoners

51 www.advertiser.ie/galway/article/52516/the-case-of-the-craughwell-prisoners

Rebellion in Galway

June 29th 1882, John H. Blake, Rathville House, Raford, Kiltullagh, Athenry.

A landlord's agent, he worked for Lord Clanricarde. He was said to have been unpopular locally as rents were high and were not reduced despite calls to do so. He was on his way to Loughrea with his wife Henrietta Frances and driver Thady Ruane when he was shot from behind a wall. Ruane was also killed and Mrs Blake was hit but survived. No one was convicted of his murder. [52]

June 29th 1882, Thady Ruane, Rathville, Raford, Athenry, Galway.

He was a servant to John H Blake. He was driving Mr and Mrs Blake to Loughrea in a horse and trap when he was shot at close range. He died almost instantaneously. No one was ever convicted of his murder. [53]

Other agrarian-related incidents.

July 1869, Attempted murder of Captain Thomas Eyre Lambert, landlord at Castle Lambert, Athenry.

Captain Thomas Eyre Lambert inherited his father's estate in 1867. Two years later he became the centre of attention nationally as he was the subject of an attempted murder. He evicted the Barrett family of Moorpark who had a large 70 acre farm. There was no apparent reason for this as they were not in arrears. Locally it was rumoured that it was because they were well-to-do tenants. In any case they went to live in Swangate in Athenry town. A few days later Captain Lambert was the subject of an assassination attempt when he was shot three

---

52 'Kiltullagh/Killimordaly as the Centuries Passed, The Land Wars in Kiltullagh 1879-1882' pp97-104
    Edited by Kieran Jordan, Kiltullagh/Killimordaly Historical Society.

53 'Kiltullagh/Killimordaly as the Centuries Passed, The Land Wars in Kiltullagh 1879-1882' pp97-104
    Kevin Jordan. Edited by Kieran Jordan, Kiltullagh/Killimordaly Historical Society.

times. He survived and raised the alarm. A son of the evicted family, Peter Barrett, who was home from London for a few days was arrested on the Galway to Dublin train that evening. He boarded at Athenry and was taken off the train at Woodford, near Ballinasloe, by Sub Constable Hayden. Peter worked as a postman in London. Hayden was going on a description of the assailant given by Lambert.

Peter Barrett was defended by Isaac Butt who had defended many Fenians over the previous years following the 1867 Rising. An initial trial took place in Galway but the jury could not agree a conviction. A second trial took place in Dublin and again the jury could not agree on a conviction. Though Barrett seemed guilty there was a lot of conflicting evidence on both sides that made a conviction unsafe.[54]

January 1909, Murder of Constable Martin Mc Goldrick in Craughwell.

Mrs Ryan a returned emigrant from the U.S.A. (where her husband had died) with a young family was given a 16 acre farm to rent by Lord Clanricarde in Templemartin near Craughwell. Tom Kenny who was the local organiser of the I.R.B. felt this land should be divided among local farmers. A reign of terror was unleashed against her including shots being fired, her hay burned, walls knocked and many people boycotting her. A row for the hearts and minds of the local people between Kenny and his supporters in the I.R.B. and the more moderate the United Irish League (U.I.L.) was also at the heart of the matter. Local middle classes, larger farmers and business owners supported Lord Clanricarde and the U.I.L. while poorer farmers and tradesmen were inclined towards Kenny's ideals.

Custom had it that unwalled farms were to return to commonage for grazing by the people of the townland. Thus,

---

54 familylambert.net Captain Thomas Eyre Lambert 1820-1919 by Ann Healy

Rebellion in Galway

Mrs Ryan's walls were knocked. These were to be rebuilt to keep her on her farm and give Clanricarde and the U.I.L. the upper hand. Two workmen were rebuilding and Constable Mc Goldrick was providing security.

Shots were fired at the party with the intention of frightening them. However, Mc Goldrick gave chase to the men who fired and they shot and killed him presumably as they were recognised.

Two men were arrested for the crime Michael Dermody and Thomas Hynes. Both were members of the I.R.B. However, both were released in May 1910 when it proved impossible to convict them. Stories of interference were rife on both prosecution and defence sides.

Both were innocent of the crime but as was often the case at the time the police were anxious to secure a prosecution. The real culprit lived uneasily with his crime for the rest of his life and never married. Dermody contracted T.B. in 1916 and died. Thomas Hynes went on to play a significant role in the 1916 Rising. Constable Mc Goldrick was just 24 when he was murdered.

The feud between Tom Kenny and the local gentry continued until 1912 when the Clan na nGael organisation, based in America, was forced to mediate between them. Kenny had hounds of the Galway Blazers Hunt poisoned in response to a prolonged campaign against him by some of the gentry and middle classes in the Craughwell area. Martin Hallinan was the leader of the opposition to Kenny and the main man in the U.I.L. This political and class struggle saw a number of violent assaults and virtual pitched battles between their respective supporters during 1911 and early 1912. Kenny was associated with the I.R.B., Sinn Fein and the G.A.A. elements while Hallinan had the support of Home Rulers, much of the clergy and the middle classes. Kenny lost his position as blacksmith to the Galway Blazers and faced financial ruin. When he poisoned the hounds the Blazers threatened to pull out of Galway. This would have been a financial disaster for the region and the businesses concerned looked for a solution to the ongoing dispute. They got Clann na nGael involved as brokers in the dispute and they with some payments to both sides managed to bring an end to it. [55]

May 1910, Attempted murder of Martin Conroy, Land-grabber at Ballintemple, Galway.

About 1910 there was serious agrarian trouble in the Ballintemple area in Castlegar three miles to the east of Galway City. A farmer Martin Conroy took over land from an evicted tenant Martin Callinan. This was seen as land grabbing by many of his neighbours. On May 20th 1910 while Conroy was sitting in his house talking to some visitors he was shot at and hit three times. He survived the attack. The next day Michael Newell from Briarhill, a known member of the I.R.B., was arrested. He lived just a mile away. He was tried for the shooting three months later but no conviction was secured. He was released on bail of £100 to be on good behaviour for twelve months. As he was constantly watched and harassed by the R.I.C. he decided to move and went to Dunboyne in Meath to work there. He later went to Mullingar and returned to Galway in 1915 when things quietened down. On his return he joined the Castlegar Irish Volunteers and was appointed Intelligence Officer. Newell took an active part in the 1916 Rising. [56]

---

55 8th -19th Century Social Perspectives, 18th-19th- Century History, Features, Irish Republican Brotherhood/Fenians, Issue 1 (Jan/Feb 2010) Vol 18.

56 W/S 342 Michael Newell.

Irish Republican Brotherhood - The Fenians

This was a secret society founded on March 17th 1858 by James Stephens from Kilkenny. He had fought in the Young Irelanders' rebellion in July 1848. This took place as the Famine was ending in Ireland. It was a hopeless attempt to rid Ireland of British control. The only real incident of any consequence was the Battle at the Widow Mc Cormack's house in Ballingarry in Co. Tipperary.

At the same time that Stephens founded the Irish Republican Brotherhoood a sister organisation called the Fenians was founded in America by John O'Mahony, also on March 17th. It was to supply the I.R.B. with officers, men, money and arms.

There was a failed I.R.B. rebellion in Ireland in 1867 when there were small engagements in Dublin, Tipperary, Sligo, Louth and Limerick. All were easily defeated by the R.I.C. and military.

There were still some old Fenians in Ireland as the 1800's drew to a close but by the 1890's membership had fallen to about 8,000 countrywide. Some of these had helped the constitutional movement organised by Charles Steward Parnell and Michael Davitt as they tried to gain improvements for Ireland. This saw Land Purchase Acts which helped farmers buy their land and improve their lot. It also saw the possibility of Home Rule for Ireland where there would be a parliament in Dublin to look after Irish affairs with the London parliament still in charge of taxation, security and Imperial affairs. However, some of the Fenian elements became frustrated by the slow progress of land reform and the stalling of Home Rule and again began to turn to the old Fenian ideal of an independent Ireland by forceful means. They were spurred on by Irish-American elements where money could be easily raised for arms for a rebellion. The Fenians in America operated under the name Clann na Gael and were very supportive of the physical force theory.

IRISH REPUBLICAN BROTHERHOOD - THE FENIANS

For many years there had been little support for this ideal even in Ireland. Indeed Parnell had managed to get John Devoy the leading member of Clann na Gael to support his constitutional politics in a venture known as 'The New Departure'. This saw the idea of a rebellion shelved in favour of parliamentary politics and the money from America backed Parnell and Davitt's efforts.

However, the rise in nationalism in the late 1800's with the advent of the G.A.A (promoting Gaelic games), the Gaelic League (promoting Irish language and culture) and the Literary Revival (promoting Irish plays and drama) saw a renewal of interest in Irish independence. No longer were some people happy with Home Rule, even if it were granted, and there was no guarantee that it would be. Thus, regardless of the Home Rule issue there was a significant number in Ireland who dreamed of an independent Republic achieved by rebellion. This was good news for the Fenians. For years they were an ageing group of older men with an ideal but with no young blood in their organisation. They certainly had no likelihood of raising an army among the youth of Ireland. Now they had a new generation many who thought the peaceful means used by Parnell and Davitt had failed to deliver.

John Redmond was now the leader of the Irish Parliamentary Party but he was continuing the methods employed for the last thirty to forty years. Home Rule finally passed in the House of Commons in England in 1912 but was defeated in the House of Lords. However, due to the Parliament Act passed in 1911 proposed legislation could only be rejected by the Lords twice. Thus Home Rule was due to be passed into law in 1914 and we would have a parliament in Ireland to look after domestic affairs.

However the new generation of nationalists reared on the stories of old Ireland, the new found enthusiasm for Gaelic Ireland, the relative failure of progress on the Home Rule front and the continued support for a rebellion from America began to look afresh at a rebellion. The older Fenians were only too glad to welcome them into the fold. Therefore, many new branches of Fenians sprang up all over Ireland in the early part of the twentieth century. These attracted a small but determined number of men to their fold especially in places like mid, south and east Galway where there were serious land issues. Despite this they still could not hope to attract enough to contemplate a rebellion. Branches were known as 'circles' and the head of each 'circle' was known as a 'centre'.

Then in 1913 they, as it were, struck it rich. The Irish Volunteers were founded in response to the Ulster Volunteers. The two were at loggerheads over the passing of Home Rule and both felt that an armed organisation would gently or otherwise persuade the British authorities to their way of thinking; the Irish Volunteers to have Home Rule passed and the Ulster Volunteers to have it rejected. Now there were thousands of men training openly, drilling and using arms and these, the Fenians felt, could be apprehended willing or otherwise for use in a rebellion. Once the sight of men with arms was evident in Ireland the whole landscape changed.

The British authorities did not quite know what to do with all these men drilling openly. The Irish Volunteers started in November 1913 and by May 1914 had an estimated 80,000 men and 180,000 by August, on the eve of World War 1. They could not hope to challenge this large group. They did attempt to confiscate the arms the Volunteers imported rather openly at Howth on July 26th but failed to do so. However, the British got an out, as a world war looked ominous, it was deemed suitable to let these men train because they would make good recruits, should they be needed, for the British army and indeed they were. However, what the British did not bargain for was that they could also be recruits for an I.R.B. army. So in a sense it became a matter of which group could make the most use of recruiting these men.

As with many things in Ireland there was a split. The Irish Volunteers split over the issue of helping the British army fight in World Wad 1. John Redmond M.P., the leader of the Irish Parliamentary Party, had also gained control of the Irish Volunteers from its founder Eoin Mc Neill. He promised that the Irish Volunteers would fight with the British army in World War 1 as he felt this loyalty would hasten the passing of the promised Home Rule when the war was over. This speech made in Woodenbridge, Co Wicklow on September 20th 1914 immediately split the Volunteer force. The majority followed Redmond to form the National Volunteers while 11,000 remained as the Irish Volunteers. These felt that if they were to fight it would be for Ireland. It was this group, again under the leadership of Eoin Mc Neill, that came under the influence of the I.R.B. Indeed without the use of the members of the Irish Volunteers that the I.R.B. picked up in the wake of the split they were in serious trouble for an army. Key positions in the Irish Volunteers were taken by I.R.B. members. Padraig Pearse was Director of Military Organisation, Thomas Mc Donagh was Director of Training, Joseph Plunkett was Director of Military Operations and The O'Rahilly was Director of Arms.

It was estimated by the R.I.C. in 1912 that there were as few as 1,660 I.R.B. members but now they had access to an additional 11,000 men if they could influence them to actually fight for Ireland and not just metaphorically do so. This was the challenge taken up by the I.R.B. over the next two years as they planned a rebellion at a time when they saw, 'England's difficulty as Ireland's opportunity'.

Events like the death of Jeremiah O'Donovan Rossa were used by Fenians to promote their cause and ideals. O'Donovan Rossa was an old Fenian from Cork who had resided in the U.S.A. for many years. When he died in 1915 it was decided to bury him in Ireland as a propaganda event. Irish Volunteer companies from all around the country attended his funeral in Glasnevin on August 1st. The I.R.B. infiltration of the Volunteers at this stage ensured that it was a real republican event. Padraig Pearse delivered the graveside oration that set a tone of defiance and fired a renewal of a nationalist spirit among most of the thousands that attended. It changed the situation in Ireland and within nine months there was a serious rebellion organised by the I.R.B. with the Irish Volunteers as their foot soldiers.

The main aim of the I.R.B. in each area was to recruit as many Irish Volunteers as possible to the Fenian cause. To do this their officers were intent on joining the Irish Volunteer companies in their area and trying to ensure that they became leading members of the organisation. In that way they could then seriously recruit suitable young men for their cause and effectively control the Volunteer movement.

When the split happened those left in the Eoin Mc Neill Irish Volunteers rather than the John Redmond National Volunteers were much more pre-disposed towards fighting for Ireland's cause than any other be it Belgium, the British crown or anti-German imperialism. Thus, the crossover between being an I.R.B. member and supporter of a rebellion or an Irish Volunteer member and wishing solely to see Home Rule implemented narrowed. Those left in the Eoin Mc Neill Volunteers were more and more disposed toward fighting for Ireland than just being the semblance of a physical force group that would do little else other than issue vague threats against Britain. As they trained, drilled and further armed themselves the resolve to fight in real terms became more evident. They were not doing mock battles around the fields of Athenry to see Home Rule or any watered down version of it introduced. The ordinary rank and file members were now more like trained soldiers who wanted independence and would fight for it. They had almost two full years from the time of the split to see where the movement was going and anyone who had any notion of what was going on and what they were doing knew that while there was no firm date set for a rebellion, that they knew of, there would be one in the offing at some stage. There is no doubt that those who chose to remain in the Irish Volunteers for the two years after the split or joined since then and paraded in Galway on St. Patrick's Day knew where the movement was heading. So while it is obvious that the Fenian, (I.R.B.) elements in a sense apprehended the Irish Volunteers so as to have an army for their rebellion it is also obvious that those who chose to be in the Irish Volunteers knew what was going on and were quite happy to go along with it. This becomes more obvious when all who mobilised after masses on Sunday April 23rd all around Galway were given the choice to leave before the action started and few if any left. Indeed all companies were stood down on Sunday evening when news of the cancellation of the rising filtered through. Thus, when they remobilised the next day anyone not wishing to partake could simply just not turn up. Those turning up on Monday April 24th certainly knew what was going on, as word was out that there was a rebellion in Dublin, and there was no doubt that this was 'the real thing'.

This is clearly demonstrated by Patrick Cooley of Clarenbridge in his witness statement when he states that the demobilisation on Easter Sunday was just a postponement of the Rising.

'We got leave to go home, we were told the
Rising was put back alright.' [57]

---

57 mspcsearch.militaryarchives.ie/docs/files//PDF_Pensions/R1/
    MSP34REF14655PATRICKCOOLEY/WMSP34REF14655PATRICKCOOLEY.pdf

Rebellion in Galway

The Irish Republican Brotherhood in Galway

The I.R.B. was very strong in Galway from the time of the Land War in the 1880's. There were branches or 'circles' in most areas and while inactive for long periods there were always a few leaders, 'centres', around who were ready to revive the movement should any opportunity present itself. Agrarian issues such as the division of landlords' estates were always to the fore in most tenants' minds. The number of murders, linked to land issues, and the huge presence of the R.I.C. within the county kept tension high. With the rise of nationalism, helped by the activities of the G.A.A. and the Gaelic League, the I.R.B. too, saw a revival in Galway.

Many young men in Galway, influenced by people such as Tom Kenny in Craughwell, joined the secret society. Many of the leading figures in the movement visited the area and they likely marked it out as a county that was willing to follow their lead. Such was the influence of Kenny, particularly in the Craughwell area, that he virtually led his own Galway 'secret society' as distinct from the I.R.B. Though he remained within the national organisation he often operated his own rules.

In November 1907 Sean Mc Bride visited Athenry and Craughwell and had meetings with Larry Lardner, Richard Murphy and Tom Kenny and in July 1909 Sean Mc Dermott spent up to nine days in the area.[58] As a result men such as James Haverty (Springlawn, Mountbellew) joined the I.R.B. in 1910, Patrick Callanan (Clarenbridge) in 1905, Stephen Jordan (Athenry) of the Town Tenants' League in 1906 and Martin Newell (Athenry) was also a member since 1908.[59] Therefore, by 1910 the police believed that there were up to 1,000 in the I.R.B. in County Galway alone.[60] Thus, it can be seen that when the Irish Volunteers were set up all around the county

---

58 Fergus Campbell *'Land and Revolution Nationalist Policies in the West of Ireland 1891 – 1921.'* pp176-177 Oxford University Press.

59 Fergus Campbell *'Land and Revolution Nationalist Policies in the West of Ireland 1891 – 1921.'* pp180-183 Oxford University Press.

60 Fergus Campbell *'Land and Revolution Nationalist Policies in the West of Ireland 1891 – 1921.'* p188 Oxford University Press.

throughout 1914 that,

> '...the leadership of the Irish Volunteer movement
> in much of east Galway was a continuation
> of the earlier I.R.B., secret society and Sinn
> Fein organisation.' [61]

The following were some of the I.R.B. cells or 'circles' in the Galway area in the early twentieth century.

Ardrahan

There was a 'circle' here but I cannot find the name of the 'centre'. It was active as there were many land issues, land-grabbing, evictions, cattle driving, etc. in the area.

Athenry

There was a small but active 'circle' in the town with Dick Murphy the 'centre' and Larry Lardner the secretary. It attracted some new young members in the early 1900's when land issues were very prominent in the town at the time.

Members included Larry Lardner, Sean Broderick and Stephen Jordan.[62] The Barrett brothers and Martin Newell were also prominent members. Athenry had a very active branch of the Town Tenants' League and though members of the I.R.B. were not supposed to join most did.[63] The I.R.B. members made sure they controlled the Irish Volunteers company when it started in the town.

> 'Sean Mc Diarmada used to attend the meetings
> every two or three months.' [64]

---

61 Fergus Campbell 'Land and Revolution Nationalist Policies in the West of Ireland 1891 – 1921.' p195. Oxford University Press.

62 W/S 714 Thomas Hynes.

63 W/S 346 Stephen Jordan.

64 W/S 346 Stephen Jordan.

Ballycahalan

Padraig Fahy was the 'centre' for the 'circle' here. He was a very committed I.R.B. man and also a leading Irish Volunteer. John Fahy from Eserkelly, Ardrahan was another member of the Circle.

Barna

Micheal O Droighneain, a teacher returned from Dublin set up a 'circle' in 1915. It had not been very active up to the Rising.

Belclare

John D. Costello joined the I.R.B. in 1913 sworn in by Liam Langley and shortly after that became the 'centre' himself. The 'circle' was involved in procuring arms and drilling.

Carnmore (Called this by Thomas Hynes but it was the same as the Claregalway 'circle')

Members according to Thomas Hynes, included Tom Ruane, Mick Newell and Brian Molloy.[65]

Castlegar

Here Michael Mulroyan was the 'centre' and the Newells were also involved. There were about 30 in the 'circle' in the early 1900's and meetings were held at least every fortnight. Land issues and suitable recruits were the main issues discussed. Again the I.R.B. members made sure they controlled the Irish Volunteers company that started in the area. It was in this area that there was the attempted murder of Martin Conway, in May 1910, on account of the accusation of his being a land-grabber. Michael Hynes an I.R.B. member was arrested but found not guilty of involvement. The Newells were blacksmiths and made pike heads at their forge.

Claregalway

<u>This was another active 'circle'</u> but I was unable to get the

65   W/S 714 Thomas Hynes.

name of the 'centre'. When the Irish Volunteers started the local I.R.B. was easily able to take control of the company. The majority of the members were active in the 1916 Rising as they were hoping to have local land issues solved.

Clarenbridge

Thomas Kilkelly was the 'centre' in the early 1900's and again there was a lot of agrarian trouble in the area. Pat 'The Hare' Callanan joined this 'circle' in 1905, sworn in by Thomas Kilkelly. He said they met every three weeks and occasionally weekly.

> 'The principal matters discussed at the
> meetings were, land division, methods to be
> adopted to compel landlords to sell holdings to
> tenant farmers, which included cattle driving,
> breaking walls and firing into the houses of landlords
> and their supporters.' [66]

Craughwell

John Newell was the 'centre' in the 1880's and his son Martin joined in 1913. They were an active 'circle' and Tom Kenny was the 'centre' prior to the Rising. They were to the forefront of activities like the murder of Constable Martin Mc Goldrick in 1909. Men from this 'circle' were responsible for murdering landlord Walter Burke and Corporal Robert Wallace in 1882. Members included Tom Kenny, Eamon Corbett and Pat Callanan. [67]

Galway

In the city there was less I.R.B. activity. The small 'circle' of about 15 members had George Nicholls as 'centre' a few years before the 1916 Rising. Meetings were irregular.

---

66 W/S 347 Pat Callanan.

67 W/S 714 Thomas Hynes.

Kilconiron

John Hannaffy was the 'centre' and there were about 15 in the 'circle'. Meetings were held once a month but some members were too old for the Volunteers so it was not a vibrant 'circle'. Daniel Kearns was in this I.R.B. 'circle'. [68]

Kinvarra

This was a real hot bed of republican activity. I did not get the name of the 'centre'. However, when Fr. O'Meehan came to the town as curate there was a large I.R.B. following willing to take part in anti-British activities.

Moycullen

Micheal O Droighneain, the teacher from Barna, also set up a 'circle' here but again it was not very active by the time of the rising. Leading members were John Geoghegan, Michael Geoghegan and P. Kyne. [69]

Mullagh

There was a very active 'circle' here as the tenants were very poor and there were a lot of evictions and many agitators were jailed including Laurence Garvey and his father.

Oranmore

Here Joe Howley was 'centre' and one of the leading lights of the I.R.B. in the county. Other members were Mick Athy and Martin Costello along with the afore-mentioned Joe Howley. [70]

Rockfield

Pat 'Hare' Callanan was the 'centre' of this 'circle'. It was relatively small with about 12 men and involved in all usual activities. Gilbert Morrissey was also a member.

---

68   W/S 1,124 Daniel Kearns.

69   W/S 714 Thomas Hynes.

70   W/S 714 Thomas Hynes.

Spiddal
This was mainly revived by Micheál O Dríógnean who was a national teacher who returned home from Dublin. Other members were Eamon Walsh and the Duignan brothers. [71]

University College Galway.
There was a reasonably active 'circle' in the college which drew on students living in Galway during college term rather than from Galway City, who would have joined locally. They were in-active during the 1916 Rebellion as it took place while they were on Easter holidays. Some of the college members were Tom Derrig, John A Madden and M. Brennan. Only one student was known to return to Galway that week, he was John A. Madden. [72]

County 'centres' (at various stages prior to the rising)
Thomas Kilkelly of Craughwell.
Tom Kenny of Craughwell.
Dick Murphy of Athenry.

National Organisers.
Archie Hernon was an organiser for the Supreme Council in Dublin but regularly visited Galway to swear in members.
Sean Mac Diarmada from 1908 was a full time organiser for the I.R.B. and he travelled the country swearing in members. He often visited the Galway area.

---

71 W/S 714 Thomas Hynes.

72 W/S 714 Thomas Hynes.

The Irish Volunteers

Eoin Mc Neill wrote an article in 'An Claideamh Soluis' on November 1st. 1913. It was written under the title 'The North Began' and suggested that the southern nationalists should set up a volunteer force along the lines of the Ulster Volunteers who had been founded in 1912. The I.R.B. took a lead from this article and Mc Neill was approached by Bulmer Hobson to act on his idea. Things moved swiftly as the I.R.B took a leading role in pushing the idea forward. A number of men, mainly I.R.B members, met in Wynne's Hotel in Abbey Street on November 11th. Among these were Bulmer Hobson, Padraig Pearse, Tom Clarke, Eamonn Ceannt, Sean Mac Diarmada, James Stritch, Harry Boland and Liam Mellows all members of the Fenians. Eoin Mc Neill was appointed the front man for the intended movement. These arranged to publicaly launch the Irish Volunteers at a meeting in the Rotunda in Parnell Square in Dublin on November 25th. The main organisational work for the launch was done by the I.R.B. as they immediately saw the opportunity presented to them of having such an organisation set up in Ireland

This launch was a huge success and was attended by over 5,000. It attracted members of all the main nationalist organisations in Ireland at the time including the G.A.A, the Gaelic League, the I.R.B. and Sinn Fein.

This new organisation spread rapidly throughout the country and the I.R.B. made sure their members were to the fore in being elected to prominent positions in the organisation. It raised finance at home but principally abroad. John Devoy in America, through Clann na Gael, raised considerable funds and these were directed towards Ireland. Roger Casement and Alice Stopford Green did likewise in England. By May 1914 there were an estimated 80,000 members and by August there were 180,000.

Erskine Childers, Bulmer Hobson, Mary Spring Rice, The O'Rahilly, Eoin Mc Neill, Sir Roger Casement and Darrell Figgis arranged for the importation of arms for the Irish Volunteers and these were purchased in Germany. They were landed at Howth aboard Childers' yacht 'The Asgard' on July 26th 1914. The consignment of 900 rifles (Mauser M1871 11mm singleshot) and 29,000 rounds of ammunition were collected and distributed by Volunteers despite the efforts of the British authorities to capture them. The frustrated military had to march back to Dublin empty handed. They were taunted by some onlookers and in the ensuing verbal exchanges tempers flared. The soldiers opened fire on the onlookers and three were killed and up to forty injured. This incident occurred on Bachelor's Walk near Sackville Street (now O'Connell Street).[73]

This action by the authorities was completely at variance with their action when the Ulster Volunteers imported their consignment at Larne. On this occasion guns were purchased from Germany through Fredrick Crawford. They were landed in Larne on the night of April 24th 1914. The consignment amounted to 35,000 rifles and 5 million rounds of ammunition and there was no army or police activity to stop the importation. Thus, the Ulster Volunteers had considerably more military hardware than the Irish Volunteers. At the time of the outbreak of World War 1 Ireland was a highly militarised society.[74]

In the summer of 1914 John Redmond wanted to take over the Irish Volunteers and he demanded control of over half of the seats on the Provisional Committee controlling the movement. In an effort to prevent a split in the movement his demands were acceded to. Of course this infuriated the I.R.B. elements within the movement.

On September 20th John Redmond spoke at a meeting of Volunteers at Woodenbridge in Wicklow and he urged all the Volunteers to join the fight and support the British in their defence of Belgium. The total numbers of Volunteers stood at 180,000 at this stage and the vast majority of them supported Redmond's call. In the region of 11,000 remained with Eoin

73 D.J. Hickey and J.E. Doherty, '*A Dictionary of Irish History 1800 – 1980.*' p232 Gill and Macmillan.

74 D.J. Hickey and J.E. Doherty, '*A Dictionary of Irish History 1800 – 1980.*' p298 Gill and Macmillan.

Rebellion in Galway

Mc Neill as he was opposed to them fighting for the British. Those who followed Redmond were now called the National Volunteers numbering some 169,000 and those who supported Mc Neill maintained the name the Irish Volunteers.

The Irish Volunteers reorganised themselves in October of 1914 with Mc Neill again at the helm as Chief of Staff. Bulmer Hobson was Quartermaster and The O'Rahilly was Director of Arms. The I.R.B. were able to infiltrate the movement at a high level and had Padraig Pearse as (Director of Military Organisation), Joseph Plunkett (Director of Military Operations) and Thomas Mc Donagh (Director of Training). These three were to be on the I.R.B. Military Council that organised the 1916 Rising. [75]

The Irish Volunteers in Galway

The first meeting to set up the Irish Volunteers in Galway was on December, 12th, 1913. It took place in the Town Hall. There was a huge crowd gathered. Martin Mc Donagh, a well-known businessman, was chairman on the night. Eoin Mc Neill and Roger Casement were among those who spoke. Many of those who attended were already members of the I.R.B and they were anxious to be associated with this group. George Nicholls 'centre' of the Galway 'circle' of the Fenians was in attendance and he and others in that secret society were among the first to join. Nicholls, Michael O Droigheáin and Dr. Brian Cusack were some of those who took names on the night of men wishing to join the Volunteers. 246 men signed up on that first night. Following this meeting there were many companies of Volunteers set up around the county in the first half of 1914.

In early 1914 companies were set up all around the county. The inaugural meeting in Athenry was on February, 8th 1914 in the Town Hall.

By May 1914 there were 3,037 Irish Volunteers in 30 companies in the county and by August there were 9,969 signed up in 110 companies. This shows the popularity of the movement

75   D.J. Hickey and J.E. Doherty, 'A Dictionary of Irish History 1800 – 1980.' p266 Gill and Macmillan.

within the county. This was no doubt aided by a push from the I.R.B. who immediately saw it as a possible force for a rebellion. Though some of these companies would be more active than others it nevertheless demonstrated the level of nationalist feeling within the county. [76]

On June 20th there was a large review of all Irish Volunteers, within the county by Colonel Maurice Moore, Instructor of the Irish Volunteers at a gathering held in Athenry. Over 2,000 attended the parade held on the 'Back Lawn' where Kenny Park is now situated.

This was before the split in the Volunteers which would come about in September 1914. Following the split the majority of the Volunteers in Galway stood with Eoin Mc Neill and pledged not to join the British war effort. Only in Galway City where there was a strong military presence did the majority of the Irish Volunteers side with Redmond and follow the National Volunteers. Though as huge numbers of young men signed up to join the army there was effectively no Volunteer movement of either branch in the city from then on. There were a few committed Irish Volunteers with a background in the I.R.B. such as George Nicolls but they had very little support. Their main activities were in anti-recruiting activities. They were poorly armed and were mainly ineffective during Easter week.

In January 1915 Liam Mellows was sent to organise the Irish Volunteers in County Galway with an eye to preparing them for rebellion at a later stage. After he arrived in the area he reorganised the Irish Volunteers on a more military footing from an administration point of view. There was one Brigade and four Battalions in the county. The Battalions were Athenry, Galway, Gort and Loughrea.

Athenry consisted of companies in areas such as Athenry, Clarenbridge, Craughwell, Cussane, Derrydonnell, Kilconiron, Killeeneen, Killimordaly, Kiltullagh, Monivea and Rockfield. **Galway** <u>area companies included</u> Barna, Castlegar, Claregalway,

76 O'Regan's Athenry – Athenry History Archive 1916 Easter Rising in Athenry and County Galway.

Galway, Maree, Moycullen, Oranmore, Spiddal.

Gort area had companies in Ardrahan, Ballycahalan, Beagh, Derrybrien, Gort, Kiltartan and Kinvarra.

The **Loughrea** Battalion had companies in Loughrea and Mullagh. [77]

Ardrahan

They were formed in early summer 1914. At first they were drilled by an ex-British army soldier called Naughton. He was paid for his time from a levy on the members. Originally there were up to 80 drilling. However, the drills were simple and straight forward with no route marches or manoeuvres. Following 'the split' in August 1914 only five supported the Mc Neill line. However, the remaining National Volunteer company disintegrated following that split.[78] As a result men in the area interested in joining the Irish Volunteers joined the Ballycahalan Company.

The company was revitalised when Liam Mellows came to the area and Peter Howley was appointed captain. There were about twenty in this company up to 1916. They took part in the November 23rd Volunteer rally in Athenry travelling by train from Ardrahan. They would frequently go to lectures given by Mellows in Hynes's mill in Gort for the companies in the Gort Battalion. [79]

Athenry

This was the main company in the county. Liam Mellows operated out of Athenry where he stayed first with Brodericks and then with Frank Hynes. This company was formed in 1914 and had great support from a host of I.R.B. men in the area. All officers and most of the members were in the secret society. Men such as Larry Lardner, Stephen Jordan, Frank Hynes, James

---

77 W/S 1,379 Peter Howley.

78 W/S 1,379 Peter Howley.

79 W/S 1,379 Peter Howley.

Barrett and Sean Broderick were the most influential. Initially they were trained by ex-British soldiers like John Naughton and Martin Holland (Houlian).[80] The company was about 70 strong and the members gave 3d a week to raise funds for training. In June 1914 the town hosted a huge Irish Volunteer rally addressed by Colonel Maurice Moore, Instructor of the Volunteers, at which over 2,000 were present. [81]

When Liam Mellows reorganised the county in 1915 Gilbert Morrissey was appointed Athenry Battalion O/C, Ned Burke Vice O/C and Sean Broderick Quartermaster. [82]

Ballinderreen

Thomas Gibbons was the captain of this company. Somehow they were overlooked for mobilisation during Easter week and took no part in the action though half way between Kinvarra and Clarenbridge. This shows how communication was a real problem during the rising and had they been notified many more companies would have risen.

Ballycahalan

Peter Deely was the initial captain but Padraig Fahy soon became captain. Parades were held twice weekly. There was some local opposition to the Irish Volunteers, no doubt relating to the split in the Volunteers and there were just about twenty members. Liam Mellows, Stephen Jordan and James Barrett often went to drill this company and usually stayed overnight in a tent. A summer camp was held here in 1915 and it was more a fun camp than a serious military training camp. There was music played and dancing in the evenings. Maybe this was a way of trying to get locals more interested in joining. Laurence Garvey from Mullagh attended this camp. [83]

---

80   W/S 446 Frank Hynes.

81   W/S 346 Stephen Jordan.

82   W/S 344 John Broderick.

83   W/S 1,062 Laurence Garvey.

The Ballycahalan Company did not officially mobilise during the rising as their captain Padraig Fahy was arrested in Kinvarra on Tuesday morning April 25th and brought to jail in Limerick. However, men from there did play a part.

'Some members turned out individually and assembled with the Ardrahan Company at Early's Wood.' [84]

Barna

There was a company started here prior to 1916 but they took no part in the rebellion. They were isolated from the main area of action and did not mobilise.

Belclare

This was a company in the Tuam area. John D. Costello was the captain. He was also in the I.R.B. Liam Langley was another member. They had a train and two carriages ready to bring them to Athenry when they got the word to mobilise. However, word did not get to them and though they assembled on Tuesday night they had to stand down as Tuam became a gathering point for police from the north and they would have been easily defeated.

Castlegar.

A company based at Brierhill was formed in the parish in early 1914. Thomas Newell was appointed the first captain. He was an I.R.B. member. The company supported Mc Neill following the split in September 1914. Most of the initial members of the company were already I.R.B. men. Early drilling was done by ex-British army men such as J. Walsh and M. Colburn these, however, were often called up for some type of duty when World War 1 broke out. By then the men in the company had learned enough to have their own instructor.

84   W/S 1,331 John Fahy.

In a reorganisation in October 1914 Brian Molloy was elected Captain, Thomas Newell First Lieutenant and Michael Burke Quartermaster. Later in 1915 Tom Courtney was appointed Intelligence Officer and Michael Newell Intelligence and Communications Officer (all were in the I.R.B.). There were now about 65 men in the company. Meetings, drilling and manoeuvres were held regularly, generally twice weekly. A collection of 5 shillings per house was made from all houses in the area and the money was used to buy arms and ammunition. After a day of manoeuvres in early January 1915 all men in the company got hats and Fr. Feeney got the rest of the money with which to secure the arms. One of these manoeuvres saw the Castlegar and Claregalway companies carrying out a mock attack on the village of Oranmore with the latter defending it. In the end they secured about 35 shotguns, mainly from local farmers, and a few revolvers. They did manage to get a few rifles from Dublin with the money collected but those with no guns had to make do with pikes supplied from Newell's forge.

By the end of 1915 the company was as ready as possible for a rebellion and while no date was set as of yet the company members knew what was ahead. The Newells had made many pike heads in their forge and these were shared with other companies like Spiddal. As 1916 dawned Alf Monahan arrived in the area and had a great deal to do with preparing the companies around Galway City including Castlegar. It was the Castlegar Company that arranged for Alf Monaghan to be spirited out of the city from under the watchful eye of the R.I.C just as he was to be deported the week before the rising.

Claregalway

The captain was Tom Ruane and other prominent members were Nicholas Kyne and Daniel Forde. This was a very active company with a large membership and they drilled regularly. They mobilised a force of over 60 for the rising and joined with Castlegar Company on Tuesday April 25th. In the lead up to the rising the company gathered a large number of shotguns and supplemented these with a number of small arms and pikes.

Clarenbridge

Eamon Corbett was captain of this company started in autumn 1914. Initially there were over 100 men at meetings of the company. They did not attend the National Volunteer review by John Redmond in the Phoneix Park in 1915 as they had supported Mc Neill and stayed with the Irish Volunteers. This was because most of the men in the company were I.R.B. men. When Fr. Henry Feeney came to the parish as curate he became a pivotal member of the company. Meetings were held in his house and bombs were made there also. The company had almost a full complement of men at the St. Patrick's Day parade in Galway on March 17th 1916. Parades were generally held twice a week and were intensified following the arrival of Liam Mellows to the area. The Flemings were also important members of this company. [85]

Coldwood

Michael Commins was the company captain of a small but determined group of which just about six mobilised for the rising.

Craughwell was known as Rockfield. (see below)

With the split in the Craughwell area due to the clashes between supporters of Tom Kenny and Martin Hallinan of the United Irish League the Craughwell branch was more in support of John Redmond. Thus the National Volunteers had a Craughwell branch and the Irish Volunteers were in the Rockfield Company.

Cussane

The captain was Patrick Kennedy of Carnaun. They did the usual drilling and training. They attended the funeral of O'Donovan Rossa in August 1915 as part of the Galway contingent. This company mobilised under Captain Kennedy in 1916 and went to the Agricultural College and joined Liam Mellows there. Pat

85   W/S 347 Pat Callanan.

Killeen of Cussane was a member of this company. [86]

Derrydonnell

This was a very active company and took part in all manoeuvres arranged by Mellows. The company captain was Michael Keane. They mobilised for the rising took up rail tracks on the Galway line and were at the Agricultural College, Moyode and Lime Park.

Dunmore

Again there was a company here but it remained inactive during the rising. Word of mobilisation did not get to north Galway and by the time they were aware of the rebellion R.I.C. from Belfast had arrived in the area making action virtually impossible.

Galway

The inaugural meeting of the Irish Volunteers in Galway was held on December 12th 1913 when a huge crowd attended the Town Hall. The officers elected were George Nicholls, Seamus Carter, Tom Flanagan and M. J. Allen. Initially up to 600 joined but eventually only about 200 were active.[87] Meetings and drilling were held in O'Donnell's Hall on Williamsgate Street. The committee formed was George Nicholls (President), Seamus Carter (Secretary) and Frank Hardiman (Treasurer) meaning that the main officers were all I.R.B. men. There were weekly parades. The first public event the company took part in was a parade on St. Patrick's Day 1914 through Galway. The company put a lot of effort into disrupting meetings that were recruiting for the British army. The most notable was when there was one in the Town Hall and the electricity wires were cut and stink bombs were released, of course this had the effect of breaking up the meeting.

At the time Redmond was seeking control of the Volunteers

86   Athenry History Archive: O'Regan's Athenry *'Athenry and the Easter Rising 1916.'* by Ronan Killleen.

87   W/S 406 Frank Hardiman.

a number of men in Galway wrote to the Volunteers' committee seeking a meeting to discuss the attitude to Redmond's intentions. Men such as Martin Mc Donagh, Martin Reddington, P. J. Mc Donnell, James Pringle and Luke Duffy were supporters of Redmond's. Following the meeting the vast majority of Volunteers gave their support to the Redmond faction which was to be called the National Volunteers. These men now began to actively recruit for the British army to fight in World War 1. Those to stay with the Mc Neill side were the I.R.B. supporters and men such as Dr. Walsh and Louis O'Dea. The company captain was George Nicolls. However, the company was in a weak and poor condition at the outbreak of the rising. To add to the problems the R.I.C. knew exactly who was in the I.R.B. and promptly arrested all the leading men and had them placed aboard the Gloucester moored in Galway Bay and from there sent to Cork. Therefore, the Irish Volunteers in the city played no part in the rising. [88]

Gort

The captain was Padraig Fahy who was a travelling Irish teacher for the Gaelic League. As such he made a lot of contacts around the county with other republicans. He was also an I.R.B. man. J. J. Gormley, and John Nelly were other prominent members. This was an active company and would have mobilised a large number of men had the guns from the Aud arrived.

Kilconiron

The captain was Patrick Coy. They mobilised about fifteen men for the rebellion out of a branch of fifty. They assembled at Moyode Castle Gate Lodge and proceeded to the Agricultural College. Most of the active members were also I.R.B. men. [89]

Killimordaly

John Craven was the company captain. They were active

88 W/S 406 Frank Hardiman.

89 W/S 1,124 Daniel Kearns.

during the rebellion with up to 30 men mobilised. They took up rail tracks near Attymon to stop trains from going between Galway and Dublin. William Kelly the company Intelligence Officer kept Liam Mellows informed as to troop movements on the Galway to Dublin line by cycling several times from Attymon to Moyode.

Kiltullagh
There was a company started here but there is little reference to it in any records in the lead-up to 1916. However, up to 12 men were arrested following the rising so it can be assumed that the area was active during the week. Arrests were made in Brusk, Kiltullagh, Killarriv and Knockatogher.

Kinvarra
There were about 40 men in this company a lot of whom were I.R.B. men. John Burke of Cahermore was the captain. Fr. John William O'Meehan, a curate in the parish, was a leading force in the company. He purchased green hats for the whole company. Liam Mellows sent for him to be the chaplain for the rebels during the rising. Padraig Fahy was to collect him in Kinvarra but Fahy was arrested by the R.I.C. at the presbytery that morning and brought to jail in Limerick. The company mobilised for three days and had a brief engagement with R.I.C. from Gort.

Maree
This was a very active company and played a leading role in the rising. The members were involved in two unsuccessful attacks on the R.I.C. barracks in Oranmore. There were about 40 members in the company. They were very active in all manoeuvres and drilling in advance of the rising.

Monivea
William Dolly was the main man in this area and a number of individual members made it to the Agricultural College for the

mobilisation of Easter week.

Mountbellew

Here James Haverty a Sinn Féiner and Fenian was the company captain.[90] It was a relatively small company and not involved in the rising as a unit.

Moycullen

Padraig Thornton was the captain of this company. They got the word to mobilise from Pat Callanan and Brian Molloy on Monday night of the rising. However, he decided against mobilising. The company was on the wrong side of Galway City from Mellows and they would have had to cross Lough Corrib to join his forces rather than risk moving a body of men through the city hoping they would go unnoticed. With little or no arms action was seen as impossible.

Mullagh

The company started in 1914. Local curate Fr. Donoghue facilitated joining and members were signed on in his house. The officers were; Captain Hubert Hanrahan, 1st Lieutenant Laurence Garvey, 2nd Lieutenant John Manning, Adjutant Michael Manning and Quartermaster Michael Finnerty. An ex-British soldier was the first drill sergeant but Hubert Hanrahan came across some drill books and took over the drilling. There were parade nights twice weekly. The company was well represented at all the Irish Volunteer meetings in the county usually held in Athenry. Liam Mellows was in the area a lot recruiting and organising drilling and often stayed over in Garvey's. The company played almost no role in the 1916 Rising as they were removed from the main action in Galway. They stood ready waiting for orders but by the time the rising was over they had not been called into action. [91]

---

90   Fergus Campbell *'Land and Revolution Nationalist Policies in the West of 1891 – 1921'* p194. Oxford University Press.

91   W/S 1,062 Laurence Haverty.

Newcastle

This was an active company with over 30 members. Michael Kelly was the captain. They were very involved in the Easter Rising, mobilised and were at the Agricultural College, Moyode and Lime Park.

Oranmore

Joe Howley was captain of this very active company. They had a large group of members. They took a full part in all training and drilling in advance of the rebellion and with the Maree Company made unsuccessful attacks on the Oranmore R.I.C. barracks on Tuesday morning and afternoon.

Rockfield

In June 1914 the Irish Volunteers started a company in Rockfield. It was originally started by Sinn Fein members in the area. Johnny Naughton was the drill sergeant. The first captain was Morgan Healy. However, Tom Kenny of nearby Craughwell felt he was unsuitable as he was not in the I.R.B. A meeting of the Craughwell 'circle' was called and it was decided the I.R.B. man Gilbert Morrissey should be captain. This was duly arranged. There were about 40 men in the company at the time. The company sided with Mc Neill following the split and took part in the review of Volunteers in Athenry in June 1914 when Colonel Maurice Moore and The O'Rahilly attended. Company parades for drilling were generally held twice weekly. [92]

Spiddal

This company was formed in early summer 1914. The officers were the local I.R.B. officers. Michael Ó Droighneain was heavily involved. Padraig Pearse conducted the first drill session for the company through Irish. Willie Pearse was also in attendance. A photograph of the new company was taken on the day but has not survived.

---

[92] W/S 874 Gilbert Morrissey.

The Gaelic Athletic Association

The G.A.A. was founded in Thurles in 1884 principally by Michael Cusack. Initially he proposed to found it in Loughrea with the help of the then Bishop of Clonfert Patrick Duggan. However, he was in poor health and he suggested to Cusack and his supporters that they approach Archbishop Croke of Thurles, which they did a year later. However, this shows the strength of Gaelic games in the county that it was in Galway that the founding of an organisation to promote this revival was being proposed.

When the G.A.A. began to function its principles were immediately adhered to throughout the county. Hurling was particularly popular especially in the mid and southern areas. This covered from Athenry south to the Clare boarder and across to the Shannon. The inaugural All Ireland hurling final featured Meelick, from the banks of the Shannon, as Galway champions against Thurles Sarsfields. This game was played in Birr in November 1887 with the Tipperary side winning by 1-1 to 0-0.

In its early days the G.A.A. had many problems and it nearly died out within the first ten years. As early as 1886 the I.R.B. sought to take control of the organisation as they saw in it an opportunity to gain control over the minds and hearts of many young athletes. They arranged a takeover of the national committee at the 1887 National Convention. They were vigorously opposed and another Convention in early 1888 restored the old order. The I.R.B. no longer controlled the organisation but they had an association with it and managed to do a lot of recruiting from among its players and officials.

In 1890 with the Parnellite split over his affair with Kitty O'Shea the G.A.A. split for or against Parnell. Though over 2,000 G.A.A. members marched at his funeral it seriously divided the organisation. Resulting from these setbacks the G.A.A. which boasted of over 1,000 affiliated clubs in 1888 had only 220 in 1892. In 1891 only six counties attended annual convention and only three in 1893.[93]   However, the movement did survive and though there was some I.R.B. interference it became G.A.A. policy that sport and politics were to be separate. This did not apply to British forces as the army and R.I.C. were banned from becoming members in 1905. At the time this made sense as many in the G.A.A. were I.R.B. members and it would be easy for the British authorities to know their business if they were in the G.A.A. together. The G.A.A. saw itself as a national cultural organisation but when it came to a choice between the British authorities and the I.R.B. there was only one winner. The revival of the G.A.A. continued in the early 1900's and by 1909 twenty five counties attended annual convention and the I.R.B. were no longer influential top figures.

The G.A.A. in Galway.

Playing Gaelic games was seen by many as a defiance of the British way of life. These were truly Irish games and very much part of the Gaelic Revival. The promotion of Gaelic games, hurling and football, soon developed along parish lines. In many areas a parish covered a large area so teams were based on church areas within a parish. Athenry was a large parish and having one centralised team would have meant a lot of travel in days when players would have to cycle too far for training. Therefore, there were teams in Newcastle, Athenry, Derrydonnell, Moyville, Cussane and Coldwood. This was duplicated in most parishes in the county.

The first County Convention was on October 24th 1886 in Athenry and local man Patrick Kelly became the first Chairman. In 1887 there were over 30 clubs represented at county convention.

The association had many difficulties in the early years with various splits. The first one was in Athenry where there were two clubs, since 1885. One organised by Patrick Kelly was objected to as it was claimed he was a 'land grabber.' The

93   M.E. Collins, *'Movements for Reform,'* p125 Edco.

National League set up a rival hurling club and it was not until 1888 that the split was resolved. No sooner was that resolved than the Parnell divorce case initiated another split, pro or anti Parnell. Much of Galway was anti-Parnell though 500 G.A.A. members from Galway attended his funeral. Again, this split seriously affected the organisation.

At this time in Galway there were Senior and Junior grades for hurling and football. Championships were played on a knockout basis and drew large crowds. Matches were regularly held at Athenry as trains could bring some of the teams. This added to the crowds and often up to 5,000 could be reported at a match. Tournaments were regularly played and one organised in Athenry in 1886 had 14 teams of 21-a-side involved. Tournaments often saw the teams led onto the pitch by local bands. They were widely reported on in local newspapers and often had a carnival type atmosphere associated with them.

The leading hurling teams at the turn of the century were Athenry, Ardrahan, Gort, Turloughmore, Oranmore, Newcastle, Peterswell, Castlegar, Craughwell, Clarinbridge, Kiltullagh and Kilconiron. Football's leading sides were Tuam Stars, Athenry de Wetts, Ballinasloe, Dunmore, Galway Sarsfields and Loughrea. Thus, you can already see a division within the county of the hurling and football areas as they are to this day.

Affiliations to the county committee often continued to be fractious and local disputes and objections to teams and players were common. There were two football teams in Tuam for a while Tuam Stars and Tuam Krugers and in Athenry you had the de Wetts and Geraldines in 1909.

In 1912 there were two county boards operating and a special convention was held in Loughrea to end yet another split. Larry Lardiner was elected County Secretary and the split was ended. As the decade ended Stephen Jordan was County Secretary in 1918, 1919 and 1920.

Therefore, it can be clearly seen that the leading G.A.A. officials in Galway were also leading members of the I.R.B. and would be the leading members of the Irish Volunteers when they were started in the county from 1914 on. One might wonder how they had the time for all these activities. However, they often had a few meetings the same night as it was mainly the same people that were involved. So when the Irish Volunteers began in Athenry it was Jordan, Lardiner, Dick Murphy and John Broderick who were involved, the I.R.B. and G.A.A. men. Again this was replicated throughout the county. Amazingly these men were also representatives to regional groups, Jordan and Lardiner as county G.A.A. delegates to Dublin and Murphy to the I.R.B. Connaught Council. The crossover between the three organisations was often blurred and this gave the members a sense of purpose that they were serving Ireland in a political, cultural and military sense.

The importance to the I.R.B. of capturing the hearts and minds of the youthful athletes of the county can be clearly seen even if the mix of politics and sport was not overtly displayed. If you look at the clubs who won County Senior Hurling Championships between 1887 and 1916 you can clearly see that they were mainly areas that were supportive of the I.R.B., and the Irish Volunteers. This shows that all three organisations tied neatly together in mid and south Galway.

County Senior Hurling Champions 1887 – 1916.[94]
Peterswell: 1889, 1898, 1899, 1900, 1904, 1905 and 1907.
Ardrahan: 1894, 1895, 1896, 1901, 1902, 1903 and 1910.
College Road, Galway City: 1892 and 1893.
Kilconiron: 1908 and 1912.
Craughwell: 1909 and 1915.
Gort: 1914 and 1916.
Meelick: 1887.   **Killimor:** 1897   **Mullagh:** 1906.
Derrydonnell: 1911 **Woodford:** 1913. **None:** 1888, 1890, 1891.

---

94 www.galwaygaa.ie/index/en/club-hurling-list

County Galway M.P.'s[95]

Following the passing of the Act of Union in1801 the Irish Parliament was joined with the British Parliament. Irish M.P.'s had to go to the British Houses of Commons and Lords in London. This arrangement lasted until 1918 when following the General Election after World War 1 most of the M.P.'s elected for Ireland refused to attend. The Sinn Fein Party succeeded in getting 73 candidates elected and they opted to set up Dail Eireann rather than attend Westminster.

In those years from 1801 to 1918 Galway had a chequered history of M.P.'s representing the county. The county was continually represented by two M.P.'s up to 1874. From 1885 to 1918 it elected four M.P.'s as follows, one each from North Galway, South Galway, East Galway and Connemara. The city or Galway Borough, as it was called, varied between one and two. Between 1801 and 1831 it was one, between 1832 and 1880 it was two and it reverted to one between 1885 and 1918. Up to 1885 the city had 22 elections and the county had 17, the difference due to various by-elections in the City Borough.

Some of the well known M.P.'s who represented Galway City before 1885 included, Lord Dunsandle, Lord Dunkellin and the Home Rulers Frank Hugh O'Donnell, Michael Francis Ward and T.P. O'Connor. The county had a myriad of colourful characters many of whom were not always that popular. Among them were Colonel Richard Martin, known as 'Humanity Dick' for his work against cruelty to animals. There was William Henry Gregory, of the 'Gregory Clause', associated with Famine Relief in 1847. He represented the county for 15 years and was married to Lady Gregory who was associated with the Irish Literary Revival and William Butler Yeats. James Daly, Lord Dunsandle, also represented the county for 21 years.

From 1885 on there were fewer M.P.'s of the landlord

---

95 'Parliamentary Election Results in Ireland 1801 – 1922.' Edited by B.M. Walker Royal Irish Acadamy.

tradition as nearly all within the City Borough and the County were Irish Parliamentary Party representatives. In the General Elections of 1885 and 1886 the I.P.P. succeeded in returning highs of 85 seats out of 105 on offer in Ireland. At this stage there were five M.P.'s for the county. Most of these were long serving and elected unopposed. In Connemara Patrick James Foley served from 1885 to 1895 winning two elections unopposed. He did fight the 1892 election and defeated a pro-Parnell candidate John Henry Joyce taking 81% of the vote. He was followed by William O'Malley who won five elections unopposed before he was unseated in 1918 by Padraic O'Máille, Sinn Fein, who took 77% of the vote. In South Galway David Sheehy held the seat for the Irish Parliamentary Party from 1885 to 1900 unopposed save for the 1892 election. In that he defeated the pro-Parnell John P. Mc Carthy taking 65% of the vote. Thereafter, William Duffy represented the constituency unopposed until he lost to Frank Fahy of Sinn Fein in 1918 polling just 14% of the turnout. In East Galway there were three M.P.'s over the 1885 to 1910 period. The Irish Nationalist Matthew Harris was followed by the anti-Parnell M.P. John Roche until he died in 1914. He was returned unopposed for most elections. When he died he was succeeded by James Cosgrave who was elected unopposed. In North Galway there were a number of contested elections. John Philip Nolan was one of just nine pro-Parnell M.P.'s in the country. Again, it shows how Galway was in many ways decidedly at odds with much of the country and many local factors continually came to the fore when looking at national issues affecting the county. He (Nolan) was briefly replaced by Denis Kilbride an anti-Parnell M.P. in 1895 but he was returned in 1900 unopposed. By that election the Parnellite split had been united under John Redmond. He was opposed by Thomas Higgins in the 1906 election but Higgins died the night of the election and was elected posthumously the next day. A few weeks later the Irish Parliamentary Party nominated Richard Hazelton as the candidate for the by-election and he was returned unopposed. He remained in the seat until 1918 when

Rebellion in Galway

Bryan Cusack was elected unopposed for Sinn Fein. On May 24th 1914 Hazelton had resigned his seat due to ill-health and on financial grounds but he was re-elected on July 21st unopposed and was therefore reinstated as M.P. after 28 days.

Therefore, it is safe to say that the power of the landlords had been broken in County Galway following the advent of the Home Rule Party (I.P.P.). The power of Charles Stewart Parnell and his political machine ensured that the M.P.'s for the county were firmly nationalist in outlook and that the interests of the Irish tenant farmer were well represented in Westminster. It was this calibre of politician that was to ensure that the issues of tenant reform and Home Rule were put firmly on the agenda in the House of Commons if not the Lords.

The Galway Borough seat was far more interesting. Between 1885 and December 1910 there were 11 elections including three by-elections. Galway M.P.'s included T.P. O'Connor, in 1885, a Home Rule M.P., though he was from Athlone. He was followed in the 1886 General Election by Captain William O'Shea, with whose wife Parnell had an affair. O'Shea used the Kitty O'Shea - Parnell situation to get on the ticket though and he never joined the Home Rule Party. He was followed in a by-election in 1886 by John Pinkerton, a Protestant tenant farmer from Antrim and a Home Rule candidate. He was returned again in 1892 and 1895 and was an anti-Parnell M.P. The Hon. Martin Morris, a Conservative, succeeded in out-voting the I.P.P. candidate Edmund Leamy by 117 votes in the 1900 election but he forfeited his seat the following year. This saw Arthur Alfred Lynch from Australia elected for the I.P.P. while away in France. However, he was tried for treason for anti-British activities in the Boer War and had to forfeit his seat in 1903 when found guilty (He was later pardoned). This opened the way for Charles Ramsay Devlin, a former Canadian M.P., to take the seat unopposed for the I.P.P. However, he returned to Canada in 1906 and once again there was an election. This time Stephen Gwynn won the by-election and held the seat until 1918 for the I.P.P. There was no Galway Borough seat in the 1918 election and following the setting up of the Irish Free State Galway County became a seven seat constituency from 1912 to 1922 and the a nine seat constituency from 1922 to 1937.

Thus, it can be seen that Galway City was completely different from County Galway when it came to elections. Martin Morris was the only native of the county to be elected from seven M.P.'s between 1885 and 1910 over 11 elections. Galway was seen as a borough where the I.P.P. often attempted to elect candidates purely by association with the party though they were not native to the county. But this strategy often failed to work as William O'Shea and Martin Morris proved. In addition, the short tenures of Devlin and Lynch were of little use to them. This succession of candidates that meant little or nothing to the city can in part be seen as a reason why it was very much a British city with little interest in national issues. Thus, the urban rural divide on political lines was rather wide and in the lead up to the 1916 Rising. There was little sympathy in the city for the land issue concerns of the rural poor and, likewise, the rural dwellers paid little interest to the unemployment concerns of the urban poor that made them join the British army.

Athenry De Wetts, Co. Senior Football Champions 1906.[96]
Front Left to Right: Mike Duffy and Leo Mahon. *Sitting Left to Right:* **Partick Kennedy, Dick Murphy,** Ned Kennedy, A.N. Other, **Charlie Whyte, Larry Lardner, and Stephen Jordan.** *Standing Left to Right:* Michael O'Malley, Jim Connor, Dick Walsh, Jack Reilly, **Martin Hynes,** Joe Kelly, Michael Shaughnessy, Paddy Fallon and Ned Ryder.
(Names in bold are known to have partaken in the Rising)

Galway, Connaught Senior Football Champions 1913.[97]
(Includes **Stephen Jordan** (Front right) and **Charlie Whyte**, Athenry).

---

96 St. Mary's G.A.A. Athenry www.athenrygaa.ie/en/club-history.html

97 St. Mary's G.A.A. Athenry www.athenrygaa.ie/en/club-history.html

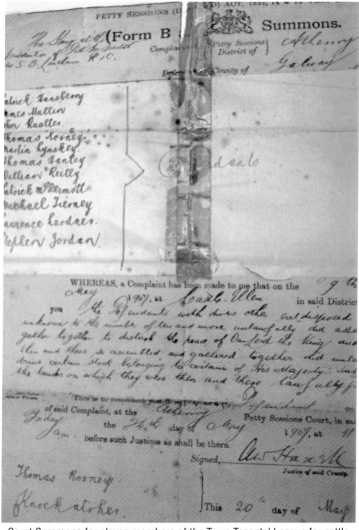

Court Summons for eleven members of the Town Tenants' League for cattle driving at Castle Ellen, Athenry in 1907.The names are, Patrick, Hansberry, James Mallin, John Qualter, Thomas Rooney, Martin Lynskey, Thomas Hanley, William Reilly, Patrick Mc Dermott, Michael Tierney, Laurence Lardner and Stephen Jordan. The last three were active in the 1916 Rising.
(Courtesy of John Jordan)

The Derrydonnell Senior Hurling County Champions 1911.
(Courtesy of the Galway GAA website).
Sitting Left to Right: Pat Heneghan and Jack Costello.
Kneeling Left to Right: **Martin Ruane, Tom Mullins,** Pat Keane (Captain),
Mike Keane, Martin Costello, Mike Freaney, and **Peter Heneghan**. ***Standing
Left to Right:*** Martin Kennedy, Mick Fahy, Mike Joyce, Andy Keane, Martin
Joyce, **Richard Higgins,** Jack Ruane and **William Higgins**.
(Bold names are known to have partaken in the Rising)

Stephen Jordan's football medals (Courtesy of John Jordan).
Left to right; Co. Championship 1906, Connacht Championships 1911/13
and 1917

Moyode Castle after which the Persse Mansion was called.

Situated near Tallyho Cross four miles east of Athenry on the Athenry Loughrea road.

Moyode Castle, Persse Mansion, Moyode, Athenry.
(Courtesy of the Connacht Tribune)

Ruins of Moyode Mansion today.

Ruins of the Bell Tower,
Moyode Mansion.

Fr. Tom Fahy, Esker,
administered to the
rebels during the rising.
(Courtesy of Declan Monaghan)

Committee - Athenry Volunteers 1914
Front Row: Pat Hynes, Joseph Rooney, John Broderick Snr. Jim Barrett, Thomas Cleary. ***Back Row:*** Frank Hynes, Stephen Jordan, Dick Murphy, Sean Broderick, Larry Lardner.
(Courtesy of St. Mary's Athenry G.A.A. website)

Tom Kenny, the blacksmith from Craughwell and prominent I.R.B. member.

Liam Mellows, the leader of the 1916 Rising in Galway.

(Courtesy of the Connacht Tribune)

The Irish Volunteers rally in Athenry June 29th 1914. They assembled on 'The Back Lawn' now the site of Kenny Park G.A.A. grounds.
This was before the split dividing the movement into the Irish Volunteers and the National Volunteers.
Estimates for the attendance range from 2,500 to 3,000.
The salute was taken by Colonel Maurice Moore of the Irish Volunteers.
The Athenry Company are said to be at the front.
(Courtesy of Councillor Gabe Cronnelly, Attymon)

Old Church Street, Athenry, in the early 1900's.
(Courtesy of Brian Quinn)

A group of Athenry Royal Irish Constabulary pictured in the back yard of their
barracks on Cross Street in 1915.
(Courtesy of Brian Quinn)

The Agricultural College, Athenry where Mellows and his forces camped
on Tuesday April 25th and there was an exchange of fire with the R.I.C on
Wednesday April 26th.
(Courtesy of Brian Quinn)

Irish Volunteers' Training Camp, Coosan, Athlone September 1915.
Back Row (left to right): Peadar Melinn (Athlone), Dick Fitzgerald (Kerry), J.J.
Burke (Dublin), J.J. 'Ginger' O'Connell (Sligo), Paul Galigan (Cavan), Larry
Lardner (Athenry), Terence Mc Swiney (Cork) and Sean Kearns (Kerry).
Front Row (left to right): Mick Spillane (Killarney), J. Morley
(Ballaghaderreen), Michael O'Buachalla (Maynooth), Billy Mullins (Tralee),
Mick Cremin (Cork) John Brennan (Roscommon) and
Mick Allis (Limerick).
(Courtesy of Councillor Gabe Cronnelly, Attymon)

(L-R) Frank Hynes, Michael Quinn and Stephen Jordan, G.A.A., I.R.B., Town Tenants' League and Irish Volunteer members. (Courtesy of Brian Quinn, Athenry)

Alf Monaghan, Second-in-command to Liam Mellows during the Galway rebellion. (Courtsy of the Connacht Tribune)

AILBHE O MONACHAIN

The memorial in Kileeneen, Craughwell from where Liam Mellows and his followers set out to attack Clarenbridge R.I.C. barracks on Tuesday morning April 23rd 1916.

IN MEMORY OF
LIAM MELLOWS
AND HIS COMRADES
WHO SET OUT FROM HERE
TO FIGHT FOR IRISH FREEDOM
EASTER WEEK 1916

The inscription on the Killeeneen memorial.

The first Killeeneen N.S. was established here.
Mr Hubert Walsh, Rosmuc, and his wife Mary Kate,
were appointed as teachers in 1885.
Hubert Walsh was a champion of the Irish language
and advances in education.
He was an ardent Nationalist.

Bunaíodh an Scoil i gCillinin sa suíomh seo.
'Sé Aodh Bhreathnach agus a bhean Máire Cáit
a ceapadh mar mhuinteoiri i 1885.
D'oibrigh Aodh go dian
diograsach ar son na Gaeilge agus dul chun
cinn an oideachais. Náisiunai den scoth a bhi ann.

Plaque erected in Kileeneen near Craughwell to mark the site of the Kileeneen National School.

Former R.I.C. Barracks, Cross Street, Athenry.

Some of the weapons used in 1916.

Rebel singleshot German Mauser rifle.

R.I.C. Lee Enfield magazine fed rifle

R.I.C. Webley revolver

Rebel pike head

Rebel single and double barrelled shotguns.

Former R.I.C. barracks Clarenbridge.

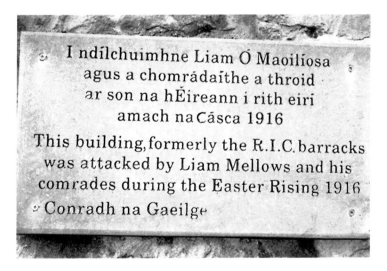

I ndílchuimhne Liam Ó Maoilíosa
agus a chomrádaíthe a throid
ar son na hÉireann i rith eirí
amach na Cásca 1916

This building, formerly the R.I.C. barracks
was attacked by Liam Mellows and his
comrades during the Easter Rising 1916

Conradh na Gaeilge

Inscription on the former R.I.C. barracks Clarenbridge.

Carnmore Cross where Con. Patrick Whelan was killed.

HMS Gloucester which arrived in Galway Bay.

HMS Laburnum which fired nine shells inland to Castlegar.

Ward's Pub Kiltullagh from where the Moyode rebels got provisions.

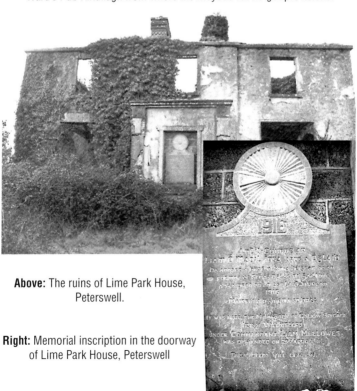

Above: The ruins of Lime Park House, Peterswell.

Right: Memorial inscription in the doorway of Lime Park House, Peterswell

Irish Volunteer prisoners, now the Irish Republican Army (I.R.A.) in
Wormwood Scrubs prison in May 1920 while on hunger strike. Larry Lardner
is seated in the second row on the extreme right.
(Courtesy of Councillor Gabe Cronnelly Attymon, Athenry)

Mellows Agricultural College, Athenry.
Site of one of the engagements with the R.I.C. in 1916.

Galway Senior Hurling Champions 1923.
Richard 'Dick' Morrissey (Rockfield) Third Row fifth from left.
Tom Kenny (Trainer, Fourth Row extreme right)
(Courtesy of Galway GAA website)

Stephen Jordan
Athenry
1916 veteran and former T.D

Mattie Neilan
Kilcolgan
1916 veteran and former T.D [98]

98   Oranmore and Athenry in 1916 Individual Accounts Irish Volunteers 1913 - 1923 By Eamon Murphy.

Statue of Liam Mellows
Leader of the Galway Rising
Eyre Square, Galway.

Statue of Joe Howley
Leader of the Oranmore Volunteers
Oranmore, Galway.

The Republican monument
in Castlegar.

Statue of Liam Mellows
1916 Rememberance Garden,
Athenry.

Stephen Jordan's service medals (Courtesy of John Jordan)
1916 and 50th Anniversary medals (left) and War of Independence and 50th
Anniversary medals (right)

Mike Athy, captain of the
Maree Irish Volunteers.

Pat 'The Hare' Callanan, of the
Clarenbridge Irish Volunteers.

(Courtesy of the Connacht Tribune)

Unveiling of the bust of Liam Mellows outside the Boys' National School in Athenry 1966.
Front Row (left to right): Miss Bridget Clasby, Mrs. Kathleen Cleary-Kennedy, Mrs. N Morrissey-Ruane, Ailbhe O Monachain, Mr. Jim Barrett, Mrs. Mary Mc Namara, Mrs Bridget Lardiner, Mrs. O Monachain.
Second Row (left to right): Stephen Jordan, James Cleary, Fr. J. Corbett, C.C. Athy, Brendan Holland, Mayor of Galway, Mrs. Una Hynes, Mrs. O Murchu, Donal O Murchu, A.N.C.A., Frank Hynes, Monsignor Thomas Fahy, Miss O Monachain, Fr. T. Hynes, and Donal Kennedy N.T. Athenry.
(Courtesy of the Connacht Tribune)

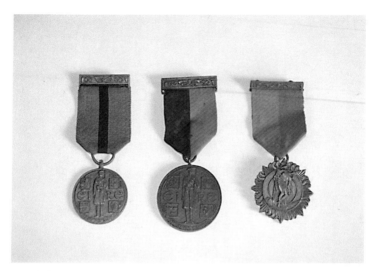

Left to right: War of Independence 50th Anniversary medal, War of
Independence medal and Cumann na mBan medal.
(Courtesy of Councillor Gabe Cronnelly, Attymon)

Cumann na mBan and Irish Volunteer veterans at the unveiling of the
Killeeneen monument near Craughwell, Co Galway in 1965.
(Courtesy of the Connacht Tribune)

Larry Lardner, Athenry.
Galway Brigade O/C.

R.I.C. Constable
Patrick Whelan

Brian Rohan,
Newcastle.

Gilbert Morrissey,
Craughwell.

Fr.Henry Feeney,
Curate Clarinbridge.

Jack Waldron,
Athenry.

Thomas Coen,
Cussaun.

Eamonn Corbett,
Craughwell.

Tom Ruane,
Claregalway.

Martin Rooney,
Craughwell.

John Rooney,
Craughwell.

Brian Molloy,
Castlegar.

All photos pp 146-148 courtesy of Relatives and Friends of Athenry 1916 - Brian Quinn

Frongoch Internment Camp, Wales.
(Courtesy of Relatives and Friends of Athenry 1916)

Castle Ellen, near Athenry, subject of
many land division disputes.
(Courtesy of Dominic Monaghan)

John J Kennedy,
Rockfield, Athenry.
(Courtesy of Brian Quinn)

Richard 'Dick' Murphy,
Athenry.
(Courtesy of Brian Quinn)

R.I.C. Constables, pictured outside
Oranmore Barracks, Galway.
(Courtesy of Paul Browne)

Liam Mellows' motorbike,
Renmore Barracks, Galway.
(Courtesy of Relatives and Friends of Athenry 1916)

Bishop Thomas Gilmartin
Bishop of Clonfert 1909-1918
(Courtesy of Tuam Diocesian office)

Pádraig Ó Fathaigh (Fahy),
Gort.
(Courtesy of Finian Ó Fathaigh)

The 1916 Easter Rising in Galway

1900

Queen Victoria paid a royal visit to Dublin from the 4th to the 25th of April. There was strong opposition to the visit in Galway.

1901

There was a census for the whole country on March 31st. The collection of all data was conducted by the R.I.C. Galway proved to being a particularly poor county with a lot of emigration. Land issues and the division of large estates among local tenants was a continual topic.

1902

According to Laurence Garvey in his witness statement farmers of Mullagh in east Galway, some four miles east of Loughrea, were extremely poor. A day's pay was 8d (pence) while rent was £2 a year per acre (there were 240d per £1). So this equated to two months wages just to pay rent for one acre of land. At one stage his father and uncle went to save the crops of an evicted woman and for this they were arrested and tried first in Carrick-on-Shannon and then in Wicklow. His father got six months in Tullamore jail for his troubles. [99]

Lord Ashtown who owned a large estate in Woodlawn evicted many of his tenants and was condemned by the Loughrea Rural District Council.

> '... in evicting his Catholic herds and workmen
> and replacing them by Orange Scotchmen .....
> .... his Lordship can find no fault to his employees
> except their religion.' [100]

---

99 W/S 1,062 Laurence Garvey.

100 Galway County Council Archives, Loughrea Rural District Council Archives Collection GOI/8/2, p421.

THE 1916 EASTER RISING IN GALWAY

On Sunday May 4th eight men were drowned of Tawin near Oranmore while fishing. Life was hard for the fishing community and such incidents were common occurrences.

1903

King Edward V11 of England visited Ireland in July and having landed in Killary Harbour between Galway and Mayo toured Connemara and arrived in Galway on the train from Clifden. His party were in Galway from Wednesday July 29th to Friday 31st. He was well received in the city and it was seen as a huge boost to tourism.

1904

There was a serious food shortage in the county making it the last year of serious famine in Galway.

1905

Sinn Féin was founded by Arthur Griffith. He proposed that any elected M.P.'s should abstain from Westminster and ultimately set up a parliament in Ireland.

1906

Stephen Jordan joined the I.R.B. in Athenry. Larry Lardner was the Secretary at this time. They were an active unit and had training and drill regularly. Seán Mac Diarmada called to the unit two or three times a month.

Laurence Garvey was part of the United Irish League movement when it started a branch in Mullagh. There was a lot of agrarian trouble in the area. There was a lot of land-grabbing as tenants were evicted from holdings. The new tenants taking the farms were not popular and often had their cattle driven off. Wall knocking and boycotting were also used against these farmers known as 'landgrabbers'

Stephen Gwynn was elected, in a by-election, as a Home

Rule M.P. for Galway becoming one of Redmond's greatest supporters.

The county continued to lose large numbers of young people to emigration as thousands went to Britain and the United States of America. The passage of most was paid for by brothers or sisters or other relatives already living there.

Indicative of the continuing land holding problems Charles O'Farrell of Dalystown Leitrim, Loughrea held 500 acres of untenanted land.[101] Such incidents caused great tension between landholders and ordinary tenant farmers who struggled to make a living.

1907

There was an I.R.B. 'circle' started in Castlegar and up to 30 men joined. Dick Murphy from Athenry was the 'centre' for County Galway at the time and he swore in Brian Molloy and others. The R.I.C. always questioned Molloy when any incidents such as driving off cattle or knocking walls happened.[102]

1908

There was a Town Tenants' League in Athenry and most of the young men joined it. Through various methods of agitation they succeeded in getting a considerable amount of land redistributed. These included wall knocking, boycotting, threatening landlords and land-grabbers. As the R.I.C. were generally unable to apprehend those who committed these acts so they took their revenge through other means. They constantly hounded those they suspected of these acts and arrested them at every opportunity for anything they could make stick. Thus suspects were arrested for drunkenness and other seemingly trivial matters.

Much of the industrial base in the county was badly

101 landed estates.nuigalway.ie
102 W/S 345 Brian Molloy.

affected by the importation of foreign goods by railway and the closure of Persse's distillery in the city was another blow to employment.

University College Galway was opened offering third level education to a small number of wealthy students.

1909

The Old Age Pension Act was passed in 1908 and people over 70 years of age were to get 5 shillings a week pension starting on New Year's Day 1909. This would be of huge benefit to many families in the county. By 1910 over 180,000 people in Ireland got the pension. It was means-tested and to get the full amount you had to earn less than £21 a year. The pension was paid on a reducing scale to no pension if you earned above £31-10 shillings a year. Uptake in Ireland was over 98% showing the poverty of the people. While not a huge sum it must be seen as against the average labourer's wage of 10 shillings a week. The pension was paid on a Friday through the Post Office. Of course there were numerous people who had aged considerably more than nine years since the 1901 Census so as to get the pension or be in line to claim it as soon as possible.

In January of this year Constable Martin Mc Goldrick was shot in Craughwell as he provided security for bailiffs who were rebuilding knocked walls on the farm of Mrs. Ryan. She got a farm that many locals thought should have been divided among small farmers to give them a liveable holding. The I.R.B. were blamed for the murder. Two men were arrested but no convictions were secured.

Land agitation continued in Galway and the R.I.C. numbers were increased. In areas where tension was high huts were built to accommodate additional police. The Fenians were spreading in great numbers around the county as land issues were to the fore in most areas.

'By May 1909, the secret society had been
established at Athenry, Bullaun, Craughwell,
Gurteen, Gurtymadden, Kilchreest, Kiltullagh,
Loughrea, Monivea, Moyvilla, New Inn, and
Peterswell in east riding, and at Ardrahan,
Gort, Kilcolgan and Oranmore in west riding.' [103]

1910

In May there was the attempted murder of Martin Conroy in the
Castlegar area. He was seen as a land-grabber. I.R.B. members
were behind the shooting.

1911

There was a nationwide census in this year taken on Sunday
April 2nd. The R.I.C. were in charge of collecting the data. The
population of the county had fallen by 5% since the last census
down to 182,224. Ballinasloe was the only area, rural or urban
to record a rise in population.[104]

A branch of the Irish Women's Suffrage League was
founded in Galway following a visit to the city by Christabel
Pankhurst.

The seriousness of the land situation can be clearly seen as
Galway was still one of the few proscribed counties (a form of
martial law was in force) in the country. Also, it was reported in
parliament that 30% of all 'boycotting' incidents in the country
occurred in Galway.[105]

1912

The local I.R.B. men in Athenry were constantly trying to
disrupt and antagonise the R.I.C. just as much as the R.I.C. were
<u>trying to exert their authority.</u> Thus the R.I.C. horse was taken

103 Fergus Campbell, 'Land and Revolution Nationalist Politics in the West of Ireland 1891 – 192.' p 188 Oxford.

104 www.census.nationalarchives.ie/exhibition/galway

105 www.census.nationalarchives.ie/exhibition/galway

for three weeks before it was left back unharmed. The tricolour was flown from the barracks chimney and the crown over the barracks door was removed and hung from telegraph wire with a £5 reward sign hung with it. Tom Cleary was the I.R.B. man mainly responsible for organising these events. Stephen Jordan in his witness statement relates these stories. These relatively minor acts of attrition between the locals and the R.I.C. added to the tension in the Athenry area and it was one of the most policed areas in the county. [106]

1913

In March the British Atlantic fleet visited Galway Bay and docked off Galway City. As a result many young men in the city joined the navy over the next year.

The Gaelic League National Convention was held in Galway, the first time it was held outside Dublin. In attendance were Sean Mac Diarmada, Padraig Pearse, Eamonn Ceannt, Eamon de Valera, Doughlas Hyde, Sean T. O'Kelly, Kathleen Clarke, Thomas Ashe, Countess Markievicz, Bulmer Hobson, Eoin Mc Neill, The O'Rahilly, Willie Pearse, Cathal Bruagh, Nora Ashe, George Russell, and Padraig O Conaire. [107] Many of the events were held in the Town Hall. This shows how Galway was perceived as a cultural capital and it furthered nationalist attitudes within the county.

The I.R.B. was very active and many were sworn in to 'circles' around the county. Many I.R.B. officials like Pádraig and Willie Pearse, The O'Rahilly and Seán Mac Diarmada regularly visited the county to speak to and encourage members.

In December the Irish Volunteers organised their first branch in Galway founding a company in Galway City. Eoin Mc Neill was at the inaugural meeting.

---

106 W/S 346 Stephen Jordan.

107 tht.ie/blog/184/Historic-Photograph-Presented-to-Town-Hall-Theatre

Rebellion in Galway

1914

Early in the year a company of the Volunteers was started in Athenry and soon there were companies in other villages such as Craughwell, Newcastle, Derrydonnell, Kilconiron, Kinvarra and Clarenbridge.

In April 1914 Cumann na mBan was started as a support group for the Irish Volunteers. Very soon afterwards branches were started in Galway and a large numbers of women in the mid and south of the county became involved in nationalist activities in what they saw was a practical way.

On June 29th there was an Irish Volunteers rally in Athenry with 2,000 to 3,000 men attending. Colonel Maurice Moore, Instructor of the Irish Volunteers, took the salute at this parade.[108] This doubled as an anti-recruiting rally against the British army and as a publicity exercise for the Irish Volunteers.

In August the Brigade in Galway got twelve rifles from the Howth gun-running incident. When they arrived Larry Lardner summoned four local companies to parade with the rifles. Athenry volunteers carried them and members from Rockfield, Newcastle and Derrydonnell were there to protect them should the police intervene. The District Inspector, Head Constable two sergeants and twenty seven men from the Athenry barracks surrounded the men. Lardner had them fire off three rounds each to show their intention to parade publicly. Following discussions with the R.I.C. they were allowed parade armed as were the Ulster Volunteers in the North. From then on the Irish Volunteers in the Athenry and surrounding areas paraded publicly with rifles and shotguns. [109]

In August following the split in the Irish Volunteers the majority in the county continued to support the Eoin Mc Neill faction of the Irish Volunteers over the John Redmond

108 W/S 346 Stephen Jordan.

109 W/S 874 Gilbert Morrissey.

National Volunteers. Companies supporting Redmond were mainly confined to Galway City and to the larger towns such as Loughrea and Tuam. Craughwell, where there was already a serious split in the nationalist community, saw a strong Redmondite company in opposition to those who were followers of Tom Kenny and thus supporters of the Eoin Mc Neill faction. Most of the rural areas in the county supported the Eoin Mc Neill Irish Volunteers and saw their role as anti-British. This would be reflective of the influence of the I.R.B. in these areas and also the attitude to British authority given the long standing land issues in mid to south Galway.

Following the outbreak of World War 1 recruits flocked to the British army, mainly in the city of Galway where the Connaught Rangers was the main regiment. They had a military barracks in Renmore, on the east side of the city. By October 1914 1,623 recruits had joined through Renmore Barracks. [110]

'When the war started in August 1914 the town of Galway went recruiting mad. It was not a question of 'will you join up?', but 'what regiment are you joining?' [111]

1915

Early in the year Liam Mellows arrived to organise the Irish Volunteers in the county. He arrived at the train station in Athenry where the Irish Volunteers were turned out to meet him. He was a slight young 23 year old and many of those who greeted him doubted his ability to whip them into shape. When he addressed them he spoke of hard work and commitment. Frank Hynes relates how he then went away with Larry Lardner to arrange digs and the crack started.

---

110 William Henry, *'Galway and The Great War.'* Mercier Press p 33.

111 W/S 447 Thomas Courtney.

'I could see the faintest trace of a supercilious
smile on some of the men. When he was finished
talking Larry and himself went off to arrange digs.
Then the smiles broke out to laughing. 'Who is the
ladeen', asked one fellow, who talks to us about
hard work?' They all enjoyed the joke, but before
the first night under his command was over they
laughed no more, they loved and respected him
after that.' [112]

While he was outwardly drilling and organising the
Volunteers as a committed I.R.B. member he was to ensure that
Galway was ready for a rebellion against the British. It was
well known to Pádraig Pearse and the other leaders in Dublin
that there was a very active I.R.B. organisation in the county
and there was constant communication with Dublin through
such people as Tom Kenny, Larry Lardner and George Nicolls
ensuring that Galway would be ready to respond to any lead
offered from Dublin.

He organised the county into a Brigade and four Battalions.
Larry Lardner was appointed Brigade Commandant, Eamonn
Corbett Brigade Vice-Commandant, Mattie Neilan Brigade
Adjutant and Pat 'The Hare' Callanan was Brigade Chief of
Scouts. There were four battalions in the brigade centred on
Athenry, Galway, Gort and Loughrea. Each of these battalions
was composed of a number of companies. [113]

When he stayed in Athenry Mellows first stayed in Sean
Broderick's house and later in that of Frank Hynes. He quickly
became respected and very popular all around mid and south
Galway. He worked hard at organising the Irish Volunteers in
the area and hardly a night went by that he did not visit a

---

112 W/S 446 Frank Hynes.
113 W/S 347 Pat Callanan.

company to train and drill the members. At weekends he held route marches, manoeuvres and mock battles.

In time there was considerable tension between Liam Mellows and Tom Kenny as the latter, who was for many years the foremost republican in the county, felt pushed out by Mellows. In the summer of 1915 Mellows wished,

> '...to hold manoeuvres on the following Sunday week between the Clarenbridge, Maree, Oranmore and Derrydonnell companies. An attempt was made by Mr. Thomas Kenny, Chairman of the County Galway Board of the G.A.A. to upset our plans, by arranging a list of fixtures to be played at Oranmore on the same day.' [114]

When asked to postpone the hurling matches Kenny refused, but the manoeuvres went ahead successfully and the hurling matches fell through.

There was a large review of National Volunteers in the Phoenix Park by John Redmond but many in Galway did not go as they favoured Eoin Mc Neill's Irish Volunteers. Some in Craughwell did attend as there was a split in that area and many under the influence of Martin Hallinan still supported the Redmond ideals.

Liam Mellows was served with a deportation order but didn't leave the country. He was arrested on July 30th and he was sentenced to three months in Mountjoy jail. Seán Mc Diarmada was there at the same time. In addition Stephen Jordan of Athenry had been charged under the Defence of the Realm Act and was sentenced to six months in jail. [115]

In August there was the funeral of Jeremiah O'Donovan <u>Rossa in Glasnevin in Dublin.</u> This was a great propaganda

114 W/S 347 Pat Callanan.

115 W/S 1,062 Laurence Garvey.

exercise for the I.R.B. companies of Irish Volunteers from all around Ireland attended in a huge publicity exercise. Companies from Galway were in attendance in full uniform and regalia. Companies from Athenry, Clarenbridge, Oranmore, Castlegar and others went by train to Dublin for the occasion. Over 400 from Galway plus a band from the city attended. Larry Lardner Brigade O/C was in charge on the day. [116]

During the summer Laurence Garvey remembers being at a summer camp for the Irish Volunteers in Ballycahalan for a week. It was really a fun camp more than anything else. Liam Mellows used to play the fiddle and local girls would come in at night for dancing.

In September there was a large recruitment rally in the Town Hall in Galway for the British army. Stephen Gwynn M.P. was the main speaker. However, it was disrupted by the I.R.B. Seamus Carter and Tom Hynes cut electricity wires and M. Allen threw stink bombs into the hall. John Hosty and Michael Kavanagh acted as scouts in case the R.I.C. showed up. This seriously disrupted the recruiting rally.

Mellows was out of jail in time for the Irish Volunteers Convention on October 31st. By November he was back in Galway. There was a huge Volunteer review on November 23rd in Athenry which he attended. Joseph O'Flaherty, an old Fenian from Loughrea, was chairman. Among those who spoke were The O'Rahilly, Lawrence Grinnell, M.P., and the priests, Fr. Connolly, Fr. O'Meehan and Fr. Feeney. Thus it can be seen that the younger clergy in the mid Galway area were in support of the Eoin Mc Neill's Irish Volunteer movement rather than John Redmond's group. Over 500 attended this rally. There were companies from Gort, Ardrahan, Ballycahalan, Kinvarra, Athenry, Craughwell, Killeeneen, Clarenbridge, Derrydonnell, Castlegar, Oranmore, Maree, Kilconiron, Loughrea, Coldwood and Galway City among others. This shows the strength of the

116 W/S 1,124 Daniel Kearns.

Irish Volunteers in the mid and south Galway regions. This rally was also seen locally as an anti-recruiting demonstration to combat the numbers who were joining the British army to fight in World War 1. At this rally Mellows was presented with a motorbike to enable him to get to drilling and training sessions in areas around Athenry as easily and as quickly as possible.[117]

Brian Molloy relates, in his witness statement, that at a meeting held in Fr. Feeney's house in Clarenbridge that month that he told Molloy, Eamon Corbett and Mattie Niland that a rising had been decided but that no date was fixed as of yet.[118]

Recruitment to the British army continued unabated throughout 1915 as rallies were held all around the county to encourage men to join the war effort. The politicians, clergy, most public leaders and prominent businessmen all supported the war effort and continually strove to increase the numbers joining up.

'The campaign was relentless throughout 1915, and to ensure that the utmost pressure was brought to bear on the public, another major recruiting rally was held in Galway. The meeting was held in Eyre Square....'[119]

On the other hand members of the Irish Volunteers opposed recruitment and continually disrupted recruiting rallies.

'In June 1915 I was charged under the Defence of the Realm Act and sentenced to six months imprisonment.' [120]

also

---

117 C Desmond Greaves, *'Liam Mellows and Irish Revolution.'* p78 An Ghlór Gafa.

118 W/S 345 Brian Molloy.

119 William Henry, *'Galway and The Great War.'* p49 Mercier Press.

120 W/S 346 Stephen Jordan.

'In or about September 1915 there was a big
recruiting meeting in the Town Hall. Mr. Stephen
Gwynn M.P. and others were to address the meeting.
We were determined to break up this meeting
so we decided ...to cut the wires. We also made
stink bombs... The gas bombs were harmless
but for the smell. The hall could not be used for a
fortnight afterwards.' [121]

1916

January

Following his release from jail in Belfast Alf Monahan was
sent to help Liam Mellows organise Galway. His main area of
responsibility was west of Galway City in areas such as Spiddal,
Barna, Moycullen, etc. He also made acquaintances with many
in Galway City and in the University.

Pádraig Pearse visited Athenry to discuss plans for
the rising with Larry Lardner and Dick Murphy. He wanted
them to hold a line on the River Suck and around Ballinasloe.
Murphy was doubtful it could be achieved due to lack of arms
and ammunition but both agreed to do all they could to help
the rising.[122]

Saturday March 17th

There was a huge parade of Irish Volunteers through the streets
of Galway as a promotional exercise and also as an anti-British
army recruiting exercise. Companies from all over the county
attended. There were companies from Ardrahan, Athenry,
Ballinderreen, Ballycahalan, Cussaun, Castlegar, Claregalway,
Clarenbridge, Craughwell, Gort, Kilconiron, Killimordaly,
Kinvarra, Maree, Newcastle, Oranmore and Spiddal. There
were up to 600 Irish Volunteers on the parade as they marched

121 W/S 714 Thomas Hynes
122 W/S 347 Pat Callanan.

through the centre of the city. However, they did not get a good reception from the townspeople where the Irish Volunteer, not to mention the I.R.B., were not very popular. There were huge number of local men serving with the British army in World War 1 their wives, girlfriends and families were less than happy to see nationalists displaying what was in effect anti-British sentiments in a public parade.

> 'At the parade held in Galway City on St. Patrick's Day,
> 1916, we received a very rough reception from the
> wives and dependents of British soldiers'.[123]

and

> 'The object of the march or military parade
> through Galway was anti-recruiting for the
> British army and perhaps a rehearsal for
> Easter week. It must have been an
> order from headquarters. Galway had no
> company of Irish Volunteers at the time.' [124]

There were R.I.C. constables from all over the county present taking note of who marched from their area and how they were armed. This information was a guide as to whom the authorities should be watching. It would also be used in the aftermath of the rising to arrest men suspected of involvement during the week. St. Patrick's Day, being a Saturday, suited a large turnout as they would have been off work.

Monday March 27th
Sometime this week word came to Galway that shortly arms would be made available for collection. People from all

123 W/S 344 John Broderick.
124 W/S 1,564 Michael Kelly.

companies were to be ready at short notice to go to the Clare-Galway border to collect them. There were no more details than that given, no doubt for security reasons. From this the members of the company knew that there would be a rebellion of some sort within a short time. It didn't deter any from giving up their involvement with the volunteers. However, they didn't hear anything concrete after that in relation to the arms and were left wondering where and when they would land.

Saturday April 2nd
Liam Mellows was deported to England in relation to his activities in the west. He was sent to Leek in Staffordshire, between Manchester and Stoke-on-Trent. He was to stay with the Morgan family who were relatives of his. As soon as he was deported arrangements were made to get him back to Ireland as the date for the Rising was set for Sunday April 23rd. Nora Connolly, daughter of James Connolly and Barney Mellows, his brother, were to go to England to rescue him. They went via Belfast, Glasgow, Manchester and Birmingham. When they got to Leek Barney changed places with his brother and Liam made the return journey with Nora Connolly. They went back to Glasgow where a priest Fr. Courtney gave him clerical clothes. From there they went to Belfast and stayed in Connolly's house in Glenalina Terrace. Denis Mc Cullough arranged transport to Dublin. [125]

Monday April 17th.
On this day Eamon Corbett, Galway Brigade Vice O/C, travelled from Galway to Dublin to discuss plans for the Rising with the leaders in Dublin. At this stage the I.R.B. military council had all their plans in place though as of yet Mc Neill was not on board.

---

125 C Desmond Greaves, *'Liam Mellows and the Irish Revolution.'* pp 81-84 An Ghlor Gafa.

The 1916 Easter Rising in Galway

Tuesday April 18th

Liam Mellows met Pádraig Pearse to discuss plans for the rising in Galway. They were to keep the British forces occupied for as long as possible in the west. This would stop them from sending reinforcements to suppress Dublin and would ensure that barracks in Athlone and maybe the Curragh would be distracted and give Dublin a better chance of success. This meant attacking R.I.C. barracks around Galway and so setting up diversions. Galway was poorly armed and had not got many of the arms landed in Howth and Kilcoole. However, the arms due in at Banna Strand were targeted for the west. They were to be brought by rail through Kerry and Limerick and on to Galway. They were to be distributed from Gort in south Galway. This would arm all of mid and south Galway. The next objective was to hold Galway as long as possible and proceed to Portumna and hold a line along the rivers Suck and the Shannon keeping pressure off Dublin for as long as possible.[126]

Eamonn Corbett, from Killeeneen, Craughwell was in Dublin to meet with Pearse to finalise the plans for the Rising and returned home to Galway late that night. [127]

Wednesday April 19th.

The 'Castle Document' appeared in Dublin newspapers naming leading Irish Volunteers, among others, to be arrested. This resulted in Eoin Mc Neill being persuaded to issue orders for a rebellion.

Liam Mellows started his journey west on a motorbike as a pillion passenger. He went through Tyrellspass and stopped at Ballymore in Westmeath where he visited Fr. Casey, an acquaintance of his to see would he recognise him in his disguise as a priest. He then continued on and crossed the Shannon at Banagher. That night he stayed in the Diocesan College in

126 C Desmond Greaves, *'Liam Mellows and the Irish Revolution.'* pp 82-83 An Ghlor Gafa.

127 www.advertiser.ie/galway/article/68870/eamonn-corbett-and-1916

Garbally in Ballinasloe with Fr. Connolly.

Bridget Walsh was met in Limerick by her sister Gretta and she bought £10 worth of bandages in preparation for the rising. They then travelled home to Craughwell.

Thursday April 20th.

Eoin Mc Neill realised the 'Castle Document' was a forgery and issued instructions cancelling his previous order to rise. The I.R.B. leaders such as Pádraig Pearse had forged in the hopes of getting Mc Neill to support the planned rising.

Bridget Walsh and Julia Morrissey travelled to Dublin by train with dispatches for Tom Clarke and came back with a uniform to be worn by Liam Mellows. While in Dublin she heard comments that Mc Neill seemed to be against the rising at this point. [128]

Mrs. Martin Conlon travelled from Dublin, by train, with a message for Michael Thornton in Spiddal. She got a loan of a bicycle in Galway and cycled out to Spiddal. She inquired from a number of people where she might find him. Eventually she met him on the road and gave him the message. She then returned to Dublin by train. She had no doubt that this message was in relation to the rising. She does not state in her witness statement what day this message was relayed but it had to be towards the end of the week as it was instructions for the rising to go ahead. [129] There was a flurry of activity regarding messages on Thursday and it is likely that she delivered it on this day. It was only after this that Mc Neill's countermanding orders cancelled the rising.

Michael Newell states that George Nicholls arrived from Dublin on the train and got off at Oranmore station where he was met by Brian Molloy and himself. The rising was set for Sunday at 7 p.m. In line with what seems to have been

128 W/S 617 Mrs. Malone (nee Brighid Breathnach).
129 W/S 419 Mrs. Martin Conlon.

the general plan for Galway companies the Castlegar and Claregalway companies were to attack the R.I.C. barracks in their local areas.

> '...the Castlegar and Claregalway Companies were
> to join together and attack and capture the police
> hut at Lydecan, which was occupied by
> about five policemen.' [130]

Thus the plan for Castlegar and Claregalway companies was to mobilise and meet together. They were then to attack and capture the R.I.C. at Lydecan where there was a hut with five men. They were then to move on to Loughgeorge where there were nine men and then to Killeen which had nine men also. They were to take the arms and ammunition in each and take the constables prisoner. They were then to march their prisoners to Oranmore.[131] Word about the rising was to be sent to Alf Monaghan who was on the run, in the Cashla area of Athenry, since he evaded police arrest earlier in the week.[132]

Miss Margaret Browne arrived from Dublin at Athenry station with a letter for Larry Lardner.[133] He was out of town and she gave the letter to John Broderick. He gave it to Larry the next day.[134] (She was later to marry Sean Mc Entee). This letter contained word of the rising being set for Sunday at 7 p.m. The Athenry Company were to capture the local R.I.C. barracks and take the constables prisoner. As it was a large barracks it was presumed, that if successful, they would capture a large amount of guns and ammunition.

130 W/S 342 Michael Newell.

131 W/S 572 Thomas 'Sweeney' Newell.

132 W/S342 Michael Newell.

133 O'Regan's Athenry Athenry History Archive – The 1916 Rising in Athenry and Co. Galway – Finbarr O'Regan.

134 W/S 344 John Broderick.

Rebellion in Galway

According to Frank Hynes,

'...the rising was to take place at 7 p.m. on Easter Sunday. It was known only to a few of us and we made arrangements in secret.'[135]

In Athenry the Irish Volunteers decided to put on a play as a diversion and this would be a cover for their attack on the R.I.C. barracks. They felt it would be easy to capture as the police allowed them to parade with firearms and doing so on Easter Sunday would be nothing unusual.

Liam Mellows got as far as Loughrea where he stayed with an old Fenian Joseph Flaherty. He was a draper and had been one of the pall-bearers at the funeral of O'Donovan Rossa. [136]

In Killeeneen there was a meeting of as many local company leaders as could assemble in Walsh's at night and they were there up to 5 a.m. on Friday morning. Eamon Corbett, Michael Kelly (Coldwood), Michael Fleming (Clarenbridge), Peter Howley (Ardrahan) and Padraig Fahy (Ballycahalan) were among the fifteen or so that were there. They were expecting news of an arms shipment but no news arrived. [137]

There was a meeting in Hynes's mill in Gort to arrange for the Irish Volunteer manoeuvres on the coming Sunday. There were representatives from all the local companies and they were instructed as to plans for the march on Sunday. All were to go to Mass, Confession and Communion. A number of company leaders were aware at this stage that there was going to be a rebellion as Peter Howley, in his witness statement, says that Padraig Fahy told him there would be. [138]

---

135 W/S 446 Frank Hynes.
136 W/S 1,562 Martin Newell.
137 W/S 1,379 Peter Howley.
138 W/S 1,379 Peter Howley.

Friday April 21st.

That morning I.R.B. leaders visited Mc Neill and persuaded him to hold a rebellion in light of the fact that they had arranged a shipload of arms from Germany which were due to land that weekend. Thus Mc Neill again changed his mind and reissued the order to proceed with the rebellion.

Roger Casement was landed on Banna Strand in Kerry from a German submarine as he arrived in Ireland with a ship load of arms and ammunition for the rising. The Aud arrived off Banna Strand but was unable to rendezvous with local Irish Volunteers to unload the cargo of arms. The ship was noticed by a British ship, the Bluebell, and arrested. The Aud was brought to Cork Harbour with its precious cargo. As it entered the harbour it was scuttled by the captain having ensured the safety of the sailors by getting them off in life boats. The failure to land the arms and ammunition was a fatal blow to the intended rebellion as it left the whole south and west without the possibility of much needed weapons. What amount of these could have been effectively distributed to the Volunteers is a matter of conjecture as is the possible effect of them having them. They were to be distributed by rail to areas in the south in Cork and Kerry and in the west to counties Limerick, Clare and Galway.

Local Kerry leaders Austin Stack and Con Collins, who were to meet up with Casement and arrange for the distribution of the arms, were also arrested and this was a severe blow to any chances of rebellion in Kerry.

Liam Mellows stayed a second night in Loughrea with Joseph Flaherty as he made his way back to be with his men in Galway for the rebellion. [139]

Saturday April 22nd.

When Eoin Mc Neill became aware of the capture of the Aud and

[139] W/S 617 Mrs Malone (nee Brighid Breathnach).

the subsequent loss of the arms and ammunition he realised it was futile to hold a rebellion. So late that night he arranged for an advertisement to be placed in Sunday's Irish Independent newspaper cancelling all Irish Volunteer manoeuvres to be held on that day. This was a last ditch attempt to ensure that the rising would not take place. However, as it was the fourth order issued by Mc Neill within five days it caused a huge amount of confusion in all areas of the country.

A meeting was held at George Nicolls' house in College Road in Galway by the main Irish Volunteer leaders. They wanted to clarify the seemingly contradictory orders coming from Dublin. At the meeting were George Nicolls, Larry Lardner, Eamon Corbett, Nicholas Kyne, Tom Ruane, Micheál O Dríógneáin, John Hosty and Pat 'The Hare' Callanan. This was virtually the whole of the leadership of the Irish Volunteers in Galway all of whom were also I.R.B members. It was decided to send John Hosty to Dublin to see any of the I.R.B leaders and to ascertain what the situation was and to report back as soon as possible. Hosty went to Dublin that night by train. [140]

When Hosty went to Dublin he did not meet Pearse but met with Eoin Mc Neill who told him the rising was off. At this stage Mc Neill was aware that the Aud had been captured and that there would be no guns for the rising particularly in the west as was planned. Thus, he dispatched Hosty back to Galway via Tipperary and Limerick and carry the news that the rising was off. He did this by train on Saturday evening. He then returned to Galway by the Limerick, Ennis, Athenry line.

According to Thomas Hynes this meeting took place on Friday, but as he was not there and Callanan was it is more likely Callanan is right. [141]

If Hosty went on the mail train to Dublin on Saturday he could get around to Tipperary and Limerick on Sunday.

140 W/S 347 Pat Callanan.

141 W/S 714 Thomas Hynes.

Liam Mellows returned to Galway and stayed in Walsh's in Killeeneen, Craughwell.

'My brother Paddy (Walsh) and Domnick
Corbett went part of the way across
country towards Loughrea to meet him
and bring him to the house.' [142]

In Clarenbridge there was a large gathering of men in Fr. Henry Feeney's house. They were waiting for word from Dublin but none arrived. Among those present were Mattie Niland (Kilcolgan), Michael Fleming (Clarenbridge), Michael Kelly and Michael Cummins (Coldwood), Pádraig Fahy (Ballycahalan) and Peter Howley (Ardrahan). It was decided at this meeting that all companies were to attack the R.I.C. barracks in their area and attempt to take prisoners, arms and ammunition. The Gort Battalion was to attack the Peterswell and Ardrahan barracks at 6 p.m. on Sunday. [143]

Sunday April 23rd.

The rising was set for 7 p.m. in the evening and there were elaborate plans prepared for each area. These were mainly known only by the top officials at Brigade and Battalion level men such as Liam Mellows, Alf Monahan, Larry Lardner, Eamon Corbett and Brian Molloy. The detailed plans may also have been known by one or two of the top officials in each company but this is hard to verify as nothing was written down and the Witness Statements in the Military Bureau give very little evidence as to what was the exact situation. However, going on the likelihood of the secrecy surrounding the rising it is most likely that such plans were not known to a large number of participants.

142 W/S 617 Mrs Malone (nee Brighid Breathnach).

143 W/S 1,379 Peter Howley.

Rebellion in Galway

'Afterwards I heard that the original plan was that
each company was to attack and capture all police
barracks in its area'. [144]

In any case the plans were to begin the rising on Sunday
evening at 7 p.m. At this time the R.I.C would generally be in a
more relaxed mood and not anticipate any trouble. It is likely
that barracks would be at their most vulnerable and be an easy
target to capture. Thus, the plan for the county was to capture
as many barracks as possible and thus capture constables and
arms and ammunition. The latter would be of significant use to
the rebellion especially as the guns had not yet landed in Kerry.
Leading up to Sunday leaders of the Irish Volunteers in the
county were still expecting a delivery of arms from someplace
in advance of the rising and were just waiting for news of where
they were to be collected from.

Irish Volunteer companies all around Galway were
mobilised for Sunday morning after mass parades. The leaders
of each company may have been aware of what was about
to happen but it is extremely doubtful if most of the body of
men and women involved knew the full extent of what was to
happen. It is obvious that the leaders would not and could not
tell all members when exactly the rising was to take place for
fear of word leaking to the authorities. It is also obvious that all
members of the companies by joining up, training and awaiting
a rising were willing to fight when the moment arrived. As many
of those involved were also members of the secret organisation
the I.R.B. they knew exactly what was going to happen at some
stage and were prepared to act on it. However, at this stage this
was just another after mass parade. Still all members had been
advised to go to confession and mass bring all their kit, arms,
ammunition and one or two days rations with them. With this
in mind it would be obvious to many that this just might be

144 W/S 344 John Broderick.

174

somewhat different. Remember that all knew that there was a likelihood of serious action at some stage and most were preparing for it since they joined the Volunteers in 1914. Those in the I.R.B. were often in the organisation in advance of 1914 and were even more prepared for action.

Athenry

On Sunday morning the Volunteers in Athenry went to mass in full gear after Cannon Canton, the Parish Priest, was consulted on the issue. After mass word was delivered that the parade was cancelled and the Volunteers were stood down.

When the rising was postponed on Sunday due to the countermanding orders of Eoin Mc Neill, Stephen Jordan and Larry Lardner went to Dublin to check out what was the situation. Both were officials in the County G.A.A and there was a convention in Dublin.[145] They used this as a cover to travel to Dublin as they had often done before. Both were usually followed by R.I.C. agents when they went to Dublin. Having attended the G.A.A. convention they were able to get some confirmation in Dublin that the Rising may happen on Monday.

'...we decided, the late Larry Lardner and myself, to go to Dublin as usual to the G.A.A. Convention and to find out the position in Dublin. We came to Dublin on Sunday and left it on Sunday night on the last train, having seen the Citizen Army mobilise and go out to take up position – at least they left Liberty Hall. [146]

---

145 mspcsearch.militaryarchives.ie/brief.aspx p38 Stephen Jordan

146 mspcsearch.militaryarchives.ie/docs/files/PDE_Membership/7/WA21%20(4)_Apdf. p10 Stephen Jordan.

Clarenbridge/Craughwell

Clarenbridge and Craughwell Companies mobilised at Killeeneen with Liam Mellows in charge. They went to mass in Roveagh church and had breakfast served by Cumann na mBan after mass. Fr. Feeney celebrated this mass. However, word then came through that the rising was off on the countermanding orders of Eoin Mc Neill. Thus, Mellows told the men that the manoeuvres were cancelled. The men were stood down and disbanded but were told to be ready for action if called on. Laurence Garvey in his witness statement says that Liam Mellows attended a hurling match in Mullagh that Sunday at about 3 p.m., dressed as a priest, and spoke to all the players. [147]

Castlegar/Claregalway

In Castlegar Brian Molloy and in Claregalway Nicholas Kyne led their men to mass and met at Carnmore Cross at 6 p.m. They were in full kit with guns and ammunition and two days rations. Castlegar had in excess of 60 men. They were armed with about 25 shotguns and the rest had pikes made by the Newells of Brierhill who were blacksmiths.

As the Castlegar Company mobilised on Sunday afternoon there were about 70 men there. They were issued with orders to attack and capture Killeen R.I.C. barracks.

> 'the Castlegar company was to attack and capture Killeen R.I.C. barracks, capture all arms and ammunition, take the R.I.C. prisoners, and proceed to Oranmore and link up with other companies there.' [148]

Again this confirms the original plan for the county which was to capture local R.I.C. barracks and attempt to get prisoners

147 W/S 1,062 Laurence Garvey

148 W/S 572 Thomas Newell.

and arms and ammunition. It also explains why Larry Lardner led his men towards Oranmore when he decided not to attack Athenry barracks. There was obviously a decision made to meet at Oranmore once local barracks were attacked and then a large presumably well armed force might think of heading towards Galway City.

They were ready to set out at 6 p.m. when word arrived that the rising was postponed. They were told to stand down but to be ready to remobilise again at short notice if required to do so. Thomas Courtney, the Company Intelligence Officer, was a member of St. Patrick's Temperance Boat Club. He had been captain since 1913 and in this capacity had access to a number of boats. He had six ready on the west side of the River Corrib to ferry the Moycullen and Spiddal Companies across to join with the Castlegar Company when the rising started.

Gort

The Gort Battalion was to mobilise at Early's Wood a mile or so from the Peterswell R.I.C. barracks. This manned by a sergeant and three constables. They were then to proceed to Ardrahan which had a sergeant and five constables. However, just as they were ready to attack word came through Thomas Fahy of Gort that the rising was suspended and to go home, which they did.[149]

Galway

John Hosty arrived back in Galway after a long day, via Tipperary and Limerick, and having met with Mc Neill in Dublin was assured the rising was definitely off. The Galway men then dispersed and hid what few guns they had.

'...and put away whatever little guns we had, 2 old German rifles, about half a dozen shotguns and 4

149 W/S 1,379 Peter Howley.

harmless revolvers, .32 and .38 with very little ammunition for either of them.'[150]

This was hardly anything you could take on the British army based in Renmore barracks and the R.I.C. with a police barracks in Eglinton Street with.

Killimordaly.

The local company of Irish Volunteers assembled for a Mass parade at Killimordaly church under the leadership of John Craven. However, they disbanded due to the countermanding despatches.[151]

Kinvarra

The local company mobilised on Sunday evening following Fr. William O'Meehan's instructions. He ordered them to mobilise, wear their volunteer hats and go to confession and communion. Half of the company mobilised at Kinvarra church and the other half at Dooras. However, they disbanded when the mobilisation was cancelled later in the day.

Monday April 24th.

Early in the morning word came from Dublin by courier on the train, that the rebellion had started in Dublin. Quickly dispatches were sent out around the county for all companies to mobilise. This most of mid and south Galway did by late evening. However, many of the original plans were abandoned as the R.I.C. was now aware of the impending rebellion.

Ardrahan/Ballycahalan

Late at night Peter Howley in Ardrahan got a dispatch from

---

150 W/S 714 Thomas Hynes.

151 mspcsearch.nilitaryarchives.ie/docs/files//PDF_Pensions/R1/MPS34REF2957Williamkelly/WMSP34REF
    2957WilliamKelly.pdf p25

Liam Mellows stating that the rising had in fact taken place. It told him that the Volunteers had mobilised in Killeeneen and were proceeding to attack the Clarenbridge barracks. He was to notify the Ballycahalan Company and they were to go to Tullyra on the Ardrahan to Gort road and hold it. They were to ensure that no military approached from the Ennis direction. Howley got his brothers William and Michael to mobilise the Ardrahan Company and he went to get the Ballycahalan Company out.[152]

Athenry

There was little activity in the area on Monday morning until word arrived to Athenry that Dublin had rebelled at 12 noon and that all Irish Volunteers were to mobilise. Miss Farrelly arrived at the rail station with word that Dublin had risen and

that Galway was to do likewise.

> 'We are out from twelve o'clock today. Issue
> your orders without delay. – P.H.P.'[153]

Commandant Larry Lardner sent James Barrett to Killeeneen to alert Liam Mellows that the Irish Volunteers had risen in Dublin and to proceed with plans for the Galway rising. He went via Clarenbridge where he stopped at Flemings and one of them took the message to Mellows. He returned with a dispatch from Mellows to be given to Lardner. This was to ensure that all companies in the area were mobilised and that communication was to be set up with Galway City.

Lardner then sent Barrett to Ballinasloe to contact Fr. Connolly and Professor Gaffney and to instruct them to set up a line of communication between Galway and Athlone. This was a difficult task and he brought John Cleary and John

152 W/S 1,379 Peter Howley.

153 C Desmond Greaves, *'Liam Mellows and the Irish Revolution.'* p87 An Ghlór Gafa.

Walsh with him. Leaving late Monday night they had to cycle the twenty six miles using back roads to avoid detection by police. They went via Mullagh as they knew Laurence Garvey, an active Volunteer there, and he could direct them how best to go to Ballinasloe.

Word was brought to Galway City about the rising in Dublin by Stephen Jordan. He travelled in to meet with George Nicholls and ensure that the men there were aware of what the situation was. They would trust him that this was the most up to date word. He went in on the 1.15 p.m. train and returned to Athenry on the last train that night, the mail train to Dublin at midnight. He was met at the station and went to the Town Hall where the Athenry Company was mobilised.

By Monday evening everyone knew that the rising had started in Dublin as the word spread around the county.

'...and the peelers started making preparations.
They called in all the peelers from the outlying
stations and occupied all the houses in the
vicinity of the barracks and made an attack
on the barracks impossible.' [154]

Larry Lardner mobilised his forces in the town and they went to the Town Hall where they generally drilled. There were a lot of men there and also a lot of Cumann na mBan members who were to support the rebels. Women such as Julia Morrissey, Annie Barrett, Bridget Clasby and Ellen Dooley were packing rations and medical supplies in readiness for the expected action. Men were arriving with what arms they could find, generally shotguns. However, late at night they were then instructed to go home and await further orders.

The difficulty now was that there had to be a change to the

[154] W/S 446 Frank Hynes.

plans that had been agreed to in advance of the rising. Initially the plan for Galway was to attack and take over all local R.I.C. barracks. This would give the Volunteers access to a vast array of guns and ammunition that would be so vital to their effort. The rising was initially set for Sunday evening when there would be the least amount of R.I.C. on duty and so capturing a number of barracks in the county may have been a distinct possibility. Now all this was changed. By the time the local units of the Volunteers mobilised the R.I.C had already known that there was a rising in Dublin and they suspected trouble in other areas around the country, particularly in Galway. Their reaction to this was swift and crucial. They withdrew all constables from outlying barracks and huts to the main barracks in the larger towns and villages. Thus in Athenry the huts at the Agricultural College and Newford were abandoned and the constables withdrew to the town. Likewise those at Bookeen and New Inn went to Loughrea. This was repeated in many areas around the county. Thus not only could the rebels not attack the huts where few were stationed they could not attack the main barracks as they were now too heavily defended.

In Athenry such was the amount of R.I.C constables recalled into the town that they took over houses in the vicinity of their barracks on Cross Street. Should the Athenry Company of the Irish Volunteers have attacked the barracks many deaths may have occurred including civilians. However, the likelihood of being able to attack a heavily armed barracks with the arms and ammunition they had was now beyond their capabilities. Thus barracks in Clarenbridge, Oranmore and Athenry were now heavily defended so by virtue of the rising happening in Dublin early on Monday it was fortunate in a Galway sense for the R.I.C. as they had reacted to it before the Irish Volunteers were mobilised and this threw the original rising plans into disarray.

Rebellion in Galway

The challenge now for the local leadership was to come up with an alternative plan as they decided that they too were going to participate in the rising. It seems that in Athenry Lardner decided to abandon the plan to attack the barracks but had little other options. He played for time and sent the men home initially and remobilised them early on Tuesday morning.

Belclare / Tuam
No dispatches were sent to the north of the county relating to the rising. Liam Langley of the Belclare Company near Tuam just happened to be in Galway on Easter Monday and heard about the rising from George Nicolls. When he returned to Belclare he informed John Costello who was Director of Organisation in North Galway of the news. They decided to mobilise their company for Tuesday night. [155]

Craughwell
In Craughwell Mellows got the word that Dublin was out from Fr. Feeney at about 2 p.m. He immediately mobilised the local company. He sent Pat 'The Hare' Callanan and Joe Fleming to mobilise as many companies as they could. They went to Maree, Oranmore, Claregalway, Castlegar and Moycullen. All these except the latter mobilised at once. They were unable to get messages to any leaders in Galway City itself. Callanan and Fleming then returned to meet Mellows near Clarenbridge at 2 a.m. on Tuesday morning.

Galway.
There was little activity in the city in the morning as John Hosty had returned on Sunday from Dublin with definite word from Mc Neill that the rising was off. However, by early afternoon dispatches were arriving from all over the place that the rising had started in Dublin. Stephen Jordan came from Athenry on the

---

155 W/S 1,330 John Costello.

1.15 train with word for George Nicolls from Larry Lardner. Maud Kyne arrived with one too. Thomas Hynes collected dispatches and sent them to Michael Thornton in Spiddal and also sent word to Moycullen. Some companies were getting two or three dispatches about the rebellion from different people. This added to the confusion in light of the word circulated on Sunday.

> 'Before 2 p.m. on Monday a despatch came to Mellows from Dublin by train to Athenry to say 'fight was on'. From there despatches were sent to the different places. Maud Kyne brought the despatch to Galway. I collected and sent despatches to Spiddal to Thornton by Mary Malone and to Moycullen to John Geoghegan. There was great confusion.' [156]

The plan in Galway that George Nicolls had made was to capture some prominent men in the city and to take over the main Post Office. However, by the time they got word of the rebellion it was too late to execute this plan as the military already had been notified of the rebellion in Dublin. They secured the Post Office and were on high alert all over the city.

Killimordaly

In the evening the company was reassembled in the vicinity of Killimordaly castle. They were mainly armed with shotguns and there were about 28 men there. They just hung around waiting for orders. Then a dispatch arrived that they were to take up the rail tracks on the Dublin to Galway line near Attymon.[157] They quickly set about this work to ensure that there could be no communication between the east and west of the country.

---

156 W/S 714 Thomas Hynes.

157 mspcsearch.militaryarchives.ie/docs/files//PDF_Pensions/R1/MPS34REF29 57Williamkelly/
    WMSP34REF2957WilliamKelly.pdf p26

Rebellion in Galway

Kinvarra

There was no action here as the Volunteers disbanded on Sunday following the countermanding orders and they were not aware as of yet about any other plans. All the men had returned home though, as with other areas, they were to remain alert as they may be needed at a moment's notice.

Tuesday April 25th.

Companies mobilised all over mid and south Galway. Liam Mellows led attacks on R.I.C. barracks in Clarenbridge and Oranmore with little success and then retreated towards Athenry Agricultural College. Leaders in Galway City were arrested and there was no mobilisation west of the city.

Ardrahan/Ballycahalan

The Ardrahan and Ballycahalan Companies were in place at Tullyra on the Ardrahan to Gort road about 11 a.m. on Tuesday morning. They had mobilised at Lime Park and had about sixteen men with a good number of shotguns and cartridges.[158] They also had two revolvers. Contact was also made with the Kiltartan and Gort companies and they patrolled between Tullyra and Gort. Thomas Mc Inerney, the chief scout (Ardrahan) and Peter Deely and John Coen were other men involved in this mobilisation.[159] The original plan to attack local R.I.C. barracks was thwarted in this area, as in many others, as the R.I.C withdrew from isolated barracks. The police in both Peterswell and Ardrahan had got word of the rebellion and abandoned their stations to go to the larger more secure barracks in Gort where there was also safety in numbers. The Volunteers remained in place all day and encountered no military or police activity. [160]

---

158 W/S 1,379 Peter Howley.

159 W/S 1,379 Peter Howley.

160 W/S 1,379 Peter Howley.

The 1916 Easter Rising in Galway

Athenry

Larry Lardner remobilised his men in Athenry in the morning and they reassembled at the Town Hall. He realised that an attack on the local R.I.C barracks was not an option due to the large numbers of constables there so he decided to lead his men towards Oranmore where he knew Mellows and indeed other companies were most likely headed. Later that evening, when they were about a mile from the village, they met with Mellows who was retreating from there due to the arrival of the R.I.C. and an army contingent from Galway. The group then decided they would head towards the Agricultural College a on the Galway side from Athenry. This large group of rebels was now made up of companies from areas like Craughwell (Rockfield), Clarenbridge, Maree, Oranmore and Athenry. They were also joined by some individuals from other areas rather than full companies as word filtered throughout the area that the rising had begun.

The rebels camped in the Agricultural College overnight. Additional volunteers joined the forces during the night and the next day. They came in from areas like Monivea, Mountbellew but most arrived singly or in twos and threes rather than in additional companies.

By nightfall there was a large number of men and women at the college. Various reports put the number at anything from 650 to 750. Additional volunteers joined the forces during the night and the next day. They came in from areas such as Monivea and Mountbellew but most arrived singly or in two's and three's rather than in additional companies. However, the extent of their arms and ammunition would suggest that there was little they could do to take on any meaningful attack on the military. Estimates as to the numbers of Volunteers vary,

'There were about 650 men. We had about twenty .303 service rifles, a few miniature

rifles and about 300 shotguns. We had a
good supply of home-made hand-grenades.' [161]

and

'The 750 men were all armed in some way. I
would say that there were about 150 rifles
of various patterns including some .22's. The
great majority of the remainder were armed
with shotguns. I saw men armed with pikes
about 20 roughly, and even a few men with
ordinary hayforks.' [162]

and

'The volunteers who were out in Galway numbered
between five and six hundred; we had about 50 full
service rifles and about thirty rounds for each rifle.
The rest were old shotguns, .22 rifles, about one
dozen pikes and a good many were not armed at all,
so if we wanted our ammunition on attacking the
barracks we had nothing to fight with after that; and
as for bombs, we made some hopeless attempts at
making bombs.'[163]

This clearly show that the rebels were very badly armed
and this severely limited their options and meant that any
further attacks on police barracks were out of the question. The
lower estimates of men for the Agricultural College on Tuesday
<u>night may not take in the Castleg</u>ar and Claregalway contingent

161 W/S 344 John Broderick.

162 W/S 1,124 Daniel Kearns.

163 W/S 446 Frank Hynes.

which did not arrive there until Wednesday morning.

Belclare/Tuam

In Belclare John Costello had mobilised his company and was ready to travel to Athenry to link up with Mellows. A railway inspector Sam Browne had a train and two carriages ready to transport the men to Athenry. However, Tuam was alive with police down from the north to help the local R.I.C. and entering the town was out of the question. Thus Costello dismissed the men who were assembled in a wood near the town and waited for orders but none ever came. This shows how difficult it was to get word around to all units and companies in such a short time frame. Also the R.I.C. communication channels, with telegraph and telephone access, were so much better and they were ahead of the Volunteers in most areas. Costello was an I.R.B. 'centre' for the region since he joined in 1913.[164]

Castlegar/Claregalway

Having reported back to Mellows at 2 a.m. in the morning, after getting mobilisation messages to a number of companies, Mellows sent Pat Callanan and Joe Fleming back to Claregalway and Castlegar to get them to join him. Thus, it was now apparent that the plan for each company to attack the R.I.C. barracks in their immediate area was abandoned. Both companies were mobilised since Monday and proceeded to join Mellows and the Clarenbridge, Killeeneen, Maree and Oranmore Companies. However, by the time they got the companies to Oranmore the group led by Mellows had attacked Oranmore barracks and were retreating from the village. The R.I.C and military reinforcements, under County Inspector George Bedell Ruttledge, had arrived and were in control of the village. Therefore, they decided to return to the Carnmore area and await making contact with the Liam Mellows group.

164 W/S 1330 John Costello.

Castlegar Company Captain Brian Molloy sent Lieutenant Tom 'Sweeney' Newell John Walsh and Pat Feeney, from Claregalway, to Athenry to meet with Mellows to ascertain what the Castlegar and Claregalway companies were to do next. They cycled to Athenry and met with Mellows late on Tuesday night.[165] As it was now about 8 p.m. in the evening Molloy had sentries posted and both companies billeted for the night.[166] The Claregalway Company billeted in the Carnmore area and the Castlegar Company in the Kiltulla area.[167]

Clarenbridge

Having assembled at Walsh's in Killeeneen Liam Mellows donned his military uniform and led his men to Clarenbridge. There they planned to attack the R.I.C. barracks located beside the village green. Road blocks were set up at either end of the village and manned so as to stop any possible reinforcements arriving. Two lorries delivering mineral water were commandeered and would be later used for transport.[168] At Mellows signal the group opened fire on the barracks. However, the police inside managed to close and lock the door and so the rebels were unable to gain entry to the building. Despite a ferocious attack on the barracks the police repulsed all attempts to capture it. They bravely refused to surrender despite the attack lasting up to three hours. It was eventually called off between noon and 1 p.m.

> 'About midday or 1 p.m. the attack was called off.
> Mellows was in full charge. No Volunteer was wounded.
> There was no R.I.C man wounded inside Clarenbridge
> barracks during the attack.' [169]

165 W/S 572 Thomas 'Sweeney' Newell.

166 W/S 347 Pat Callanan.

167 W/S 345 Brian Molloy.

168 The Rising County Galway 1916, *The Connacht Tribune* Sat. April 9th 1966

169 W/S 1,564 Michael Kelly.

Four R.I.C. constables from Kilcolgan, one mile from Clarenbridge to the south on the Gort road, arrived during the attack. They may have been reinforcements or arriving into the barracks having abandoned their own. One constable, David Manning was wounded at a check-point as he approached the village. He and the three others were taken prisoner and kept with the rebels for the rest of the week.

Galway

Thomas Courtney, Intelligence Officer for the Castlegar Irish Volunteers, was a postman and he went in to work in the main Post Office in Eglinton Street at 5.30. The R.I.C. were there all night as word had come to the telegraph office about the Dublin Rebellion. He now planned to go out to Castlegar and spread the word that Galway was in the hands of the military and police and for all Volunteers to be careful or they would be arrested. On the pretext of delivering letters to Renmore Army Barracks he cycled out to Newell's in Brierhill to alert Mick Newell. Newell then sent him to Moycullen to get that company to cross the Corrib and link up with Castlegar. He was captain of the Temperance Rowing Club and he had six boats ready to use to ferry them across. He got no response in Moycullen and there were no Volunteers there who were going to join the rebellion.

Following his visit there he returned through Galway City hoping to see some of the Galway Volunteers. He met with Micheál Ó Droighneain and just passed him on the street not wishing to arouse suspicion that might lead to his arrest. However, before he could meet him in secret Ó Droighneain was arrested and put on board a ship in Galway Bay with the other Galway leaders who were arrested.

Courtney then returned to Spiddal but knew very few there and had no success in mobilising any Irish Volunteers. He returned to Galway which was now crawling with military, police and Special Constables who were sworn in to help defend the town. By evening he befriended two local youths Christy Monaghan (St. Patrick's Avenue) and Paddy Heffernan (Foster Street) who would help him during the week by compiling lists of Special Constables and minding the boats on the Corrib when he was away. Late that night he crossed back to the east side of the river to head to Castlegar and report on the day's events. He slept that night in Small's of Killoughter where Mrs. Catherine Small fed him. Smalls were very supportive of the rebels' activities. [170]

The authorities moved at once to arrest the main Irish Volunteer leaders and people suspected of being I.R.B. members. Thus,

> '… George Nicolls, Tommy Flanagan, Johnny Faller, Seamus Carter, Frank Hardiman, Padraic O Maille and Professor Steingeberger (Professor Steingeberger was a German Professor of Languages) – they were bundled off to a destroyer in Galway Bay.' [171]

Micheál Ó Droighneain arrived in from Spiddal to the city to see what was going on and he was also arrested and put on board the Guillemot, a military ship anchored in the bay. Thus the rebels were quickly paralysed in Galway City and no activity took place there. Thomas Hynes relates that only three from the city took part in the rising,

> '…a boy named Mc Dermott, J. Corbett and another.' [172]

In the afternoon there was a meeting called for the Town Hall to decide what to do to ensure the safety of the city. Over

170 W/S 447 Thomas Courtney.

171 W/S 714 Thomas Hynes.

172 W/S 714 Thomas Hynes.

100 people attended and a Committee for Public Safety was set up. It was under the chairmanship of Martin Mór Mc Donagh. There was to be a curfew between 5 p.m. and 8 a.m. All public houses were ordered closed. The Post Office was taken over by the military so as to ensure what happened in Dublin would not be repeated in Galway. The National Volunteers were firmly on the side of the authorities and their leader in the city, Captain J. P. Mc Neill ensured they would play a role patrolling the city. These were armed and under military command. Special constables were sworn in to help patrol the city and ensure its safety. The Committee for Public Safety held daily meetings to review the situation. [173]

Kilconiron

The company was mobilised, by captain Patrick Coy, early in the morning having got a dispatch the night before that the rising had begun. Only about fifteen of a company strength of fifty turned out. This would show that not all wished to rebel. It most likely reflects that those in the I.R.B. were most likely to rebel while those only in the Irish Volunteers may not have been as happy to do so. Their assembly point was the Gate Lodge of Moyode Castle. They received a dispatch telling them to proceed to the Agricultural College and they did so. Other Volunteers included Daniel Kearns and Patrick Naughton.

Killimordaly

This company broke into a rail-yard shed and got equipment to take up rail lines. They took up three sections between Attymon and Woodlawn. They were then to remain in the area and observe and send any information of importance to Liam Mellows. Thus, they stayed in the area and did not head towards Athenry. They remained in the area that night, though

---

173 www.historyireland.com/20thcentury-contemporary-history/the-most-shoneen-town-in-irelandgalway-in-1916/

some did go home for food. [174]

Kinvarra

Pádraig Fahy was sent to Kinvarra by Liam Mellows to get Fr. William O'Meehan to mobilise the local company. He was in a car driven by 'Sonny' Grady that came from Athenry. Fahy also brought Tom O'Dea and Martin 'Sonny' Morrissey with him. Once Kinvarra were mobilised they were to return with Fr. O'Meehan to Clarenbridge.[175]   However, the local R.I.C., backed up by other constables from Gort, were waiting near the presbytery watching the priest who was known to be an avid republican. They had been expecting trouble in Kinvarra since they knew of the rebellion in Dublin. Thus, when Fahy, who was well known to them, appeared he was arrested following a struggle.[176] Fahy's companions escaped and returned to Mellows in Craughwell. Fahy was brought south to Limerick where he was jailed.

The R.I.C. abandoned their barracks and moved to Gort as word broke to them of the rising in Dublin. They took all their arms and ammunition with them and closed up the barracks.

Moyode

The rebels arrived at the Athenry Agricultural College by evening having been mobilised since early morning. Some of the group had unsuccessfully attacked both Clarenbridge and Oranmore R.I.C. barracks and now found themselves with little in the way of plans. At this stage there were ten companies gathered at the college in addition to other individuals or small groups of men who had drifted into the college. The companies

---

174 mspcsearch.nilitaryarchives.ie/docs/files//PDF_Pensions/R1/MPS34REF2957WilliamKelly/WMSP34REF2957WilliamKelly.pdf p26

175 The Rising Co. Galway 1916 'Connacht Tribune,' Sat, April 9th, 1966.

176 C Desmond Greaves, 'Liam Mellows and the Irish Revolution.' p88
    An Ghlór Gafa.

were, Athenry, Clarenbridge, Craughwell (Rockfield), Cussane, Derrydonnell, Kilconiron, Maree, Monivea, Newcastle and Oranmore.

Mullagh

Michael Manning from Mullagh accompanied James Barrett, John Cleary and John Walsh from Mullagh to Ballinasloe to meet with Fr. Connolly and Professor Gaffney. Having delivered the dispatch they cycled back to Athenry where they reported to the Agricultural College at 1 a.m. on Wednesday morning following their round trip of some sixty miles.[177]   This was an arduous cycle over that distance and trying to ensure that they were not arrested by the R.I.C. who may have encountered them. Given that news of the rebellion in Dublin may have been in the hands of the local police they would be very suspicious of men not local to the area.

Oranmore/Maree

Early in the morning the Oranmore and Maree companies were mobilised on the dispatch of Pat Callanan the previous evening. This was about 4.00 a.m. in the morning. The joined together under the leadership of Joe Howley (Oranmore) and Mike Athy (Maree) and stuck with the original plan of attacking the local R.I.C. barracks. The combined strength of the two companies was up to 100 men. About 10.00 a.m. they attacked the barracks at Oranmore which was defended by about five policemen. Another five constables were on patrol around the town with Sergeant Healy. The attackers were unable to gain entry to the barracks or indeed force the police to surrender. On hearing the gun fire Sergeant Healy and the patrol returned to the barracks but as it was too dangerous to attempt to gain entry. Instead they went into Constable Smyth's house across the road. The

---

177 W/S 343 James Barrett.

rebels proved unable to capture this house either.[178]   Thus it showed that without sufficient arms it was virtually impossible to capture an R.I.C. barracks. It also shows the great courage of the R.I.C., who came under very heavy attack, to hold out in their barracks and the house and resist surrendering. This attack lasted for about quarter of an hour.

There was one Irish Volunteer injured by gunfire during this attack.[179] Remarkably just one R.I.C. constable was injured during the attack, he was Constable Joseph Ginty a 44 year old with 21 year's service.

While in the Oranmore area the rebels cut telegraph wires and dismantled rail lines on the Dublin side of the town.

'Oranmore and Maree companies mobilised
early on Tuesday morning and attacked
Oranmore Barracks unsuccessfully, the attack
lasted only about quarter of an hour or so.
The men dismantled the Post Office telephone,
the cabin at the Oranmore railway station and
tore up some of the rails on the railway line.' [180]

Having failed to capture the barracks they eventually gave up trying. At this stage they abandoned the attempt to capture the barracks and headed towards Clarenbridge where they knew Mellows and his forces were.

Both groups, which now involved companies from Craughwell, Clarenbridge, Maree and Oranmore, again decided to attack the Oranmore barracks. There were now up to 180 men in the rebel group. However, their renewed attack was not anymore successful. The rebels also attempted to blow a hole

178 The Rising Co. Galway 1916, 'The Connacht Tribune.' Sat. April 9th 1966

179 The Rising Co. Galway 1916, 'The Connacht Tribune.' Sat. April 9th 1966

180 mspcsearch.militaryarchives.ie/docs/files/PDE_Membership/7/WA21%20(4)_B.pdf. pdf p74
    Michael Costello

in the bridge over the river on the road out of the town going towards Galway. This was to impede reinforcements that may come from Galway. However, this was only partly successful and did not destroy the bridge. Also a scout, Michael Commins, was sent to the railway station outside the village to watch for reinforcements coming from Galway. [181]

In due course these did arrive. A group arrived by road, R.I.C. constables under County Inspector Ruttledge and ten Connacht Rangers under Captain Sir Andrew Armstrong. These set up a machine gun on the bridge and carefully proceeded on foot up the village. Ruttledge led this force into the village and towards the R.I.C. barracks. At the sight of this contingent the rebels who had now called off the attack on the barracks and Constable Smyth's house retreated. As the British forces advanced Mellows, with a few chosen men, covered the retreat of any rebels left in the village. Ruttledge was rewarded with the King's Police Medal for his bravery under such fire. Another group of military had arrived by rail from Galway and were disembarking at the station a mile outside the town. Michael Commins returned with this news to Mellows as he was pulling out of Oranmore. [182]

The Castlegar and Claregalway units who were to join Mellows in Oranmore now had to re-access their situation as the Mellows' group had left Oranmore. They sent scouts to meet up with him to seek instructions. The rebels left Oranmore via the Dublin road and made their way towards Athenry. A few miles outside the village they met up with Larry Lardner on his way from Athenry to meet with them. Lardner, with Athenry men and others him, had declined to attack the Athenry barracks as there were so many police in it and they had also taken over residential housing in the vicinity of the barracks.

---

181 The Rising Co. Galway 1916, *The Connacht Tribune.* Sat. April 9th 1966

182 The Rising Co. Galway 1916, *The Connacht Tribune.* Sat. April 9th 1966.

Rebellion in Galway

Both groups now proceeded to the Athenry Agricultural Station situated in Ballygarraun West a mile west of the town. Here they set up camp for the remainder of Tuesday. There were now a large number of rebels on the move and they stretched for up to quarter of a mile while on the road.

> 'They marched in company first. Then they had scouts out in front, cyclists, some on foot and some on horseback, and the main body marching were some in cars, some in vans.' [183]

The group assembled at the Agricultural College on Tuesday night comprised of companies from Athenry, Clarenbridge, Coldwood, Cussane, Derrydonnell, Kilconiron, Maree, Newcastle, Oranmore and Rockfield (Craughwell). Men from other areas were there as individuals rather than as full companies.

Other companies in the field by Tuesday night were Claregalway and Castlegar who were both billeted near Carnmore crossroads. In addition to these men from Ardrahan, Ballycahalan, Belclare, Gort, Killimordaly, Kinvarra and Mullagh were also standing mobilised in their localities ready for orders.

There were a good number of Cumann na mBan women accompanying the men all day since they left Killeeneen early that morning. When they reached the Athenry Agricultural College food was commandeered to feed the men. The Cumann na mBan women were accommodated in the college buildings themselves. That night the men slept in sheds and other barns belonging to the College. Sentries were posted and men took shifts on duty.

---

183 mspcsearch.militaryarchives.ie/docs/files/PDE_Membership/7/WA21% 20 (4)_Bpdf.pdf p75
    Martin Neilan

Rockfield

At 5.30 a.m. Gilbert Morrissey got a dispatch from Liam Mellows that there was fighting in Dublin. He was to mobilise his company and meet Mellows at the College. He duly mobilised the Rockfield Company and headed to the College when they were all assembled.[184] There had been a split in the Craughwell area between the supporters of Tom Kenny who followed Eoin Mc Neill's Irish Volunteers and Martin Hallinan's supporters who followed John Redmond's National Volunteers.

Wednesday April 26th.

An R.I.C. constable was killed, by the rebels, in an engagement at Carnmore crossroads. There was a brief engagement between the rebels and the R.I.C at the Agricultural College and following this they retreated to Moyode manor house. Galway City was completely controlled by the military and R.I.C. reinforcements arrived and Belfast. The poorly armed rebels were now unable to attack any R.I.C. barracks.

Ardrahan/Ballycahalan

The Ardrahan Company and some men from Ballycahalan, Kiltartan and Gort still held the road at Tullyra under the leadership of Peter Howley. They were visited by Chief Scout Thomas Mc Inerney who told them that both Kinvarra and Clarenbridge R.I.C barracks had been attacked. In reality Kinvarra barracks was empty and the constables gone to Gort. Howley was impatient for news from Mellows and he sent William Thompson to find him and to get further instructions. He returned later in the evening with the dispatch that they were to stay in position.[185]

---

184 W/S 874 Gilbert Morrissey.

185 W/S 1,379 Peter Howley.

Rebellion in Galway

Athenry/Moyode

In the morning there was an exchange of fire between some rebels at the College and R.I.C. from Athenry barracks who had approached the College to ascertain the strength of the rebel forces. Eamon Corbett took charge of a number of men who ventured out of the college to engage the R.I.C. The police were driven back with no casualties on either side. The R.I.C. group numbered up to ten men.

> 'There were about 20 to 30 men picked out to
> engage the 9 or 10 Peelers coming in.' [186]

Following this exchange there was a war council was held between Mellows and the company captains to discuss what to do next. It was decided that the current position would be too difficult to defend. It was on relatively flat land with little cover. In addition it may have been thought to be within the range of the shells fired from the sloop, the Laburnum, and a danger to the forces there. They were also bounded by R.I.C. forces to the east, at Athenry, as well as military forces in Galway to the west and so moving out of that immediate area would have made good sense. A meeting was called by the leaders to discuss the situation. Among those at this meeting were Liam Mellows, Eamon Corbett, Mattie Niland, Tom Ruane, Larry Lardner, Fr. Harry Feeney and Dick Murphy.

Following the meeting Liam Mellows and his fellow officers decided to abandon the Agricultural College as it would be too hard to defend and marched to Moyode Castle some five miles away to the south east. Thus, the rebels left the college at 4 p.m. with a large entourage of cars, lorries, bicycles, horses and carts and people walking to proceed to Moyode. They went through the townlands of Mulpit, crossed the Athenry/Craughwell road

186 mspcsearch.militaryarchives.ie/docs/files/PDE_Membership/7/WA21%20(4)_Bpdf.pdf p2
    Martin Newell

at Boyhill and proceeded to Deerpark. The entrance lodge to Moyode Demesne was near Tallyho cross. They arrived there on Wednesday evening.

Again, Pat Callanan was sent on a scouting mission this time with Willie Newell. They were to go to meet the Moycullen Company and bring them to Moyode. However, when they got to Moycullen they failed to find Pádraig Thornton and the company had not been mobilised nor had a message been sent to Spiddal for them to mobilise. It would be Thursday before they got back towards Moyode.

All the R.I.C. prisoners that had been captured were brought with them including the injured Constable David Manning. A large number of cars, carts and horses that were commandeered were also brought. As much food as was possible was also taken. This included cattle and sheep that were to be slaughtered to feed the large number of volunteers and Cumann na mBan members in the entourage. Some scouts were sent ahead to ensure that if any military were met word would be passed back to the main group.

Members of Cumann na mBan like Gretta Walsh, Mary Corbett were also in the group. Some of the Cumann na mBan detoured to cycle to the town of Athenry, some two miles away, to make arrangements to get food, tobacco and cigarettes for the men from the locals. The vast majority of the local townspeople were in support of the rebels and were more than happy to supply food to the men.

On the way to Moyode the group also made an effort to commander any food they could. A lorry carrying a load of flour from Galway to Farrell's Bakery in Loughrea was intercepted and taken. The flour was distributed to local families to be baked into bread and then the loves were sent to Moyode.

Moyode

The rebels reached Moyode about 7 – 8 p.m. and set up camp.

Sentries were posted on all approaches to the house with each company providing men for this duty.[187]

Moyode Castle and Demesne belonged to the Persse family. The house had been constructed about 1820. In the 1870's the family owned about 1,800 acres in County Galway. However, they sold some of this in the Land Judge's court in 1888.[188] There was none of the family in residence at the time. It was being looked after by a caretaker so there was no problem gaining entry to the estate.

That evening priests from Esker Redemptorist monastery, two miles away, heard the Volunteers had arrived and Fr. Tom Fahy and others went to Moyode and heard confessions from the men. [189]

Castlegar/Claregalway

Having returned the previous night from Oranmore where they knew there to be a large number of R.I.C. and other military the companies got what food and rest they could.

At about 3 a.m. the scouts, Tom Newell, John Walsh and Pat Feeney, returned from the Agricultural College with the message that the companies were to join Mellows there. They were to bring whatever food and horses and carts they could with them. With this in mind Brian Molloy roused his men and had them moving towards Athenry through Carnmore cross by 4 a.m. They noticed a young girl on Kiltulla hill waving a white apron. She was Bina King hoping to alert them as to a large number of approaching cars.

At first the rebels thought these were Irish Volunteers coming from Galway to join them but it soon became apparent it was a large military force. There were up to 15 cars in all, most open topped. They contained in excess of sixty men both R.I.C.

187 W/S 1,564 Michael Kelly.

188 N.U.I. Galway Estate Record Landed Estates Database.

189 W/S 383 Very Rev. Dr. Fr. Tom Fahy.

under the command of District Inspector Heard and military under the command of Captain Bodkin. They had ventured out of Galway to make a reconnaissance of the area to the east of the city in an effort to ascertain the movements of the rebels.

Captain Molloy reacted quickly and placed men behind walls at the crossroads for cover. Most were in the vicinity of Cooney and Grealish's houses. At once a fire fight ensued between both sides. The police and military got out of their cars and also took cover. The rebels opened up with shotguns but a lot of them were too far away to hit any targets, however, they fired anyway. The military responded with intense fire. District Inspector Heard and Constable Patrick Whelan who were closest to some of the rebels and Whelan shouted at them to surrender as he knew most of them anyway. However, in calling on them he inadvertently put his head too far above the wall and was shot. He was hit by a shotgun blast and killed instantly.

When Whelan was shot and others wounded the police and military retreated back towards Galway. They did try a flanking movement but Molloy, on seeing this, was able to head it off with a section of his men. Brian Molloy states that another constable was wounded in this exchange.[190]

In addition to Constable Whelan's death statements from several Irish Volunteers claim other British forces were wounded during the engagement and put the total number at up to thirteen. It may have been military who were wounded as only one R.I.C. man was named as wounded. He was Constable Hugh Hamilton, a 31 year old with 9 years' service.

The whole exchange lasted for almost half an hour. The rebels then regrouped and moved on towards the Agricultural College near Athenry. The military and police returned to Galway City.

---

190 W/S 345 Brian Molloy.

Rebellion in Galway

Cumann na mBan

A number of Cumann na mBan members gathered up provisions and took them by cart to Moyode to help feed the men there. Bridget Walsh from Killeeneen was among these.

Galway

Very early in the morning a sortie of six cars from Renmore Barracks under Sir Andrew Armstrong and Captain J.J. Bodkin joined District Inspector Heard of the R.I.C., with nine cars and headed to the east of the city to look for rebel activity.

Thomas Courtney returned to Galway City to wait on the Salthill/Barna side in case arms were landed on the Galway coast for the rebellion. He learned that the town was well defended and the police and army had machine gun posts set up on the roads leading to Tuam, Athenry and Oranmore. There were rumours that the rebels were all set to march on the city to capture it. A huge number of Special Constables were sworn in to help defend the city but they were not given arms.[191]

He was contacted by his brother, David, met him and told him a man was at their house to see him. When he went there the man told him there was a submarine seen off Spiddal and would he know if it was a German one to land arms. By the time he got to Spiddal he was disappointed to learn from a former navy reserve that it was a British light draft anti-submarine boat. He couldn't go back to the Castlegar side with news that night as he met lads he knew from the boat club. Both were Special Constables and would have been suspicious had he hurried away. One of them, Jack Liston, constantly questioned him about any lads he knew from the country. He had to go to his own house that night accompanied all the way by the constables.[192]

The Laburnum arrived in the bay from Cork by 10.00

191 W/S 447 Thomas Courtney.
192 W/S 447 Thomas Courtney.

a.m. During the day Mr. Leslie Edmunds, an official with the Congested Districts Board, came on board the ship and around 2.30 p.m. the ship's guns fired nine shells inland.[193] They landed in the region of Castlegar. Edmonds was able to direct the gunners where to fire. It is unclear as to the purpose of the firing. It is most likely that it was as a warning as to what could be done rather than to cause death of destruction. No doubt the shells could have been fired to hit specific targets if so desired. It did create panic among the locals but no one was killed or injured neither were these shells of any specific danger to the rebels at this juncture.

It can be assumed that this brief firing was to frighten the rebels from attacking Galway should that have been part of their plan. On the other hand it might be to lull them into a false sense of security that the gunners couldn't get their range. In conversation with some sailors Thomas Courtney got some information to pass on to Liam Mellows.

'Those shots, he explained, were to 'cod' the
Shinners....The shots already fired were to
make the Shinners think that they were not able
to get the range of the road, etc....... I then
went to Castlegar, direct route, and sent
on the information to Moyode Castle.' [194]

Later in the day a group of 150 R.I.C. constables arrived by car from Belfast to help the authorities in Galway and these were welcomed by all the townspeople.[195] These were to supplement those already in the city.

---

193 W/S 374 Micheal O Droighneain.

194 W/S 447 Thomas Courtney.

195 www.historyireland.com/20thcentury-contemporary-history/the-most- shoneen-town-in-irelandgalway-in-1916/

Rebellion in Galway

Killimordaly

The local volunteers were still standing-to waiting for any further orders and keeping an eye on any possible movement along the Dublin-Galway railway.[196]

Kinvarra

The company mobilised in the Clonasee area, a mile south of the town, about mid-day. The company captain was John Burke of Cahermore. Word was out that the rising had started in Dublin since Monday. Therefore anyone who assembled in Clonasee was under no illusion as to what they were letting themselves in for. While they may have been kept in the dark as to when the rebellion was starting the vast majority were willing to fight when the day came and were no doubt training with this in mind.

> 'Our company knew nothing of the coming
> Rising.'.... It was not until Wednesday morning
> that I heard of the Rising in Dublin. .... When I got
> to Clonasee, most of the company was
> mobilising.'[197]

Fr. O'Meehan was the mainstay of the company but he advised anyone not wishing to take part in rebellion to step out and go home, none left. From there the company marched into the town and collected up what guns and ammunition, mainly shot guns, they could. They then made their way to the townland of Northampton, a mile south east of the town, where they had good information they could secure more guns. This was on the road towards Gort. As they proceeded along the

196 mspcsearch.nilitaryarchives.ie/docs/files//PDF_Pensions/R1/MPS34REF2957Williamkelly/
    WMSP34REF2957WilliamKelly.pdf p27

197 W/S 1,173 Michael Hynes.

road they encountered an R.I.C. patrol on bicycles. They were constables from Gort, along with those from Kinvarra who had abandoned their barracks in the town, on Tuesday. This was in line with policy, when word of the rebellion in Dublin broke, of bringing all small isolated units into bigger towns. No doubt they were on a reconnaissance mission to see what was going on in the area. This chance encounter took place about 3 o'clock.

The R.I.C. dismounted and both sides traded shots for a short time. No one was killed or wounded on either side. The R.I.C. then remounted their bicycles and retreated towards Gort. The rebels did not follow them but returned to Kinvarra. They went to the R.I.C. barracks which was abandoned. However, they did not enter it as they knew there would be no guns or ammunition there. [198]

The company then proceeded to Dungora, a mile outside the town, on the Ardrahan road. Here they were fed with bread and beef donated by businesses in the town. Mrs. Tyrrell and Mrs. O'Dea supplied the bread from their bakeries and Michael Leach the beef from his butcher shop. [199]

By the time they had eaten it was after 5 o'clock and they decided to go to Moyode Castle where they knew Liam Mellows and his troops to be. However, they had only reached Ballinderreen when a scout met them and they were instruced to return to Kinvarra. They remained mobilised that night and billeted in houses around the town. The fact that people put them up, feed them and gave them guns and ammunition would suggest strong local support for the group. This seems to have happened willingly rather than out of fear.

Mullagh

In the evening, Laurence Garvey arrived at Moyode having cycled from Mullagh to join the rising. He knew from James

198 W/S 1,173 Michael Hynes.

199 W/S 1,173 Michael Hynes.

Barrett that the Athenry area had mobilised as he had passed through Mullagh on his way to Ballinasloe early on Tuesday morning. Garvey stayed Wednesday night and met with all the main leaders.[200] Though some Volunteers had mobilised in the area there was no action of any kind in the Mullagh area.

Thursday April 27th.

The rebels remained at Moyode and requisitioned food and supplies locally. There was another engagement with the R.I.C. though there were no injuries on either side. There was little action in any other areas of the county. Rumours of approaching British forces intensified as scouts reported back to Moyode but it was hard to know what was truth or fiction.

Ardrahan

The Ardrahan Company was still in position guarding the road from Ennis and Gort. At this stage they had heard that the rebels were now at Moyode so they continued to hold their

position watching for any military activity coming from the south.[201] While they had relatively small numbers they would hope to stall any military advance while they would send word to Mellows of any approach.

Ballinasloe

Laurence Garvey was sent to Ballinasloe, by Liam Mellows, to bring another dispatch to Fr Connolly and he cycled back through Mullagh to do so. He met the Mullagh Company on his way and instructed them to stay mobilised and wait for orders. He returned to his house on Thursday night and set out for the rebel camp early on Friday morning.[202]

---

200 W/S 1,062 Laurence Garvey (He mixes up the days slightly as he has the rebels in Moyode on Tuesday night.).

201 W/S 1,379 Peter Howley.

202 W/S 1,064 Laurence Garvey (He must have gone on this trip on Thursday as the rebels were not in Moyode on Wednesday morning as he states in his statement)

Bushfield

Four scouts on their way from the Oranmore area towards Moyode became aware of the many false rumours abounding about various British military activities. Knowing them to be false they sent word to Mellows of the up-to-date situation as they knew it to be. Mellows instructed them to set up an outpost at Bushfield. This was on the Oranmore to Athenry road at Derrydonnell Cross some three miles from Oranmore and seven from Moyode. This was to ensure they would know of any military activity in the area due east of Galway and be able to alert Mellows if necessary.

There were four men at this outpost, Thomas Furey, Roger Furey, Pat Flanagan and Pat Callanan. Between them they had little in the way of arms and ammunition.

'We had two shotguns and a revolver between us, ten or twelve shotgun cartridges and six rounds of revolver ammunition.' [203]

Castlegar/Claregalway

As 'The Hare' Callanan and Willie Newell returned from Moycullen via Castlegar they called on Fr. John Moran, the local curate, and he gave them two Webley revolvers.[204] These were R.I.C issue revolvers. This shows Fr. Moran's support for the rebels. Callanan then went on to set up the outpost at Bushfield.

Cumann na mBan

Cumann na mBan still played a vital role in cooking for the men and ensuring they were fed. The women who accompanied the rebels continued to collect and cook food. They went miles arranging for food to be cooked by locals and then collecting it

203 W/S 347 Pat Callanan.
204 W/S 347 Pat Callanan.

and bringing it back to Moyode. This shows the local support the rebels had in the area.

> 'I went into the village and got two young fellows, Mick Mulkerns and John Joe Kennedy, and they helped me to collect food. I went into the village of Caherquin and got food from the neighbours there. Yes, I got an ass and cart and we went out to Moyode that evening.'[205]

Galway

The Gloucester arrived from Cork accompanying a troop transport ship with up to 200 marines. These were belonging to the Royal Munster Fusiliers. They disembarked and marched to Renmore Barracks.

> '....a company of Munster Fusiliers arrived by ship into Galway docks. They marched to Renmore Barracks with a large supply of guns and ammunition.'[206]

These got a huge welcome from the people of the city who now felt a lot safer.[207]

Thomas Courtney made his way to the docks to see what was going on there when he heard there were British naval ships arriving. There he and with a sailor named Stark, whom he knew, and a driver called Thomas Murray. Stark was a Galwayman serving on a ship moored in the docks and Murray was a driver for Leslie Edmunds, the official in the Congested Districts Board

---

205 mspcsearch.militaryarchives.ie/docs/files//PDF_Pensions/RS/MSP35REF1981BRIDGETRUANE/
WMSP34REFBRIDGETRUANE.pdf p33.

206 Galway Independent/Renmore in Irish Hands.

207 www.historyireland.com/20thcentury-contemporary-history/the-most-shoneen-town-in-
irelandgalway-in-1916/

who had directed the firing towards Castlegar the previous day. He managed to persuade them and other sailors, they having got permission, to go for a drink and he endeavoured to get as much information from them as possible. They did not know he was an Irish Volunteer Intelligence Officer. In relation to the firing of the shells he found they were using 4 - inch guns, which were relatively small, for most destroyers. The shells that had landed had hit nothing of significance and were well away from villages and houses. This was deliberate to 'cod' the Volunteers into believing that they could not hit specific targets. Then, if the rebels attacked towards Galway they could make direct hits to within five square yards if necessary. The naval commander Hannon was assisted by Edmunds, as he knew the area had maps of it, and could hit what they wished once the gunners got the range required. When he had solicited this information Courtney left, assuring Stark he would let his wife know he was fine. Courtney cycled to Castlegar so as to meet scouts who would then pass on all this information to Mellows. These details included troop strengths, movements of police, special constables and military within the Galway City area. A line of communication had been set up all over the area to get information to and from Moyode.[208]

He later cycled back home, changed and went back into Galway. There he was arrested and brought to the Eglinton Street R.I.C. barracks. He was questioned by police, including District Inspector Heard, about being a member of the Irish Volunteers. Eventually, he was able to persuade the police he was not in the Volunteers and he was released. Also a known Volunteer, named Conroy, who was also arrested stated that he knew Courtney only as a postman. This also helped him get off. He promptly returned home had something to eat and went on the run.[209] Following the sending of word to Cork for help

208 W/S 447 Thomas Courtney.
209 W/S 447 Thomas Courtney.

a company of Royal Munster Fusiliers, numbering about 200 landed in Galway and

Killimordaly

The company was still in the area of the Attymon rail station and guarding the roads watching out for any police or military activity. However, there was no activity and they just waited around. Some went to and from their houses for food during the day. [210]

Kinvarra

The rebels, under the leadership of John Burke and Fr. William O'Meehan, seem to have got no further instructions from Liam Mellows in Moyode. They remained mobilised during the day but grew impatient as the day wore on. By evening time most had disbanded and returned home.

> 'On Thursday night some of the Volunteers went home as they did not wish to impose on their neighbours.' [211]

Moyode

When they got to Moyode each company was detailed to be responsible for getting provisions for their group. Sentries were posted at all points leading to the mansion grounds to ensure the safety of the area. The rebels numbered in the region of 700 men at this stage. Some additional men had arrived who were not with a specific company but took it upon themselves to join the rebellion.

> '...men were sent out with big Patrick Kennedy and his horse and cart on foraging expeditions, (Kennedy

210 mspcsearch.militaryarchives.ie/docs/files//PDF_Pensions/R1/MPS34REF2957WilliamKelly/WMSP34REF2957WilliamKelly.pdf p27

211 W/S 1,173 Michael Hynes.

belonged to the Kilconiron Company), of how Miss Greally took charge of the baking of bread...' [212]

Later in the morning Liam Mellows was anxious to find out what was the situation in the area surrounding Moyode. There were various rumours about military activity in the area and British forces were said to be marching towards Moyode. He organised a trip towards Ballinasloe to survey the situation for himself. Stephen Jordan recounts the following in his witness statement,

> 'Early on Thursday morning Mellows brought J. Cleary, myself and a number of others to reconnoitre the surrounding district. He called at several homes making enquiries as to the movements of police and military.' [213]

They went as far as New Inn on what was then the main road towards Ballinasloe and onto Athlone and Dublin. New Inn is about nine miles to the east of Moyode. When they reached New Inn they headed for the R.I.C. Barracks but found it to be undefended. When they went inside there were two women there. Upstairs was an ill R.I.C. sergeant, husband of one of the women. Mellows questioned him at length in relation to police activities. The R.I.C. had been instructed to abandon the barracks and bring all arms and ammunition with them and go to the Loughrea barracks. As he was too ill to travel he was left there hoping that he would come to no harm.[214] The party left the sergeant in the barracks and returned to Moyode. They didn't encounter any police or military in the area on their return journey.

212 W/S 345 Brian Molloy.

213 W/S 346 Stephen Jordan.

214 W/S 346 Stephen Jordan.

Again, the priests from nearby Esker Redemptorist Monastery visited Moyode. Fr. Tom Fahy and Fr. Mc Namara heard confessions and gave absolution to the men. While many priests were not always in agreement with the activities of the rebels they were anxious that they would receive the sacraments. Thus it can be seen that there was considerable support within the local clergy for the movement. When arriving at Moyode these priests would have met up with Fr Henry Feeney who was accompanying the rebel group on their activities since mobilising on Monday night.

Several times during their stay at Moyode Tom Kenny, the I.R.B. activist visited to speak with Mellows. He did not agree with the rebellion as he felt the time was not right and they were poorly armed. However, Kenny did not take an active part in the rebellion. As said previously, Kenny was somewhat put out by the arrival of Mellows in January 1915 as the organiser for the Galway area. Liam Mellows had significant military training of which Kenny had none and thus in the lead up to the rebellion was seen by most as the more important leader of the Irish Volunteers and even the I.R.B. element within the mid, south and east Galway areas. Kenny insisted that there was a large group of military about to descend on Moyode. An argument ensued between them. There was serious discussion between these and the company captains as what to do. Many were of the opinion that Kenny was just trying to frighten them in an effort to get the rebels to disband. During the argument Mellows temporarily handed over command to Larry Lardner but he (Lardner) would not disband the men and Mellows assumed control again after about an hour.

'During our stay in Moyode, Tom Kenny came
several times on horseback and had discussions
with Mellows.' [215]

215 W/S 1,562 Martin Newell.

and

'He handed over command to Larry, but Larry
would not disband them. Liam after about
hour tookover again and called for volunteers to
go out the roads to see if there were any soldiers.' [216]

It was the responsibility of each company to get their own
food. Parties went out locally for food and provisions. Many
returned with cattle to be slaughtered. James Barrett recalls,

'I went out with a couple of foraging parties.
On one occasion I was sent out to get some
cattle for slaughtering. I brought back 21
of the finest bullocks to be got anywhere.
They were the property of the Daly's
of Dunsandle, however, none of them were
slaughtered. I went on another occasion
to Mr. Ward, Publican and Grocer, of Kiltullagh,
for tea, sugar and tobacco. I gave him a receipt
for the goods which we took. I told him if we
won we would pay for them, but if we lost he
would lose very little. When commandeering
provisions, etc., we went only to wealthy shopkeepers
and big farmers.' [217]

When Stephen Jordan returned from the trip to New
Inn he went with a party of men to commandeer food. They
went to the farm of Joseph King, a large farmer in Rahard,
some three miles away. This was just two miles to the east
of Athenry, thus showing that the rebels felt they were safe
to operate in this area free from interference by the police.

216 W/S 446 Frank Hynes.
217 W/S 343 James Barrett.

However, on this occasion the R.I.C. had a party of men in the area and they attacked the men as they filled two carts with potatoes. They had made a sortie out from Athenry towards Moyode, on bicycles, when they came across the men. They were no doubt seeking to gather information on the activities of the rebels when they inadvertently came across the party loading potatoes. The rebels opened fire on the R.I.C. and they returned fire. The sides exchanged fire for ten minutes or so before the R.I.C. party withdrew towards Athenry. Liam Mellows and the men at Moyode heard the firing and two or three cars were dispatched to the aid of their comrades. By the time Mellows and the reinforcements arrived the police had retreated. Though Mellows and his carloads of men pursued the police they reached the safety of the town before he was able to engage them in a fight.

In the evening Liam Mellows and Alf Monahan assembled all the men, except those on sentry duty, in the grounds of the house. Mellows, realising that many were not sufficiently armed and others may have had a change of mind in relation to the act of rebellion addressed them. He said that if anyone felt he wished to go he could do so and no ill would be felt towards him. Some did leave, estimates were up to about 200, especially those poorly armed. Thus, men and women were afforded the opportunity to go home if they wished without any disgrace. However, many of these were to return early on Friday morning though no reason is given for this. [218]

At the end of the day there was still a large contingent of men in the vicinity of Moyode Castle. No sentries had reported any unusual activity that night and there was no known activity by the British military or R.I.C. overnight.

Mullagh

The Irish Volunteers in this locality continued to be at the

218 W/S 1,562 Martin Newell.

ready if called upon but no word came. They generally went about their work during the day but met in the evenings in case they were needed.

'Mullagh Company remained 'standing to' from Monday to Friday.' [219]

and

'There were 12 shotguns in the company during Easter week.' [220]

The company was to destroy the bridge at Banagher at the crossing point between Galway and Offaly if ordered to. They never got any orders.[221]

Friday April 28th.
The rebels moved to Lime Park House near Ardrahan as many rumours circulated that a large military force was set to close in on them. News arrived that Dublin had surrendered and the rebels became uneasy as to what to do.

Ardrahan
Late in the evening this company, led by Peter Howley, received a dispatch ordering them to Lime Park House near Peterswell to act as an advance party ahead of the rebels moving there from Moyode. Thus they left their post on the Gort Ardrahan road and proceeded there. This was a distance of about three miles.

---

219 W/S 1,062 Laurence Garvey.

220 W/S 1.062 Laurence Garvey.

221 W/S 1.062 Laurence Garvey.

Rebellion in Galway

Bushfield

Pat 'The Hare' Callanan, Roger and Thomas Furey and Pat Flanagan continued to man the outpost on the Ornamore-Athenry road at Derrydonnell. They saw no activity that threatened the rebels at Moyode. They sent word to Mellows updating him that there was no danger from this area and he instructed them to continue monitoring the area and to do their best to slow any advance along that road, should it occur.

Galway

The city was well secured and military, R.I.C and Special Constables continued to patrol the town. Up to twenty of the arrested prisoners were transferred to HMS Snowdrop and on to Cobh from where they were ultimately sent to Dublin.

Killimordaly

Word came to Attymon that a military train was on its way from Dublin with soldiers and was heading for the Galway region. William Kelly who was the second-in-command and the chief dispatch rider went to Moyode to report this news to Mellows. When he arrived he was sent back to try to find out where they going to, Galway or Loughrea. There was a branch line from Attymon to Loughrea passing through Dunsandle station at Kiltullagh. This could bring the soldiers to within four miles of Moyode. He returned, the six or so miles, to Attymon station to find the train had just pulled in and was taking on water. To get over the broken lines the train must have brought a repair crew onboard. He enquired at the station, from Robert Powell who worked there, as to their destination. Powell told him they were going to Loughrea. He counted the carriages and guessed that there were between 400 and 500 men on it. Quickly he returned to Moyode to report to Mellows and Monahan. They told him to return to Attymon and disband the company, go home and hope to avoid arrest. He got back late that night to

Attymon and did as he was ordered. He stayed at home that night.[222]

Thus it was quite obvious that rumours of large amounts of military heading towards the rebels in Galway were not just rumours and that these well-armed soldiers would have been easily able to defeat the poorly-armed rebels should an engagement follow. It is also obvious that Mellows and Monahan were aware of this whether or not they gave all of this up-to-date information to all the company leaders and men still in Moyode.

> 'On Friday evening we got word from one of
> scouts who were watching the railway, that 900
> soldiers were in Attymon and were
> marching on Moyode.'[223]

With this contingent of troops advancing it was obvious that Moyode could not be defended. It may also explain why they moved southwards towards Clare so as to put distance between themselves and this rumoured British force. However, it also begs the question, was Mellows willing to sacrifice all in a large battle with the authorities, regardless of the outcome, so as to make a name for the rebels in the west?

Kinvarra

There was no further action in the area as no dispatches had arrived from Liam Mellows. The company was stood down and all the Volunteers went home.

---

222 mspcsearch.militaryarchives.ie/docs/files//PDF_Pensions/R1/MPS34REF2957Williamkelly/
   WMSP34REF2957WilliamKelly.pdf p44

223 W/S 446 Frank Hynes.

Rebellion in Galway

Moyode

Again men from Moyode were active in going out to the surrounding areas to get food. Cuman na mBan members with the men cooked food and the men were in general well fed. The priests who accompanied them continued to hear confessions and gave general absolution.

Early in the morning Liam Mellows sent Fr. Tom Fahy to Galway to see Bishop Dr. Thomas O'Dea and to find out what they could about the situation regarding the military in Galway City.

'On Friday morning Fr. Thomas Fahy came to Moyode Castle and after consulting Fr. Feeney and the Brigade officers he cycled to Galway City to get news about Dublin.'[224]

Rumours continued to abound as to what the plans of the military might be. Various rumours reached the camp as men came and went for food. Some of the men who departed the camp on Thursday evening returned and they no doubt had various stories also. Among the rumours circulating were that the British army were planning an attack from the direction of Ballinasloe twenty miles to the east.

Word came through from Craughwell that some of Redmond's National Volunteers, heretofore against the rising, wished to now join the Moyode rebels. Gerry Deely and Martin Newell were sent to meet with these men but on arriving were informed that they would not join.[225]

'One report stated that the British were about to launch a large scale attack with British military from Loughrea, R.I.C. from Athenry and military

224 W/S 298 Alf Monahan.
225 W/S 1,562 Martin Newell.

from Galway City.' [226]

While in Moyode Liam Mellows and Alf Monahan felt happy that their efforts had meant something. They had succeeded to some degree at attracting the attention of the British who could not concentrate all their forces on Dublin.

'Poorly armed as his forces were, the Galway
Volunteer leaders had no hope of doing anything
else.' [227]

At this stage there was another military council held among the leaders to decide what should be done. It now seemed clear that they could not take on any British military in a battle and hope to succeed. Their original plans, to attack and capture several R.I.C. barracks and take prisoners and capture arms and ammunition, were also in disarray. When the R.I.C. abandoned rural outlying barracks and huts and withdrew into towns such as Athenry and Loughrea they were now too well secured for the rebels to attack. The abortive attacks on Clarenbridge and Oranmore had shown this. In the absence of any written records it is difficult to see what plans unfolded as the days progressed. They could head south towards Clare hoping that people would rise there and join them or they could head towards Portumna and the Shannon hoping likewise. However, it seems more likely at this stage that they just hoped to keep a distance from the military and move to any area that might offer some security and be reasonably feasible to defend if attacked. It must be remembered that at this stage they had a very limited supply of arms and that as a result of engagements at Clarenbridge, Oranmore, Carnmore, the Agricultural College and Rahard their supply of ammunition was considerably less

226 W/S 346 Stephen Jordan.

227 W/S 298 Ailbhe O Monachain (Alf Monahan).

than when they started out the previous Monday.

As the leaders thought over these issues they held several meetings throughout Friday and eventually it was decided to move again. They moved southwards heading towards Clare as it is most likely Mellows had it in mind that should that county have risen he could link up with them. The remaining group of volunteers left Moyode Castle late at night as they headed south towards Gort. After leaving Moyode they passed through Ballywinna and Caheradangan, moved east of Craughwell through Ballymanagh, Monksfield and Moneen and on to Lime Park House between Ardrahan and Peterswell. They wished to avoid Craughwell as there was a large force of R.I.C. stationed there and there was considerable support among some locals for the police. They marched through the night using back roads and boreens to reach their destination.

Lime Park was a large house belonging to the Persse family though it was not occupied at this time. There were about 450 to 500 men and women left with Mellows and Monahan at this time as a number of others had decided to go home.

'If I were to be exact I would be putting it at 450 – 500'[228]

and

'I think there would be about 500 men. That is
a very rough guess of mine because I couldn't
well remember.' [229]

Many of these had no guns or other arms or were now very low on ammunition considering that shots had been fired on a

---

228 mspcsearch.militaryarchives.ie/docs/files/PDE_Membership/7/WA21%20 (4)_Bpdf.pdf p93
    Martin Neiland

229 mspcsearch.militaryarchives.ie/docs/files/PDE_Membership/7/WA21%20 (4)_Bpdf.pdf p4
    Martin Newell

number of occasions. It was now also going to be increasingly difficult to feed the men and keep such a large number of men in the field.

> 'Our supplies were run down – because we had
> nothing. We had nothing except some raw flour.
> We had no stuff, no ammunition.'[230]

Various rumours reaching the camp about the possibility of military action against the group also played a part in lowering morale. The fact that they now seemed to be just moving from place to place rather than taking a pro-active stance, as they did on Tuesday and Wednesday, also had an effect on morale. Tensions were also creeping in as Tom Kenny had showed up a few times in Moyode and urged them to disband.

Peter Howley guarding the road to Gort with his Ardrahan Company was sent a dispatch from Moyode ordering them,

> '...to leave Tullyra and to act as advance guard
> for the main body to Lime Park.' [231]

James Barrett was a rearguard scout for the march to Lime Park. He was overtaken by Fr. Fahy and Fr. Martin O'Farrell as they returned from Galway and caught up with the Volunteers. Fr. Fahy told him that there were 200 marines landed in Galway and that they would be sent against the rebels and that they had best go home. By the time he arrived in Lime Park, having completed his scouting duties, he said the decision was already taken to disband and go home or on the run. A number of R.I.C

230 mspcsearch.militaryarchives.ie/docs/files/PDE_Membership/7/WA21%20 (4)_Bpdf.pdf   p98
     John Broderick

231 W/S 1,379 Peter Howley.

prisoners were in the kitchen and the food that was cooked was left to them. [232]

When Fr. Tom Fahy and Fr. Martin O'Farrell caught up with the rearguard group as they proceeded towards Lime Park. Fr. Fahy was returning from Galway where they had travelled to in order to see Bishop O'Dea and to ascertain what was the position in Galway City as to troop movements.[233] He was now accompanied by Fr. O'Farrell. They had news that the rising in Dublin was virtually over and that Pearse was about to surrender. [234]

Dublin was in flames and the leaders and most of the rebels were being rounded up and arrested. This was a serious turn-a-round in events and had serious implications for the rising in Galway. Therefore, the priests were of the opinion that further resistance was futile. They were aware of the large numbers of troops that had landed in Galway from Cork, up to 200 men. The Laburnum was capable of firing shells inland for some distance and there was the possibility that troops could be sent from many other parts of Ireland to engage the Galway rebels, particularly as Dublin was on the verge of surrender. They now knew for sure that there were troops and police all over Galway in places such as Tuam, Loughrea, Ballinasloe and Attymon just waiting for the orders to attack the rebels in south Galway.

The main body of rebels had reached Lime Park late on Friday night and discussions began on what to do next. Initially discussions began between Liam Mellows, Alf Monahan and the priests Fr. Fahy and Fr. Feeney. The priests were of the opinion that continued resistance was pointless. Dublin had surrendered and now the full weight of the military and police would be unleashed on Galway. Mellows was of the opinion that they would all be rounded up and killed anyway and that it

232 W/S 343 James Barrett.
233 W/S 343 James Barrett.
234 W/S 1,564 Michael Kelly.

would be better to die fighting than to surrender. The opinions of the priests must be seen as being more of military reasoning than clerical interference. Fr. Fahy and Fr Feeney along with many other priests had been loyal supporters of the movement and their advice could not now be seen as clerical opposition and interference. Ultimately, Fr. Fahy persuaded Mellows to bring in the company leaders into the discussions. [235]

Saturday April 29th

Early in the morning after Fr. Fahy outlines the situation to Mellows and the company leaders a vote is taken and it is decided to disband and return home or go on the run.

Bushfield

At about 3 a.m. Pat Callanan decided to disband the outpost he had set up at Bushfield as a lookout for any activity in the area that could be relayed to Mellows. He had been made aware that the rebels were likely to move from Moyode on Friday evening but had not received any word as to what was happening or where they may have gone. As he and the three others with him decided to go towards Moyode to see what was afoot they met others on their way from Lime Park. These said that the Volunteers had been disbanded and were all on their way home or going on the run. Callanan sent those with him home and went on the run himself. [236]

Lime Park

There were fourteen to fifteen men, in addition to the two priests, at the crucial meeting held at Lime Park House to decide what to do in the changing circumstances the rebels now found themselves. Both Fr. Tom Fahy and Fr. Martin O'Farrell, who had arrived from Galway with Fr. Fahy, had the latest

235 W/S 298 Ailbhe O Monachain (Alf Monahan).

236 W/S 347 Pat Callanan.

information and were anxious that this would be given to all the leaders so that an informed military decision could be made. Those gathered at this meeting were as follows; Liam Mellows, Alf Monahan, Larry Lardner (Brigade O/C), Eamon Corbett (Clarenbridge), Martin 'Mattie' Neilan (Clarenbridge), Frank Hynes (Athenry), Nicholas Kyne (Claregalway), Tom Ruane (Castlegar), Joe Howley (Oranmore), John Broderick (Athenry), Michael Fleming (Clarenbridge), Michael Cummins (Coldwood), Michael Kelly (Newcastle), Michael Newell (Clarenbridge), Brian Molloy (Castlegar), Fr. Henry Feeney and Fr. Tom Fahy. These were mainly the various company commanders, from the Brigade, and they felt responsible for the fate of their men.[237]/[238]

Initially Liam Mellows fell asleep when the meeting was called in the front room of the house. He had barely slept for three days. Alf Monahan spoke on not disbanding or surrendering as he was of the same mind as Mellows. The priests spoke of the hopelessness of the situation. Frank Hynes woke Mellows so that he could give his opinion before the final decision.

> 'When Liam understood the situation he apologised for having slept and now he said, 'I brought out the men to fight, not to run away. If they disband now what will happen. They will be shot down like rabbits without a chance of defending themselves. I refuse to disband them. I hand over command to anyone who wants it.' [239]

Various points were put before the decision was taken. Mellows felt he had already put it to the men in Moyode that if they wished to leave and go home they could and some did.

237 W/S 345 Brian Molloy.

238 W/S 1,379 Peter Howley.

239 W/S 446 Frank Hynes.

Those here now wished to fight on. He also felt that they would be arrested anyway and should die fighting. Mellows said that the R.I.C. had free rein in many localities while the rebels were in Moyode and that they would already know who was missing from their homes and be ready to arrest and imprison them at least. He also pointed out that they held a number of R.I.C. prisoners and these men could easily recognise many of the leaders and men and this would speed up the capture of the rebels if they disbanded. Fr. Feeney approached the R.I.C. prisoners on this issue and succeeded in getting them to agree not to help with the recognition of any rebels in the ensuing roundup should the men disband and go on the run.

> 'After deliberations these six R.I.C. men
> gave an undertaking they would give no information
> to their authorities, which undertaking I was glad
> to be afterwards authentically assured, was
> honoured.' [240]

On the other hand, it was seen that the position was hopeless, the British military was about to advance from all sides. Munster Fusiliers, had landed in Galway, Belfast R.I.C., were in the Tuam/Galway area and up to 900 soldiers were approaching from Attymon/Loughrea side. They would be easily surrounded and killed as their lack of arms and ammunition would render it a hopeless task to hold out. In addition, there were many men in Lime Park that had virtually no arms at all. It was suggested that should they disband they could hold on to what arms and ammunition they had and use them later when another rising could be arranged. There was some talk of breaking up into smaller units and fighting a guerrilla war but again the lack of suitable arms meant this was unlikely to work.

---

240 W/S 383 Fr. Thomas Fahy.

'...he (Fr. Fahy) formed the opinion in the end
that the position was becoming more and more
hopeless: and he thought that if the military were
allowed to surround us it would be wholesale
massacre which he did not want.' [241]

Following intense discussions involving all those named a
vote was taken on how to proceed.

'Twelve officers voted for immediate disbandment,
Mellows and I against.' [242]

In all the meetings involving the leaders, the officers and
priests lasted through various stages for up to four hours.
Eventually at about 3 a.m. it was decided to disband. Liam
Mellows did not wish to address the men and asked Fr. Fahy
to do so.

'I asked Mellows to convey the decision to the men.
He begged myself to do so, saying that he was
reluctant to ask a single one of them to go away. I
then addressed the men, telling them the decision
and advising them to break up immediately and
save their equipment for another day. Mellows did
not address the men.' [243]

Many of the men who were now in Lime Park probably
still wished to fight on, however, it was increasingly obvious
that there was not much point. They had little food, poor guns
and less ammunition. They had already taken part, over the

---

241 mspcsearch.militaryarchives.ie/docs/files/PDE_Membership/7/WA21%20 (4)_Bpdf.pdf p101
    Martin Neilan.

242 W/S 298 Ailbhe O Monachain (Alf Monahan).

243 W/S 383 Very Rev. Dr. Tom Fahy.

week, in seven engagements and that saw a serious amount of ammunition used. They were shortly going to be faced with various British forces of far superior strength and as they deliberated these forces were heading towards Lime Park. Still there were some prepared to fight on despite the prospect of an attack by the British military.

'He (Fr. Fahy) asked them would they go home or fight and they shouted that they would fight.' [244]

However, due to more persuasive arguments, they finally disbanded.

'Finally, Alf Monahan got permission from Mellows to disband them and he did.' [245]

It is easy to say that they should have fought on but to what effect. The far more common sense strategy was now to disband and see if they could hold on to their guns and maybe look to the future and fight another day.

Following the disbandment Liam Mellows, Alf Monahan and Frank Hynes went on the run together. They first went to William Howley's house in Lime Park where they had some breakfast, cooked by his daughter Bridget. They left there at about 7 a.m. and went to Patsy Corless's in Ballycahalan.[246] From there they went towards the Sliabh Aughty mountains on the Galway-Clare boarder and they hid out there for some months until they were able to get away safely. During that time they received great local support from the people of the area.

---

244 mspcsearch.militaryarchives.ie/en/collections/online-collections/military-service-pensions-collection/ search-the- collection/easter-rising-1916/aplicants-at-action-sites Nicholas Kyne p42

245 mspcsearch.militaryarchives.ie/en/collections/online-collections/military-service-pensions-collection/ search-the- collection/easter-rising-1916/aplicants-at-action-sites Nicholas Kyne p42

246 W/S 1,379 Peter Howley.

Rebellion in Galway

Aftermath

In Dublin there was a huge amount of destruction as much of the centre of the city was destroyed. Over 1,000 citizens were wounded. There were 230 civilians, 132 British soldiers/police and 64 rebels killed during the exchanges.[247] A few other military personnel were killed principally in Ashbourne where two rebels also died.

In Galway, over the next few weeks, there was a general round up, by the R.I.C. and British military, of hundreds of suspects. Up to 400 were arrested and of these 328 were eventually sent to jail in Britain.[248] They knew who they were looking for and tracked down most of them pretty quickly. Here is a selection of what happened to some of the participants in the weeks following the rebellion.

James Barrett went on the run and evaded capture for about three weeks. After his arrest he ended up in Frongoch until August 1916.[249]

John Broderick was on the run for a number of months before he got a job in Maynooth College from priests who were sympathetic to his cause.

Pat 'The Hare' Callanan escaped to America in August with **Eamon Corbett** after hiding out in the Galway area for a number of weeks. [250]

Thomas Courtney stayed on the run after the rising for about a fortnight. He then managed to get a doctors certificate saying he was sick and returned to work in the post office. He was paid for the time he was off even though the overseer Mr. Meally (a Protestant and a Loyalist) had a very good idea what he was up

---

247 www.bbc.co.uk/history/british/easterrising/aftermath/af01.shtml

248 www.historyireland.com/20thcentury-contemporary-history/the-most-shoneen-town-in-irelandgalway-in-1916/

249 W/S 343 James Barrett.

250 W/S 347 Pat Callanan.

to. Meally had a regard for, as an Irishman, what Courtney had done to try to help his country. [251]

Fr Tom Fahy was able to return to Maynooth College where he later arranged employment for some of the leaders who were on the run, John Broderick, Alf Monahan and Frank Hynes. [252]

Fr Henry Feeney went on the run and evaded arrest. He first went to Mount Melleray and then to America. [253]

Laurence Garvey was arrested the week after Easter but released after questioning. He was re-arrested on May 10th and taken to Loughrea, Athenry and then Richmond Barracks in Dublin. He was eventually interned in Frongoch and released in August 1916. Laurence was the only man from Mullagh who was interned. [254]

Peter Howley He and his brothers were arrested at their house on Saturday evening, April 29th. There were about sixty R.I.C. constables in the party including many down from Belfast. The Howleys were eventually sent to Frongoch. [255]

In Kinvarra there were a series of arrests in early May when a number of suspects were rounded up and sent to jail. However, the younger ones including **Michael Hynes** and **James Picker** were released within a fortnight. [256]

Following the disbandment **Stephen Jordan** went on the run along with **Dick Murphy**, the Fenian 'centre' in the Athenry Circle. They were arrested in Tuam, in June and eventually deported to England and jailed in Frongoch. Stephen was released at Christmas and returned to Ireland. [257]

---

251 W/S 447 Thomas Courtney.

252 W/S 344 John Broderick.

253 W/S 383 Fr. Thomas Fahy.

254 W/S 1.062 Laurence Garvey.

255 W/S 1,379 Peter Howley.

256 W/S 1.173 Michael Hynes.

257 W/S 346 Stephen Jordan.

William Kelly was arrested at his house in Killimordaly and sent to jail in Nutsford in Scotland being released in November 1916. [258]

Tom Kenny, though not directly involved in the rising, was one of the most wanted men in the county. He escaped to America where he remained for a few years before returning home to Craughwell.

Frank Hynes, Liam Mellows and Alf Monahan They went on the run together in south Galway when the rebels disbanded. Eventually Liam Mellows escaped to America via Liverpool. Alf Monahan and Hynes got jobs in Maynooth College through the sympathetic Fr. Tom Fahy. All three avoided arrest despite the police and military combing the countryside for them.

Larry Lardner was on the run for three months before he was arrested. He was jailed for a short time but re-arrested and sent to jail in England for a year in connection with the German Plot.

Brian Molloy brought his men back to Brierhill in Castlegar and they disbanded. He went on the run to Connemara but was arrested after a week or so. He was sentenced to death but it was commuted to ten years in jail. He spent time in jail in England and was released in May 1917.[259]

Gilbert Morrissey and his three brothers (**John, Martin** and **Patrick**) who were active in the rebellion went on the run but were shortly rounded up and arrested. They were sent to Richmond Barracks in Dublin and on to Scotland. From there he was sent to Frongoch. He was released in the general amnesty in December of 1916.[260]

Fr. William O'Meehan continued as curate in Kinvarra before

---

258 mspcsearch.nilitaryarchives.ie/docs/files//PDF_Pensions/R1/MPS34REF2957Williamkelly/
    WMSP34REF2957WilliamKelly.pdf p64

259 W/S 345 BrianMolloy.

260 W/S 874 Gilbert Morrissey.

going to Rahoon in Galway in 1919.[261]

Tom Ruane returned to the Castlegar area and went on the run but he was arrested and sent to Frongoch in Wales.

There was a group of twelve from around Athenry, later referred to as 'the Twelve Apostles', that were kept in jail until mid 1917. These men, **Thomas Barrett** (Court Lane), **Michael Donoghue** (Slieveroe), **Mortimer 'Murty' Fahy** (Slieveroe), **John and Michael Grady** (Church Street), **John 'Jack' Hanniffy** (Slieveroe), **Martin Hansberry** (Rahard), **Michael Higgins** (Coshla), **Patrick 'Patch'** and **Thomas Kennedy** (Slieveroe), **Peter Murray** (Derrydonnell) and **Charlie Whyte** (Caherroyan) were considered among the most dangerous and subversive in the county.

---

261 W/S 1,034 Mrs. Mary Leech (nee O'Meehan).

What the Papers Said.

All the local and national newspapers were outraged at the rebellion and reports, articles and editorials reflected this fact. Unanimously they condemned the rising and its leaders for their actions. They claimed that there were virtually none in the country that supported a rebellion at this time especially as most of our efforts were aimed at supporting the war effort for World War 1. It was also notable that most newspaper articles claimed that the rebels were aided and supported by Germany and that the rebels were supporting Germany as much as seeking independence. Additionally, the rising was seen as a Sinn Féin rising and the blame for organising it was laid squarely at their feet.

Wednesday April 26th **The Connacht Tribune (Galway City)**
This was the lead page of the Connacht Tribune of Wednesday April 26th (though the paper is wrongly dated April 25th)[262]

IS IT INSURRECTION?
ALLEGED GENERAL "RISING"
IN IRELAND
The Irish Volunteers
WILD RUMOURS FROM DUBLIN
REPORTED SEIZURE OF GOVERNMENT OFFICES
GALWAY ISOLATED
POSTAL AND TELEGRAPHIC COMMUNICATION CUT OFF AND RAILWAY LINE TORN UP.
TWO LOCAL ENGAGEMENTS
AT ORANMORE AND CARNMORE
POLICE CASUALTIES
Strange Scenes in Galway Yesterday

---

262 www.nli.ie/1916/pdf/7.14

Also

Incidents at Oranmore
POLICE BARRACKS RUSHED AND
STATION SIGNALS BROKEN

SHOTS EXCHANGED

*BETWEEN FORCES OF THE CROWN
AND THE VOLUNTEERS*

Also

Bloody Work!
BATTLE AT DAWN THIS MORNING
AT CARNMORE

Constable Whelan, Eglington Street, killed.

There was also an Editorial in the paper in relation to the activities ongoing since the beginning of the week. In it comments were broadly sympathetic to the aims of the rising, viewing the participants as well-meaning but misguided. It also stated that if they had sought help from Germany, as they were rumoured to have, the leaders should at the very least expect to hang.

Friday April 28th   **The Daily Express (London)** [263]

**'Both Sir Edward Carson and Mr John Redmond expressed
their detestation of the outbreak.'
'Whole Country Placed Under Martial Law.'**

---

263 www.nli.ie/1916/pdf/7.14.pdf

'The revolt has spread from Dublin to other places in the south and west – particularly the west. In order not to hamper military precautions the names of these localities have not been disclosed.'

Tuesday May 2nd   **The Belfast News Letter (Belfast)** [264]

'The latest news about the Sinn Fein rising is good. On Sunday General Maxwell informed a group of Press representatives that the back of the rising was broken, but not yet over....'

Thursday May 4th   **Irish Independent (Dublin)** [265]

'No terms of denunciation that pen could indict would be too strong to apply to those responsible for the insane and criminal rising of last week...'

However, as the week passed and the executions mounted the attitude changed somewhat and questions began to be asked and reported on as to whether or not there was an overreaction by the authorities. The public reaction to the executions was beginning to see the leaders as martyrs

Wednesday May 10th   **The Irish Times (Dublin)** [266]

'In the House of Commons on Monday Mr. Redmond asked the Prime Minister to put an immediate stop to the execution of rebels in Dublin...'

---

264 www.bbc.co.uk/history/british/easterrising/newspapers/index.shtml

265 www.bbc.co.uk/history/british/easterrising/newspapers/index.shtml

266 www.bbc.co.uk/history/british/easterrising/newspapers/index.shtml

The Easter Rising also made the news in the United States though most of the information would have come from British sources through the cable link from Clifden to Newfoundland. First reported on Tuesday April 25th the story made the front page of the New York Times for 14 days in a row despite being in competition with World War 1 news.[267] The news was not always accurate but with censorship in place from Britain that is not surprising.

Wednesday April 26th   **New York Times (New York)**

TROOPS CRUSH REVOLT IN DUBLIN
TAKE POST OFFICE SEIZED BY RIOTERS;
MANY KILLED IN STREET FIGHTING

WIRES FROM CITY ARE CUT

But Government Says Trouble Is in Hand and
Has Not Spread

Friday April 28th   **The New York Times (New York)**

IRISH REVOLT SPREADS WEST AND SOUTH
WHOLE ISLAND NOW UNDER MARTIAL LAW;
COLONIAL IRISH ROUSE AGAINST REBELS
DUBLIN STILL CUT OFF

and also

Carson and Redmond Join Against Revolt;
Urge that No Political Use Be Made of It

---

267 The 1916 Easter Rising made the front page of the New York Times 14 days in a row

Rebellion in Galway

Thursday May 4th   **The New York Times (New York)**

FOUR IRISH REBEL LEADERS EXECUTED; THREE OTHERS GET 3 YEARS IN PRISON; BIRRELL RESIGNS AS IRISH SECRETARY

CASEMENT'S TRIAL SOON

*Pearse, Clarke, Mc Donagh
and Probably Connolly
Shot in Tower.*

At home, in Britain and in the United States in the days during and immediately after the rising most of the media reaction was against it. However, it must be remembered that the majority of newspapers were published and run by those with links and leanings to the authorities and their outlook was firmly pro British and establishment.

The Royal Irish Constabulary

This police force was founded in 1836 as an armed force by Thomas Drummond. It was given the title Royal following its role in suppressing the revolt of the Irish Republican Brotherhood (The Fenians) in 1867.

The force was mainly manned by Irish Catholics from the tenant farmer class. It is estimated that 75% of the force was Catholic. However, it was mainly the ordinary constables who were Catholic with the officers making up most of the remaining 25% belonging to Protestant religions. It was really a police force doing a soldiers job. Pay was poor, promotion was slow and conditions were tough. Constables were not posted in their own county that of their wife's or one in which they had relations. A constable was moved frequently so as not to develop a close relationship with the locality in which he served. You could not marry until you had served over seven years and your bride had to be approved by the authorities. Constables were confined to their barracks at night, had no vote in elections, had to under-go military training and had no recognised leave or holidays.

Constables or their wives were not allowed to engage in trade or partake in selling produce. Neither could their wives engage in certain trades, like dressmaking or take in lodgers. Indeed at one time constables were not allowed to enter public-houses in a social capacity.

The force was an armed force. They were issued with Webley revolvers and the .303 Lee-Enfield rifle. By 1900 there was little discernible nationalist activity and more often than not constables did not go around armed. They generally had a baton and handcuffs. As a result target practice became an annual requirement to ensure they were familiar with the weapons. They wore a dark green uniform and a flat peaked cap. Recruits and officers were trained at the R.I.C. headquarters in the Phoenix Park in Dublin.

Officers were mainly drawn from the Protestant religion and were recruited by open civil service examination. They were likely to be less sympathetic to nationalist ideals than the rank and file Catholic constables. Many were university graduates and a good deal were former army officers. Many of this officer corps were members of the Freemasons. There was some level of promotion prospects for officers and elevation to District Inspector or County Inspector after some twenty years' service was generally as high as most ever went.

At times the force was unpopular as it assisted with evictions and was considered an agent of British surveillance and control. This was especially true in areas like Galway where there was considerable discontent during the Land War. Much of the information going to Dublin Castle in relation to Land League and other more subversive activities was supplied by the vigilance of R.I.C. constables. They had to furnish Dublin with lengthy reports on a regular basis.

In addition to their usual duties the R.I.C. were charged with the responsibility of collecting the 1901 and 1911 census statistics.

Young men joining the force did so as a job and it was an alternative to emigration mainly for second and other sons that were unlikely to inherit the family farm. Being stationed in Ireland in what was a mainly peaceful country while being less adventuresome was likely a lot safer than being stationed abroad in some war torn country with the British army.

The numbers grew steadily throughout the late 1800's and in 1870 stood at 12,000. In the 1901 census there were 1,600 R.I.C. barracks and 11,000 in the force.[268] Attracting new recruits grew more difficult in the early 1900's. Morale was low, pay and conditions continued to be poor, the job was often unpopular locally and people with an interest in a military lifestyle

268 Eircom.net/~celtichistories/constabulary.htm

were more attracted to the army. Numbers were falling and resignations and retirements were forbidden under the Police (Emergency Provisions) Act of 1915 unless you were enlisting in the armed forces to serve at the front in World War 1. [269]

In 1901 Sir Neville Francis Fitzgerald Chamberlain was appointed Inspector General of the R.I.C. He was a military man and had served in India. He is credited with inventing the game of snooker while in India. He was appointed at a difficult time as there was an upsurge of nationalist organisations in the country. Most of these such as the G.A.A., Sinn Fein, The Gaelic League and later the Irish Volunteers were focused on a greater freedom for Ireland either politically or culturally. Added to this were the renewed activities of the I.R.B. in many areas such as Galway. Also the rise in tension between the Irish and Ulster Volunteers as they armed themselves and took opposing sides in relation to the proposed passing of Home Rule in1914. This brought the R.I.C. into greater conflict with people in their localities. From 1913 on after the forming of the Irish Volunteers it was a regular occurrence to see armed men and indeed women parading on the streets of towns and villages around Ireland. Indeed it was hoped by many that as World War 1 looked ominous and then indeed broke out that these men would get good training on weapons and drill that would prepare them to volunteer for service with the regular British army.

Chamberlain did let Chief Secretary Augustine Birrell and Under Secretary Sir Matthew Nathan know that there was a rumour about that guns were to be landed on the south coast of Ireland coming up to Easter of 1916 but between them it was dismissed. The Royal Commission into the 1916 Rising, the Hardinge Commission, did exonerate the R.I.C. in relation to all its dealings with the rising but nevertheless Chamberlain had resigned in the wake of the rising. Birrell and Nathan also

269 Policing in Ireland warwick.ac.uk.../Ireland/constabulary.htm

resigned.

There were a total of 14 R.I.C. officers and 3 Dublin Metropolitan Policemen killed during the rising. Eight of these died during or as a result of the Battle of Ashbourne. Constable Charles Mc Gee was shot in Castlebellingham in Co. Louth, Sergeant Thomas Rourke and Constable John Hurley were shot in Tipperary trying to arrest I.R.B. men, Constable Christopher Miller was killed in Dublin, Head Constable William Nelson Rowe was killed in a siege of the Kent house in Castlelyons in Co. Cork and Constable Patrick Whelan was shot at Carnmore in Galway as he confronted a group of rebels. All three D.M.P. men, Constables James O'Brien, Michael Lahiff and William Frith, were shot and killed in Dublin. [270]

Following the 1916 Rising four gallantry medals were awarded to R.I.C. members. Two of these were for action in Galway and two for action during the Battle of Ashbourne. Those in Galway were to County Inspector George Bedell Ruttledge and Sergeant Thomas Reilly and for the Ashbourne engagement to Sergeant William O'Connell and Constable Eugene Bratton. [271]

Royal Irish Constabulary in Galway.

At the time of the 1916 Rising Galway was in the Western Division of the R.I.C. The County Inspector was George Bidell Ruttledge and he was aided by two District Inspectors one for West Riding, George Bennett Heard, and one for East Riding, Edward Miles Clayton. Due to the level of agrarian related violence, the activities of the Irish Volunteers and the I.R.B. Galway had the most number of R.I.C. constables per head of population of any county in Ireland at that time. The R.I.C. generally rented a building, barracks, in local towns and

270 www.policememorial.org.uk/index.php?page=royal-irish-constsbulary

271 irishconstabulary.com/topic/786#.VR1OxvzF_h5

villages where they felt a presence was needed to maintain public order. Huts were sub stations set up in areas where there was an increased likelihood of disturbance.

Between R.I.C. barracks and huts there were 93 stations in Galway at the time of the 1911 census. Of these at least 38 were in areas that were to be directly the focus of the 1916 Rising. Athenry had Cross Street in the town and Newford and Ballygarraun outside the town in areas where there was tension over land issues. These returned 30, 13 and 5 constables respectively. Craughwell had two barracks in the town with 16 and 12 constables. There were barracks in Rathgorgin, Bookeen and Hollypark with 10, 11 and 4 men stationed there. These were all within four miles of Kiltullagh which was near both Loughrea and Craughwell. Loughrea had two barracks on Barrack Street with 18 men in one and 3 in the other. Oranmore Barracks, at Innplot, had 11 R.I.C. men and Kinvarra had 13.[272] This showed the level of police presence in the mid to south Galway area.[273] When you compare this to Galway City where Eglinton Street barracks had 20 men while Lenaboy in the Salthill region had just 3 you realise the serious view taken by the authorities to the mid Galway region at the time.

By 1916 Galway was one of the few proscribed counties in the country. There were serious disturbances throughout the county and it had a large number of R.I.C. personel in areas where trouble was expected. The barracks or huts that were in the area most affected by the Rising were;

Ballyconnell (Ballycahalan), **Ballygarraun** (Athenry), **Barrack Street 1** (Loughrea), **Barrack Street 2** (Loughrea), **Bookeen** (Kiltullagh), **Castletaylor** (Ardrahan), **Colmanstown** (Tiaquin), **Craughwell Town 1, Craughwell Town 2, Cross Street** (Athenry), **Cuilmore** (Peterswell), **Cummer** (Cummer), **Derrybrien North** (Derrylaur), **Eglinton Street** (Galway

272 1911 Census Ireland.

273 http://winters-omline.net/RIC-Barracks-1911/Galway/

City), **Glennaloghaun** (Monivea), **Gort Town, Gortmore** (Turloughmore). **Hollypark** (Moyode), **Innplot** (Oranmore), **Kilchreest** (Kilchreest, Loughrea), **Killafeen** (Kilbeacanty), **Killeely More** (Drumacoo, Kilcolgan), **Kinvarra, Laghtgeorge** (Claregalway), **Lecarrownagappoge** (Kilreekill), **Lenaboy** (Galway South Urban), **Lickerrig** (Moyode), **Lydacan** (Carnmore), **Military Barracks** (Gort), **New Docks Street** (Galway East Urban), **Newford** (Athenry), **New Inn** (Aughrim), **Newtown** (Kilcolgan), **Rathgorgin** (Kiltullagh), **Rathwilladoon** (Beagh), **Rinmore** (Galway East), **Spiddal Town** (Spiddal), and **Vicar Street** (Tuam). [274]

The R.I.C. in Galway was ever vigilant and kept a close eye on all known republicans. These were often closely followed when they left their areas as it was assumed they were making contact with other republicans and likely to do things that would lead to disaffection. When G.A.A. members such as Stephen Jordan, Tom Kenny or Larry Lardner travelled to Dublin for meetings they were followed and notes taken as to where they went and whom they met. At least one R.I.C. man from each barracks was present in Galway on St. Patrick's Day 1916 for the Irish Volunteers march through the town. The purpose of this was to take notes as to who was there and how they were armed and the R.I.C. was able to use this information so as to arrest them in the wake of the 1916 Rising.

During the Rising the Galway R.I.C. played a pivotal role and it was they rather than the military that faced the rebels in all the encounters. There were attacks on barracks at Clarenbridge and Oranmore with a constable wounded in each encounter. They showed great bravery in these encounters as the barracks came under intense fire when defended by just a few men. A constable was shot dead in the battle at Carnmore Cross (Constable Patrick Whelan) and the R.I.C. had exchanges

274 http://winters-online.net/RIC-Barracks-1911/Galway/

of fire with the rebels at both the Agricultural College, Athenry and Moyode Castle. Thus, the following R.I.C. officers and men should be mentioned in relation to their roles in the Rising.

Given that most of the rank and file constables were local men from farming backgrounds conflicts of interest often occurred. Thus, we see that Nora Haverty aunt of James Haverty of Springlawn, Mountbellew married an R.I.C. constable. James Haverty was an I.R.B. man and captain of the Mountbellew Irish Volunteers' company. He was jailed in 1916 for his activities while his uncle in law, John Brennan from Roscommon, had risen to the rank of Head Constable in the R.I.C. Nora was an aunt and James a brother of my paternal grandmother Ellen, who married Stephen Jordan, one of the leaders of the Rising, in 1919.

Killed
Constable Patrick Whelan

In 1916 he was a 34 year old single man attached to Eglinton Street Barracks, Galway.[275] He was a farmer's son, as were many R.I.C. members. In the census of 1911 there is a P.W., a single man stationed in Williamstown north Co. Galway. As he is a Kilkenny native it may be him. The R.I.C. only gave initials for their constables in the census.

In 1916 he was a 34 year old attached to the Galway Barracks. Early on Wednesday morning the 26th of April a large group of R.I.C. constables were mobilised to move out of Galway City to see could they ascertain the position of the rebels. They encountered a group of rebels at Carnmore Cross. In the engagement that followed Constable Whelan was killed as he called on the rebels to surrender saying he knew most of them anyway. He had 8 years and 6 months service in the force.

He was the first R.I.C. officer to be killed outside Dublin during the Rising. He is buried in Bohermore Cemetery, Galway.

275 Jim Herlihy,' A Short History and Genealogical Guide The Royal Irish Constabulary.' Four Courts Press.

1911 Census

18 Williamstown Town (Kilcroan, Galway).

P W (26) Constable R.I.C.

Wounded

Constable Joseph Ginty

He was a 44 year old with 21 years 4 months service in the force. He was wounded in the defence of the Oranmore Barracks when it was attacked by the Oranmore and Maree Irish Volunteer companies on Tuesday 25th of April.

Constable Hugh Hamilton

He was wounded in the engagement in Carnmore when the R.I.C. confronted a large group of rebels. He was 31 and had 9 years 10 months service.

Constable David Manning

He was wounded in Clarenbridge when he was captured at a check-point as he arrived during the attack on the R.I.C. barracks. He was approaching the barracks which was under attack on a bicycle when he was asked to surrender. In the confusion he was shot and wounded. He was a 32 year old with 10 years service.

Constable Martin Meany

He was on an N.C.O.'s training course in Portobello Barracks in Dublin when the rebellion broke out. He was wounded taking part in an attack on the South Dublin Union. Aged 26 he had 4 years 2 months service.

- Most witness statements from Irish Volunteers present at the engagement at Carnmore Crossroads on Wednesday April 26th testify to up to 13 R.I.C. being wounded. However, this is not referred to in R.I.C. reports.[276][277][278]

Gallantry awards.

The King's Police Medal was awarded to two members of the R.I.C. for service in Galway during the rebellion.

County Inspector George Bedell Ruttledge

George Ruttledge was born in Co. Fermanagh in 1863. He rose rapidly in the R.I.C. He was appointed a District Inspector in 1889 and a County Inspector in 1911. He was District Inspector in the Kinsale region, according to the 1901 census. He married Winifred Herbert in 1895 but was a widower by the age of 38. He was a member of the Church of Ireland. In 1911 he was stationed in Mullingar and living with his 14 year old son Derek and a maid Mary Melia. His son was born in Tipperary showing how the force were constantly moved in line with policy ensuring they did not become too close to people in the locality. He held a medal from 1903 issued in relation to the visit of King Edward V11 to Dublin. He served in the force from the early 1880's to his retirement in 1920.[279]

At the time of the 1916 Rising he was County Inspector for Galway and the security of the county was his responsibility.

The Oranmore barracks was attacked on the morning of Tuesday 25th April by rebels from the Maree and Oranmore areas. The R.I.C. constables successfully repulsed the attack. Word was sent to Galway for reinforcements. However, the rebels were determined to make a second attack on the barracks

---

276 Brigade Activity Reports Easter Week 1916 County Galway (A/21/4/A) p27.

277 W/S 447 Thomas Courtney.

278 W/S 345 Brian Molloy.

279 Jim Herlihy, 'Royal Irish Constabulary Officers, A Biographical Dictionary and Genealogical Guide 1816 – 1922.' Four Courts Press.

when Liam Mellows arrived from Clarenbridge later in the day. Eventually reinforcements arrived from Galway under the command of County Inspector George Ruttledge.

They arrived by train from Galway and proceeded towards the R.I.C. barracks. Ruttledge led his men up the town to the barracks and under fire succeeded in driving off the rebels.

He received his award on January 1st 1917 with the following citation, 'for displaying conspicuous courage and ability during the rebellion he was entirely responsible for the security of County Galway. While commanding the police in the county he attacked and dispersed large bodies of rebels'.[280]

1901 Census
8 Compass Hill, Kinsale, Co. Cork.
George Bedell Ruttledge (36) District Inspector R.I.C.
Kate Keatinge (40) Servant.

1911 Census
Harbour Street, Mullingar, Co. Westmeath.
George Bedell Ruttledge (48) District Inspector R.I.C.
Derek Stewart Ruttledge (14)
Mary Josephine Melia (21) Servant.

Constable Thomas Reilly
He was a Catholic born in Cavan in 1879. In the 1901 census a T.R., originally from Cavan, is stationed in the Phoenix Park R.I.C. Training Depot. This may well be Thomas Reilly as the R.I.C. often gave initials only in census returns. Aged 22 he is the correct age to be Thomas Reilly. In the 1911 census he was a 32 year old stationed in Lisnaskea, Fermanagh. He was married to Janie (24) with a 2 year old son James.

He was stationed in Kinvarra in 1916 and was sent to watch Fr. O'Meehan at the outbreak of the rising. Fr O'Meehan was

280 irishconstabulary.com/topic/786#.VR1OxvzF_h5

a known subversive. Patrick Fahy a driver and two others showed up at the presbytery in Kinvarra to bring him to serve as Quarter-Master to the rebels. When they arrived Reilly was able to arrest Fahy and he was brought to Limerick Jail and then on to Dublin.

On 17th May 1917 Reilly was presented with his medal for gallantry and £5 war stock. The citation read, 'For displaying conspicuous gallantry in arresting and disarming a leading rebel whose capture early in the Rising was of utmost importance.'[281]

1911 Census
46 Main St., Lisnaskea, Fermanagh.
Thomas Reilly (32) Const. R.I.Constabulary, Janie (24).
James (2).

Other Awards

The Constabulary Medal, a First Class Favourable Record and a Grant from the C F Fund was granted to the following in light of their activities during the rising in the Galway area. Their years of service are given in brackets. The awards were presented at a ceremony on July 27th 1916.
Sergeant Isaac Reid (1888 – 1920), Acting Sergeant Samuel Mc Carthy (1893 – 1921), Constable Patrick Smyth (1891 – 1921), Constable Patrick Mc Shane (1895 – 1922), Constable Daniel Foley (1896 – 1920), Constable John Conlon (1898 – 1922), Constable Anthony Barrett (1901 – 1922), Constable Michael Lavelle (1906 – 1920), Constable James Hannon (1908 – 1922), Constable Peter Heffernan (1914 – 1920) and Constable John Shea.[282]
All eleven were from the Galway West Riding area.[283]

---

281 irishconstabulary.com/topic/786#.VR10xvzF_h5

282 Jim Herlihy, 'A Short History and Genealogical Guide The Royal Irish Constabulary.' Four Courts Press

283 irishconstabulary.com/topic/1577#VRb5b_ysXh4

Rebellion in Galway

District Inspector George Bennett Heard 1870 - 1961

He was born in Kilmallock, Co Limerick in 1870. Both his father Alexander and brother William were District Inspectors. In 1893 he married Cecilia Black. Heard was appointed a District Inspector in 1892 and a County Inspector in 1916. He was awarded a medal for the visit of King Edward V11 in 1903 and a Certificate from the Irish Police and Constabulary Recognition Fund. He became Commandant of the Phoenix Park Training Depot from 1920 to 1922 when he retired. He died in Ballinter, Co. Meath in 1961. [284]

In 1916 George Heard was the District Inspector for west Galway known as West Riding. He accompanied the group of R.I.C. to look for rebels to the east of Galway City early on Wednesday morning April 26th. He was with Constable Whelan when he was shot dead. He was encouraging him to call on the rebels to surrender. Heard was a Limerick man married to Cecilia with two girls Cecilia and Phyllis. Aged 46 at the time and had previously served in Dublin and Waterford. He was a member of the Church of Ireland.

1901 Census

71 Main Street, Cappoquin, Co. Waterford.

George Bennett Heard (31) District Inspector R.I.C.

Cecilia Heard (28)

Cecilia (6), Phyllis (5).

Lillian Byrne (26) Servant, Mary Condon (20) Servant.

1911 Census

1 Eglinton Street, Galway City.

George Bennett Heard (41) District Inspector R.I.C.

Cecilia Heard (38)

Cecilia (16), Phyllis (15).

Mary Condon (30) Servant, Bridget Brennan (18).

---

284 Jim Herlihy, 'Royal Irish Constabulary Officers, A Boiographical Dictionary and Genealogical Guide 1816 – 1922.' Four Courts Press.

District Inspector Edward Miles Clayton

He was born in Kildare in 1863 and was first married in 1892 and later in 1896 to his second wife Sylvia. He was appointed a District Inspector in 1888. In 1903 he received a service medal for the visit of King Edward V11 and in 1910 a Certificate from the Irish Police and Constabulary Recognition Fund. Following his role in Galway in 1916 he gained promotion and he served as Divisional Commissioner of the Munster No 2 Division in 1920. He retired from the force in 1922. [285]

He was D.I. for east Galway (East Riding) in 1916 and was well aware of most of what was going on in his area in places like Ballinasloe, Mullagh and Loughrea. A member of the Church of Ireland he was originally from Co. Kildare. Aged 52 in 1916 he was married to Sylvia with two children William and Muriel. He had previously served as a County Inspector in Down and was recorded there in both the 1901 and 1911 census.

1901 Census

4 Newry Road, Banbridge, Co. Down.

Edward Miles Clayton (38) District Inspector R.I.C.,

Sylvia Clayton (29).

William Paget L' Estrange (3) and Muriel (1).

Maria Mercer (32) Servant, Mary Anne Hart (25) Servant.[286]

1911 Census

55 Saul Street, Downpatrick, Co. Down.

Edward Miles Clayton (47) County Inspector R.I.C.

Sylvia Clayton (39)

Muriel (11).

Bridget Martin (21) Servant.

---

285 Jim Herlihy, 'Royal Irish Constabulary Officers, A Boiographical Dictionary and Genealogical Guide 1816 – 1922.' Four Courts Press.

286 All census data on R.I.C. members from the 1901/1911 Census, Ireland.

The British Military and Other Officials
in Galway in 1916.

By 1916 there were technically five armies in Ireland and there were four of these in Galway. There was the official British army, the National Volunteers (under the leadership of John Redmond), the Irish Volunteers (under the leadership of Eoin Mc Neill) and the Fenians or Irish Republican Brotherhood (a secret society). In addition to these there was the Ulster Volunteer Force in the northern counties.

The Connaught Rangers.

The main British army regiment in Galway was the Connaught Rangers. This unit was originally raised by the Earl of Clanricarde in 1793. They were also known as the 88th Regiment of Foot. They recruited mainly in Connaught. Originally they were active under the Duke of Wellington in the campaigns fought against Napoleon. They served in Spain, Egypt, the Crimea and South America.

In 1881 they were amalgamated with the 94th Regiment of Foot. Both battalions now became known as the Connaught Rangers. This unit spent just twelve years in Ireland between 1881 and 1914. They continued to serve in India and also in South Africa where they fought in the Boer. They played a very active part in World War 1 seeing action in such area as Ypres, Gallipoli and the Somme.

In Ireland their headquarters was Renmore Barracks in Galway City. On the outbreak of World War 1 the unit was sent originally to England and then to France. They were not stationed in Renmore at the time of the 1916 Rising. However, there may have been some of their reservists or retired members who were recalled serving in the barracks on an individual basis.

This regiment would later hit the headlines in relation to

a mutiny of some of its soldiers in India in June 1920 when they protested about the British army's treatment of the Irish during the War of Independence. Three soldiers died as a result of the mutiny and another, James Daly from Tyrellspass in Westmeath, was executed by firing squad for his part.

Following the foundation of the Irish Free State the unit was disbanded on July 31st 1922. Subsequently many of its members joined the Irish Free State army and fought in the Irish Civil War 1922 – 1923.

Renmore Barracks – Dun Ui Mhaoliosa.

The Board of Ordnance acquired land in Renmore in 1852 with the construction of a new military barracks in mind. At a meeting on August 4th 1852 it was stated,

> ' Leases to the Board of Ordnance of 73 statute
> measures of Renmore lands; also a strip of land
> for a road; also a strand opposite the land of low
> water mark; all at the yearly rent of £70 (£76,
> today) which included receiver's fees: Term ten
> thousand years from 1st May 1852.' [287]

The barracks was built by the Colleran Brothers from Dublin between 1876 and 1880 and was a state-of-the-art building when completed.[288] It had bed space for 176 soldiers in addition to married quarters, a sergeants' mess, officer quarters and an armoury. Works were overseen by Lieutenant R.E. Wilson. There was a workforce of 2,000 men who spent a month on and a month off so as to maximise the amount of local employment. When the barracks was completed the Royal Irish Fusiliers were first to move in. Later the Connaught Rangers were resident there and it was to become their base barracks when the Royal Irish moved out. [289]

---

287 Galway Independent/Renmore Barracks Foundation.

288 History of Renmore Barracks – Renmore History Society.

289 Galway Independent/Renmore Barracks Foundation.

Rebellion in Galway

During the Easter Rising the Connaught Rangers were gone to France and the Barracks was used primarily as a recruiting station. On Wednesday April 26th during the Galway rising six cars from the barracks joined the R.I.C as they went on a reconnaissance mission to the east of the city. Commanders from the barracks Sir A. Armstrong and Captain J.J. Bodkin joined them. It was on this sortie that Constable Patrick Whelan was shot. On Thursday 27th a force of Munster Fusiliers from Cork, who landed at Galway docks, marched to the barracks to support the troops there.[290]

British Military and other Officials.

Captain Sir Andrew Armstrong
see Appendix 5 page 355

Commander W.F. Blunt.
He was the commander of HMS Gloucester when it patrolled Galway Bay in April 1916. She arrived on Thursday 27th escorting a transport ship with a company of Royal Munster Fusiliers aboard. She received a number of prisoners and passed them on to HMS Snowdrop on Friday.

Commander Blunt was in charge HMS Hawke when, on September 20th 1911, she was in collision with RMS Olympic, sister ship of the Titanic. The planned voyage of the Olympic was cancelled and her captain Edward J. Smyth was thus available to captain the Titanic on her maiden and final voyage. Commander Blunt was somewhat sidelined as a result of the incident but was promoted on the outbreak of war and appointed commander of the HMS Gloucester. [291]

---

290 Galway Independent Renmore In Irish Hands.

291 The Royal Navy in Galway/joemulvey

Captain J.J. Bodkin.

He was attached to the 3rd Battalion of the Connaught Rangers as a reserve officer during World War 1. He was promoted Captain in January 1915 and was given recruiting duties with the Home Service in Renmore Barracks. He was stationed there until June 1918. He was at Carnmore Cross on Wednesday April 26th with men from Renmore Barracks when Constable Patrick Whelan was shot.

Admiral Sir Lewis Bayly 1857 – 1938.

It was he that was in charge of the Atlantic Fleet when the 1916 rising broke out. Stationed at Cobh, in Cork, he immediately sent ships to Galway and Clifden to support local troops and R.I.C. He also arranged the transport of up to 200 Munster Fusiliers to Galway.

He was the commander of the Royal Navy in Cobh in Cork Harbour for most of World War 1. He was appointed in 1915 and served there until 1919. From 1917 he was in charge of the Anglo-American fleet following the U.S. entry into the war. He organised convoys of supply ships so as to minimise their sinking and this proved very successful. He retired from the navy in 1919 and died in London in 1938.

'The brilliant but sometimes cantankerous Bayly
had overall operational command of the combined
Anglo – American naval forces from July 1915
until the end of the war,' [292]

Leslie Edmunds 1873 – 1922.

He was a British born government official who was Oxford educated. He worked for the Congested Districts Board in Ireland and is recorded in the 1901 census in Ballaghederreen,

---

292 www.independent.ie/lifestyles/cobhs-forgotten-war-remembered-26546549.html

Mayo and in 1911 in Galway City. He was married to Laura in 1900 and they had five children.

During the 1916 Rising in Galway he was one of the leading figures in the defence of the city. He collaborated with the R.I.C. and Naval Commander Francis Hannon to arrest leading republican figures and confine them on ships moored in Galway Bay. He supervised the firing of shells inland, from the Laburnum, to frighten the rebels. Following the rebellion he did work for the Admiralty in addition to his work with the Congested Districts Board.

On Monday July 25th 1922 while travelling with his chauffeur, John Jordan aged 19,[293] both were killed as they stumbled across an I.R.A. ambush of the Irish National Army during the Civil War.[294] The ambush took place at Carnmore to the east of Galway City near where Constable Patrick Whelan was killed in April 1916.

1911 census.

Palmyra Crescent, Galway West Urban.

Leslie Edmunds (38) Inspector Caryenter Bistrict Bc. *(should read, Congested Districts Board)*

Laura (38).

May (10), Laura (8), Patricia (6), Rita (4), Derek (2).

Margaret Dooly (32) and Delia William (20).

Commander Francis W. Hannon.[295]

He had retired as naval commander in Galway in August 1914 but came out of retirement to command the Galway naval base in the wake of the war. He was in command when the 1916 Rising broke out. In association with the R.I.C. the leading members of the Irish Volunteers were arrested on Tuesday 25th and put on board the Guillemot. In association with the

293 www.irishmedals.org/civilians-killed-civil-war.html

294 johnny-doyle.blogspot.ie/2014_04_01archive.html

295 www.historyireland.com/20th-century-contemporary-history/galway-916/

military and the R.I.C. he was in charge of co-ordinating the defence of the city with the military and the R.I.C. Also, under Article 10 of the Defence of the Realm Act he ordered that all public houses in the city close and under Article 13 that there be a curfew from 5.00 in the evening until 8.00 in the morning.[296] He supervised the firing of shells inland towards Oranmore and Castlegar on Wednesday from the Laburnum. He along with Leslie Edmunds directed where the shells were to be fired.

He received a Distinguished Services medal in April 1917.

The British Navy in Galway Bay.

When the rising in Dublin spread to Galway on Monday April 24th military authorities became alarmed. There was a British naval base at Cobh in Cork and a large number of ships were based there particularly since the outbreak of World War 1. These were usually used to protect convoys of merchant ships bringing supplies to Britain and to counteract German naval presence in the Atlantic. A decision was taken to send reinforcements from Cork to Galway and a force of naval vessels was dispatched to insure that as much as could be done to secure the west would be undertaken. Ships were sent to Galway City and more to Clifden. Those sent to Clifden were to defend the transatlantic cable from there to Nova Scotia in Canada that carried Morse code messages to the Americas. Among the ships that were in Galway Bay for during week were the following:

The Guillemot.

A converted trawler she arrived in Galway Bay on Tuesday April 25th. This ship had been converted to a mine-sweeper. The first group of arrested Volunteers in Galway were put on board so as to remove them from the city ensuring there would be no chance of them being rescued. They spent Tuesday night on the ship and were transferred to the Laburnum on Wednesday morning.

The Laburnum.

She was launched in 1915 having been built by Charles Connell and Co. in Scotstoun, Scotland. She was an Acasia-class sloop had a crew capacity of 77 and was armed with two x 12 pounder guns and two x 3 pounder anti-aircraft guns. She served in World War 1 and was transferred to the New Zealand navy in 1922. She was eventually scuttled in Singapore during World War 2.[297]

This ship arrived off Galway on Wednesday morning April 26th and anchored off Mutton Island a mile or so from the city. Immediately prisoners who had been arrested the previous day such as Micheal O'Droighneain, Frank Hardiman, George Nicolls and Padraig O'Maille were transferred to her and were kept aboard until Friday evening. By 2.30 p.m. on the day of arrival the ship's guns fired shells inland. According to the ship's log book it fired nine shells.

> '1.30 p.m. Hands employed as requisite.
> 2.20 p.m. Hands to action stations.
> Fired 9 rounds (5 common, 4 lyddite) from
> after guns in direction of the rebels advancing
> Galway Town.'[298]

An official from the Congested Districts Board Leslie Edmunds and Commander Hannon, of the navy, gave directions as to where to fire.

'…while observers were on the roof of the

---

297 J.J. Colledge, Ben Warlow, *'Ships of the Royal Navy: The Complete Record of all Fighting Ships of the Royal Navy.'* Chatham Publishing.

298 The Easter Rising on the Bay 1916 antAlantach.

Railway Hotel (now the Meyrick in Eyre Square) to report results.'[299]

No damage was reported and it is likely that the shots were to make the rebels aware of what could be done if necessary. Thomas Courtney relates in his witness statement that he had conversations with a sailor from the ship and that he said the guns could be as accurate as the gunners wanted them to be.

'One of the sailors who I then knew was a gunner said: 'When I have the range I can drop a shell into five square yards.' [300]

The rebels may initially have had plans to advance on Galway had they captured arms in a number of R.I.C. barracks. However, when that plan failed they were unlikely to attempt this. Given that they now knew that a number of war ships had arrived in Galway and could fire inland they were definitely not going to attack the city.

The Gloucester.

H.M.S. Gloucester was a Town-class cruiser built by William Beardmore and Co. of Glasgow in 1909. Its guns included 2 x 6", 10 x 4" 4 x 3 pounder guns, 4 machine guns and 2 x 18" torpedo tubes. She could accommodate a crew of up to 480 sailors. The ship took part in the Battle of Jutland between Britain and Germany off Denmark in May 1916 and was then posted to the Mediterranean and east Africa. It was sold for scrap in 1921. [301]

In 1916 she arrived off Galway on Thursday April 27th as a show of force.[302] She escorted a transported ship with up to

299 W/S 406 Frank Hardiman.

300 W/S 447 Thomas Courtney.

301 J.J. Colledge, Ben Warlow, '*Ships of the Royal Navy: The Complete Record of all Fighting Ships of the Royal Navy.*' Chatham Publishing.

302 John de Courcy Ireland, '*The Sea and The Easter Rising.*' p 25 Dun Laoghaire Maritime Institute of Ireland.

200 marines from Cork to bolster the local forces in the face of the rebellion. These marines marched out to Renmore Barracks following their disembarkation. These were a company of the Royal Munster Fusiliers. On this trip she was under the command of Commander William Frederick Blunt. When the marines disembarked prisoners were put on board.

A Troop Transport Ship.

Frank Hardiman relates in his witness statement that the Gloucester arrived on Thursday April 27th escorting a transport ship that had up to 200 marines to strengthen the local military and police forces. These were Royal Munster Fusiliers forces sent from Cork.

> 'In the distance we saw the cruiser
> 'Gloucester' entering the Bay and escorting
> a troop ship with a British regiment on their
> way to Galway.' [303]

The Snowdrop

HMS Snowdrop was an Azalea-class sloop built in 1915 in the McMillan yards, Dumbarton in Scotland. She was manned by a crew of up to 79 and was armed with two 4" guns and three 3 pounder anti-aircraft guns. The Snowdrop had a short lifetime being sold for scrap in 1923.[304]

She arrived in Galway Bay in mid week. On the evening of Friday April 28th over twenty men who had been arrested in the city, Dunmore and Tuam were transferred to her. She then set out for Cobh with these prisoners from where they were eventually sent to Dublin.

---

303 W/S 406 Frank Hardiman.

304 J.J. Colledge, Ben Warlow,'*Ships of the Royal Navy: The Complete Record of all Fighting Ships of the Royal Navy.*'Chatham Publishing.

Personalities in the Galway Rising.

Barrett Family, Athenry.

Michael and Mary Barrett from Court Lane had twelve children nine of whom lived to adulthood. Five of the family were active in the Easter week rebellion, Jim, Michael, Thomas, Christy and Annie. Annie was a founder member of Cumann na mBan and the boys were all founder members of the Irish Volunteers when they started in the town in 1914.

Jim was the most active of the brothers and was on the Volunteer organising committee. He was in the I.R.B. from 1913 sworn in by Dick Murphy. On Easter Monday he brought the dispatch from Larry Lardner to Flemings in Clarenbridge and returned to Athenry with one from Liam Mellows. He then was sent to Ballinasloe with a dispatch for Fr. Connolly. He did not get back to Athenry until late on Tuesday night and went straight to the Agricultural College. John Walsh and John Cleary were with him on the journey. All five Barretts were in Moyode and Lime Park.

After the rising Jim went on the run and was arrested after three weeks. Michael was sent to Frongoch and Thomas to Wormwood Scrubs. Thomas was detained until mid 1917.

Following the Civil War all four brothers continued the family trade as painters while Annie emigrated to England and married there. Her younger sister Nellie also married an Englishman. Jim remained single while Christy married Delia Kenny and Thomas married Maimie Reilly. Michael was married, prior to the rising, with four young children. Thomas and his family lived in Ballydavid, Christy in Caheroyan and Jim remained in the home house in Court Lane.

Jim and Christy were heavily involved in handball in Athenry, Christy as a gifted player and Jim mainly as an administrator and largely responsible for securing the site of the new handball alley near Kenny Park.

Rebellion in Galway

Jim Barrett 1884 - 1973
Michael Barrett 1886 -
Thomas Barrett 1890 -
Christy Barrett 1892 - 1976
Annie Barrett (Allum) 1894 - 1977

1901 Census

135 Athenry, Co. Galway.

Michael Barrett (35) Painter, Mary (30).

Maria (19), **James (17) Apprentice Painter, Michael (15) Apprentice Painter**, Bridget (13), **Thomas (11) Scholar, Christy (9) Scholar, Anne (7) Scholar** and Ellen (3).

1911 Census

9 Court Lane, Athenty, Co. Galway.

Michael Barrett (50) Painter, Mary (53).

Thomas (21) Painter, Christy (18) Painter, Annie (14) Scholar, Nellie (12) and Margaret (9).

1911 Census

13 Caherroyan, Athenry, Co. Galway.

Bridget Kenny (45) Servant, Mary Anne Kenny (23), Patrick Kenny (19).

Michael Barrett (24) House Painter (Lodger), Rose Barrett (20).

Joseph (3), Teresa (2) and Christopher (1).

Kate Grace (28) Cook Domestic Servant.

Sean Broderick   1890 – 1953

He was born in Athenry where his father John was a building contractor. John and Lizzie Broderick had ten children of three of whom died young. When the Irish Volunteers were founded in the town, in 1914, both father and son joined. John, 76 at the time, was elected President and Sean a Lieutenant. The company trained regularly and sided with Mc Neill after the split. Sean took an active part in the 1916 Rising. He was one of the officers present at the crucial meeting when the decision to disband was taken. Following this he went on the run and ended up in Maynooth College where Fr. Tom Fahy secured him a job. He returned to Athenry in 1917 following the release of the prisoners from Frongoch.

He was again active in the War of Independence and at the time of the Civil War he was a supporter of the Anglo-Irish Treaty. He became very active in politics and was elected to the fourth Dail in 1923 as a Cumann na nGaedheal T.D. He served continuously in the Dail for the Galway area until his defeat in the 1943 election. Thus, he served in the Dail from to 4th to the 10th inclusively. He served initially as a Cumann na nGaedheal T.D. and after 1933 as a Fine Gael T.D.

1901 Census

43 Athenry

John Broderick (55) Builder, Lizzie (45).

William (15), **John (11) Scholar,** Christopher (9), Hanoria (7), Julia (5). Delia Hamilton (30) and Thomas Barrett (20).

1911 Census

2 Church St., Athenry.

John (65) Builders Contractor, Lizzie (50).

William P. (25), **John J. (20) Builder**, Nora P. (16), Julia J. (13). Annie Carley (18).

Eamon Corbett 1890 - 1945

He was from Killeeneenbeg near Craughwell. Having joined the I.R.B he later became a chief organiser for the Irish Volunteers. He was in close contact with Padraig Pearse in the lead-up to the 1916 Rising. He was active in the rising up to the disbandment at Lime Park. He escaped to the U.S.A. following the rising but returned in 1918. He was active in the War of Independence but was arrested and spent time in jail in England. He later became a Fianna Fail T.D. serving the Galway constituency following his election in a by-election in

1935. Having lost his seat in the 1937 election he was elected for Galway West in 1943 but he did not contest the election called for the following year. He was also Chairman of Galway County Council.[305]

1901 Census

1 Killeencenbeg, Killeely, Co. Galway

Thomas Corbett (58) Farmer, Mary Corbett (42).

Thomas (16), Honoria (14), Patrick (2), **Edmond (11) Scholar,** Mary (9), John (7) and Dominick (5).

William Duffy 1865 – 1945

From Loughrea he was returned as an Irish Parliamentary Party M.P. for South Galway in 1900 and remained in Parliament until his defeat in the 1918 election. In that election he lost to Frank Fahy of Sinn Fein gaining just 14% of the vote. He was a John Redmond supporter. He joined the short-lived National League Party (1926 – 1931) founded by William Redmond. He was one of their eight T.D.'s following the June 1927 election but he did not run in the September election of the same year.

During World War 1 he was an avid supporter of recruitment to the British army. Loughrea was, in the main, a very pro-British town unlike most of the rural areas surrounding it and much of this was due to the support given to Duffy.

He was very involved in the G.A.A and with Michael Cusack he was on the deputation that visited Dr. Patrick Duggan Bishop of Clonfert in the early 1880's with a view to forming an association to promote Gaelic games. Dr. Duggan declined the offer of patronage and Dr. Croke Archbishop of Cashel took up the offer. Duffy later served as G.A.A. County Secretary for Galway but resigned due to the Parnellite split. [306]

---

305 www.advertiser.ie/galway/article/68870/eamonn-corbett-and-1916

306 Galway Advertiser The Crucial Match That Loughrea Lost.

Personalities in the Galway Rising

Thady Duggan 1898 – 1973

Thady was typical of the young men from rural county Galway that joined the Irish Volunteers from 1914 on. He was from a farming background and lived in Montiagh South, Claregalway. From a family of six children born to Michael and Mary Duggan he had four older sisters and a younger brother. Both his father and mother died in their early 40's in 1906 and 1909 respectively. This left Thady as the head of the household in the 1911 census as he inherited the farm as the oldest boy. In his mid teens he joined the Irish Volunteers and may also have been a member of the I.R.B.

He was an active participant in the rising mobilising on Monday morning and was at the engagement at Carnmore where Constable Whelan was shot. He fired several rounds from his shotgun. Thady was with the rebels for the whole week at Athenry, Moyode and Lime Park. He managed to avoid arrest following the rising while he was on the run for six weeks. During the War of Independence he was again active in the Claregalway area.

Thady married Margaret Duggan in the 1921 and they had six children. However, she died in 1936 aged 36. Thady retired from farming in the 1950's and his son John inherited the farm. In the late 1950's the family moved to Kildare in a Land Commission farm swap and Thady moved with his son's family. Eventually, the family moved back to Galway in 1973 and Thady died shortly after going to live with them in Portumna.[307]

1901 Census

22 Montiagh South, Claregalway.

Michael Duggan (40) Farmer, Mary Duggan (37).

Bridget (14), Mary (12), Margaret (9), Ellen (6), **Thady (3)** and James (1).

---

307 Interview with Sean Duggan

Rebellion in Galway

1911 Census.
1 Montiagh South, Claregalway.
Timothy (Thady) Duggan (14) Farmer
James (11), Mary (23) and Margaret (19)

Frank Fahy 1880 – 1953.

From a family of 11 children his father John was a teacher in Kilchreest near Loughrea. He was later educated in Mungret College Limerick and University College Galway. He did an Arts degree and taught Latin, Science and Irish in Castleknock College, Dublin. Later he taught in Tralee C.B.S. where he met his wife Anna Barton, a metal artist. She was a Cumann na mBan member.

He played a role in the activities of the Rising and took the anti-treaty side in the Civil War.

He qualified as a barrister in 1927 and was also General Secretary of Conradh na Gaeilge for a time.

In 1918 he was elected to the First Dáil and was a member of every Dail up to the 14th. Initially he was a Sinn Féin T.D. and later a founder member of Fianna Fáil in 1926. Following his election as Ceann Comhairle (Chairman) of the Dáil in 1932 he held the position for 19 years until Fianna Fáil lost the 1951 election.

Padraig Fahy 1879 – 1976

Padraig was born in Gort in south Galway. He was a fluent Irish speaker and was a travelling Irish teacher with the Gaelic League. He would have been a member of the I.R.B at this time. This enabled him to be in contact with a lot of activists following joining the Irish Volunteers in 1914. He was a close friend and associate of Liam Mellows and one of the main organisers in the south Galway area. On the Tuesday morning of the rebellion Mellows sent him by car to Kinvarra with three others to bring Fr. O'Meehan to Craughwell to act as Quarter-

Master to the rebels. However, the group was confronted by some R.I.C. constables and Fahy was arrested and brought to Limerick Jail. Following the Rising he was jailed in England for a time. He was active in the War of Independence and arrested during it but escaped. He took part in several ambushes during the war. He was on the Anti-Treaty side in the Civil War. Later he became a teacher and also worked as a Health Board official for the Galway County Council.

1911 Census
2 Lurgan, Ballycahalan, Galway.
Bridget Fahy(71) Farmer.
Michael (31), John (29), **Patrick (27) Teacher of Irish Language**, Brigid (33) and Mary (22).

Stephen Gwynn 1864 – 1950 [308]

He was born in Rathfarnham, Dublin. His father John was a Church of Ireland clergyman and his mother was Lucy Smith O'Brien, daughter of Young Irelander William Smith O'Brien. Stephen was educated in Oxford University and spent time in France as a young man. When he returned to Ireland he became involved in politics. He was also a noted writer, biographer, novelist and journalist. From his activities as a writer he developed an interest in Irish and was an active member of the Gaelic League. He was elected M.P. for Galway in a by-election in 1906 and served until 1918. He was an ardent supporter of John Redmond's. On the outbreak of World War 1 he joined the army though over 50. He served with the Connaught Rangers at Messines and the Somme and was awarded the Legion of Honour. Gwynn opposed conscription in Ireland in favour of voluntary service. Following the demise of the Irish Parliamentary Party he founded the Irish Centre Party in 1919. In later life he devoted himself to writing and wrote an important biography of John

---

308 Stephen Gwynn (1864 – 1950) – Ricorso.

Redmond.

Stephen is not returned in either the 1901 or 1911 census as he was in London at the time. He is buried in Tallagh cemetery.

Joe Howley 1895 - 1920

He was a native of Oranmore whose father died when he was about two. His mother remarried William Keane. He joined the Irish Volunteers in 1914 and soon became a leading member. On Tuesday April 25th the Oranmore Company joined with the Maree Company and attacked the Oranmore R.I.C. barracks. They failed to capture it and again a later attack with the help of Liam Mellows and his units was similarly unsuccessful. He was arrested and jailed after the rebellion. He was a main I.R.A. organiser during the War of Independence. On a visit to Dublin in December 1920 he was shot by members of the Cairo Gang, a British army under-cover unit. There is a statue to him in Oranmore unveiled in 1947.[309]

1901 Census

10 Oranmore, Co. Galway.

William Keane (36) Shop keeper, Mary Keane (30)

John Rabbitt (29), **Michael G Hawley (5) Scholar,** (This should read Michael J Howley) and Patrick Burke (14).

Frank Hynes 1886 - 1970

He lived in Cross Street in Athenry. Liam Mellows stayed with the family for a time when he lived in Athenry. He went on the run with Mellows and Monahan after the rebels disbanded in Lime Park.

They spent a few months in the mountains between Galway and Clare being fed by local sympathisers. He eventually was brought to the Shinrone area of Offaly and then to Maynooth

---

309 Galwayindependent.com/20120229/news/talking-history-52945.html

where he got a job in the College. He got great support from clergy who had republican leanings. Eventually they arranged for him to go to work in Cork. He became involved with the I.R.A. in Cork and fought in the War of Independence there. He was arrested in 1918 and spent some time in jail. He took no part in the Civil War.

1901 Census

184 Athenry, Co Galway.

Patrick Hynes (48) Contractor Builder, Mary Hynes (50).

Thomas (23), Martin (22), Mary Kate (19), **Francis (15) Apprentice** and Winefred (14).

Stephen Jordan 1887 - 1975

Born on January 1st 1887 to Mark Jordan and Mary Burke he was the eighth of eleven children. His father was a shoemaker and the family lived in Davis Street, Athenry. Three of his siblings died as children and his elder brother Michael (30), also a shoemaker, died in 1904 of T.B. His father died in 1904 aged 56 and his mother in 1909 aged 59. The 1901 census returns shows both parents and five children including 11 year old Stephen. By 1911 both his parents were dead as was his brother Michael, his eldest brother William had inherited a farm in Tiaquin and four of his sisters had emigrated to America. Stephen was now living in the family home with his sister Monica who was four years younger.

Stephen was very active in nationalist organisations being a member of the G.A.A. the Irish Volunteers, the I.R.B. and the Town Tenants' League. He was an accomplished footballer and won county championships with Athenry De Wettes in 1903, 1904 and 1906. He also played for Galway for a number of years, winning Connaught titles with them in 1911, 1913 and 1917.

He took an active part in the 1916 Rising as Adjutant of the Athenry Company and went on the run following the rising. He turned himself in, in May, and was jailed in Frongoch until December 1916.

Following his release from prison he was elected a Sinn Féin councillor, for the Loughrea area and he served as Chairman in 1920. However, he was jailed for ignoring the official British justice system by facilitating Sinn Féin courts to operate justice within the county. He spent almost a year in jail for this. In the continuing troubles in Ireland he played a role in the War of Independence and the Civil War, on the Republican side. He was to spend a number of terms in jail around this time.

He was County Secretary of Galway G.A.A. for many years starting in 1918 and was still there in the early 1920's. He also served as County Chairman for a time. He filled these roles during the War of Independence and Civil War when keeping the G.A.A. going was particularly difficult. He was a noted referee officiating in several All-Ireland football and hurling finals at both senior and minor levels. He also refereed League finals and the first All-Ireland camogie final, which was played in 1932 between Galway and Dublin, with the latter winning.

Stephen was a publican, a shoemaker and a County Council foreman at various stages of his life. Stephen served as a Sinn Féin local county councillor for a number of years before becoming a T.D. for Fianna Fáil from 1927 to 1937. In later years he was secretary of the Athenry Agricultural Show for 27 years and a caretaker for Kenny Park G.A.A. grounds for many years in the 1960's and early 1970's.

In 1919 he married Ellen youngest sister of James Haverty, a leading I.R.B. man, from the Mountbellew area, and a participant in the rising. They had eleven children, the ninth Willie being my father.

Stephen died on September 15th 1975 aged 88 and is buried in the New Cemetery in Athenry.

1901 Census
Davis Street, Athenry, Co. Galway.
Mark Jordan (54) Shoemaker, Mary Jordan (48).

Sarah (22), Michael (20), Katie (18), **Stephen (14) Shoemaker's apprentice,** Monica (8).

1911 Census

Davis Street, Athenry.

Stephen Jordan (22) Shoemaker, Monica Jordan (19) sister.

Tom Kenny 1878 - 1947

Tom Kenny was born in Ardrahan in 1878. The family later moved to Craughwell where he made a decent living as a blacksmith. He is returned in the 1901 census as a 24 year old living with his father Matthew (60) a blacksmith, his mother Bridget (55) and his sister Nonie (19). In the 1911 census he was returned as a 33 year old living with his widowed mother and there is a boarder Thomas Mc Inerney (26) also a blacksmith. So obviously there was work for a second man following his father's death.

Tom was the main mover in the Irish Republican Brotherhood in the Craughwell area and was 'centre' for Galway. He swore many young men in the area into the I.R.B. He was involved in the I.R.B. at the time of the shooting of Constable Martin Mc Goldrick in 1909. At the time and for a number of years afterwards there was a bitter dispute between him and the I.R.B. on one side and the more moderate U.I.L. on the other. Kenny was in a sense replaced by Liam Mellows in the run up to the 1916 Rising and played no active role in the rising. He publicaly stated that without arms it was never going to succeed. He did visit the rebels at Moyode Castle and spoke to Liam Mellows hoping to get him to send the men home as he felt it was the wrong time for a rebellion and they were poorly armed.

He escaped to America following the Rising and stayed there for a number of years. Here he associated with Jim Larkin and returned a committed socialist following the Civil War.

When he returned he continued his association with his other great love, the G.A.A. and he was the trainer of the first Galway senior hurling team to win an All-Ireland, defeating Limerick in the final. This delayed 1923 final took place in 1924. He had been County G.A.A. Chairman in 1915 and spend many years as a delegate to Central Council. The G.A.A. grounds in Athenry, Kenny Park, are called after him.

He was involved in the Soar Eire movement in the early 1930's and died in 1947.

1901 Census
Craughwell, Galway.
Matthew Kenny (60) Blacksmith, Bridget Kenny (55).
Thomas (23) Blacksmith, Nonie (19).

1911 Census
Craughwell, Galway.
Bridget Kenny (70).
Tom (33) Blacksmith, Thomas Mc Inerney (26) Blacksmith.

Larry Lardner. 1883 - 1936

Larry Lardner was born in Athenry in 1883 to William and Bridget Lardner. They had a pub and shop in the town on Chapel Lane now Church Street. William's brother Michael also had a large business in the town with several employees. In 1901 Lawrence (18) lived with his widowed mother, then 38 years old, and his brother James.

He was a noted footballer with Athenry De Wetts winning Galway senior county championships with them in 1903, 1904 and 1906. He was G.A.A. County Secretary in 1912. There had been a split in the county the previous year with two county conventions held and he was involved in healing this split. He was also secretary of the Athenry branch of the Gaelic League for a time.

Larry was very active in local politics from an early age

and was sworn into the local I.R.B. Circle by Dick Murphy in the early 1900's. Murphy was later on the Connaught Supreme Council. He was an active member of the Town Tenants' League like many other I.R.B. men. This group had some success in getting land distributed among local farmers and townspeople when some local estates were sold.

Following the rising he went on the run and was arrested after three months. He was rearrested upon his release at the prison gates as a suspect in the German Plot and spent a year in Lincoln Jail in England.

During the War of Independence he was arrested and sent to Wormwood Scrubs prison where he was instrumental in aiding Eamon de Valera to escape. He was on hunger strike for a time while in jail there.

Following his revolutionary activities he was a very active member of the local community. He was secretary of the Sack Factory committee set up to bring this factory in the town. Larry was also active in bringing the sugar beet factory to Tuam in the late 1920's and he also served as secretary of the Athenry Agricultural Show for a number of years before his death.

He died at the age of 53 on April 23rd 1936 and was accorded a military funeral. He was survived by his wife Bridget and daughter Kitty. Larry Lardner is buried in the New Cemetery in Athenry. [310]

1901 Census
Athenry, Co. Galway.
Bridget Lardner (32) Widow, Publican.
Lawrence (18) Shop assistant, James (11).
Mary Lynskey (40) Seamstress, Bridget Lynskey (30) Seamstress.

---

310 Commandant Larry Lardner – 1916 Rising, War of Independence by Finbar O'Regan. O'Regan's Athenry, Athenry History Archive.

1911 Census.

1 Church Street, Athenry, Co. Galway.

Bridget Lardner (54) Shop Keeper, Dressmaker.

Lawrence (28) Publican's assistant, James (22).

Bridget Lynskey (44) Servant.

Martin 'Mor' Mc Donogh 1860 – 1934.

He was a businessman in Galway who owned a substantial number of businesses around the town. He was the son of a small farmer from Connemara who amassed great wealth for his family. He was educated in universities in London and Galway. Eventually he built up a large business empire in the city. Among his assets were a general merchants store, a flour-mill, a saw-mill, many houses, a shipping company and he started a munitions factory during the Great War. He was totally opposed to the 1916 Rising and helped to organise the special constables to support the military and police defend Galway.[311]

Martin was a member of most boards and committees in Galway City, the Harbour Commission, the Galway Race Committee, the Board of Guardians, the Urban District Council and many more.[312] He became a politician in 1927 when he was elected as a Cumann na nGeadheal T.D. in the June election. He was returned in September 1927, 1932, and 1933. He died in 1934.

He is returned in the 1901 and 1911 census living with his brothers, sisters and servants. His 65 year old father is living with him in 1901.

1911 Census

4 Flood St. Galway East, Urban.

Martin Mc Donogh (40) General Merchants etc. and All manufacturers,

311 Mr. Galway': Martin 'Máirtín Mór' – WorldPress.com by Dr. Jackie Uí Chionna

312 Journal of the Galway Archaeological and Historical Society, *The Rising of the Moon: Galway 1916'* p124 Una Newell.

Thomas (38), Michael (34), Mary Anne (36), Katie (32).
Bridget Derrane (26), Barbara Nee (22), Julia Grealy (24), John Moran (40) and Matt Lydon (24).
Gertrude Mc Aleenan (30) niece.

Liam Mellows 1892 – 1922[313]

He was born in Hartshead Military Barracks in Ashton-under-Lime near Manchester in England. His father's family, though Irish in origin, had a long tradition of joining the British army. His mother was Sarah Jordan from Wexford. William, now a Company Quartermaster Sergeant, was transferred to Dublin in 1895 and the family moved from England. The then three year old went to live in Wexford with his grandparents. He was ill at the time and it was felt that the country air would be better for him. It was here he was first introduced to the republican tradition and there were many stories about the 1798 Rebellion told to him. Later when his family were moved to Cork he went to live with them there. He attended military school with his brother Fredrick at Wellington Barracks. When the family returned to Dublin in 1900 he attended military school at Portobello Garrison School where his father hoped he would become an army officer. Liam's mother was very musical and influenced all the children to play. Liam had a keen interest and played the fiddle. He left school in 1907 and became a clerk, first in the Junior Army and Navy Stores and then in Messrs. Goodbodies, a supply company. His refusal to join the army disappointed his father who was now retired on a good pension.[314] In 1911 having read a copy of 'Irish Freedom' (the I.R.B. newspaper from 1910 to 1914) he went to Thomas Clarke's shop and joined the I.R.B. He later met James Connolly and took on socialist ideas.

Liam was a founder member of the Irish Volunteers in

313 D.J. Hickey and J.E. Doherty *'A Dictionary of Irish History 1800 – 1980'* pp 343 - 364 Gill and Macmillan.

314 C Desmond Greaves *'Liam Mellows and the Irish Revolution'* pp 33 – 40 An Ghlór Gafa.

Rebellion in Galway

November 1913. He was sent to Galway in early 1915 to organise the west for the rebellion. In this task he was most efficient organising a brigade and companies around Galway and training the Volunteers in military matters. He spent time in jail in 1915 but on his release continued his very methodical work.

Shortly before the Easter Rising he was re-arrested and deported to England where he was staying with relatives in Leek, near Stoke. However, his brother Barney went over to impersonate him and he returned to Galway just in time for the Rising. He led a large contingent of up to 700 men from Monday to Saturday during which they attacked Clarenbridge and Oranmore R.I.C. barracks. They disbanded early on Saturday morning as British forces were about to close in on them. Mellows went on the run with Alf Monahan and Frank Hynes. Eventually he escaped to America where he stayed for four years. He spent some time in jail there as he was suspected of subversive activities. He was an organiser of Eamon de Valera's fundraising tour in 1919 – 1920 before returning to Ireland. On his return he was I.R.A. Director of Purchases during the closing year of the War of Independence. [315]

While in America he was put forward as a Sinn Féin candidate in the 1918 general election and he was returned as T.D. for both East Galway and Meath.[316] In the general election of May 1921, for the Second Dáil, he was returned as a T.D. for Galway.[317] This was held during the War of Independence and all Sinn Féin-nominated candidates were returned unopposed in the twenty six counties.

Following the signing of the Anglo-Irish Treaty in 1921 he was one of the most ardent opponents of it in the debates which followed. When Sinn Féin split over the Treaty he took the <u>Republican side and was in the</u> Four Courts in Dublin when

315 C Desmond Greaves 'Liam Mellows and the Irish Revolution' p 223 An Ghlór Gafa.

316 C Desmond Greaves 'Liam Mellows and the Irish Revolution' p 165 An Ghlór Gafa.

317 C Desmond Greaves 'Liam Mellows and the Irish Revolution' p 245 An Ghlór Gafa.

it was attacked by the Provisional Government troops at the start of the Civil War. He was arrested in July and interned in Mountjoy prison. As the Civil War saw the situation in the country deteriorate at an alarming rate hundreds were being killed. The Republican forces named a government in opposition to the Provisional Government and named Mellows Minister for Defence though he was in prison.

On December 7th 1922 Sean Hales T.D. a supporter of the Provisional Government and Patrick O'Malley were shot on Ormond Quay in Dublin. That evening the Free State Cabinet met and decided on their reprisal. A Republican prisoner representing each province would be executed. Mellows was selected as the Connaught representative. The others were Rory O'Connor, Dick Barrett and Joseph Mc Kelvey.[318] They were executed by firing squad the following day, December 8th.

Liam Mellows is honoured in many ways in Galway. The Irish Army military barracks in Renmore in now called Dún Ui Mhaoliosa. There is Liam Mellows Hurling Club in Galway City, a statue of him in Eyre Square, the Agricultural College outside Athenry is called Mellows College and there is Mellows Street in Tuam, to name but a few.

1901 Census
2 St. Joseph's Terrace, Ballyhooly Road, Cork.
William Joseph (42) Staff Quarter Master Sergeant Army Pay Corps, Sarah Mellows (35).
Jane (14), **William Joseph (8) Scholar**, Fredrick (6), Herbert (5).

1911 Census
21 Mount Shannon, Usher's Quay, Dublin.
William Joseph (52) Army Pensioner, Sarah Mellows (45).
William Joseph (18) Bookkeeper, Fredrick (16), Herbert (15).

---

318 C Desmond Greaves *'Liam Mellows and the Irish Revolution'* p 385 An Ghlór Gafa.

Rebellion in Galway

Alf Monahan 1889 - 1967

He was a fluent Irish speaker born in Belfast in 1889 to a nationalist family. In the 1901 census he was living in Riley's Place with his father Robert, mother Johanna, two sisters and three brothers. Both his parents were dead by 1911.

He joined the I.R.B. and the Irish Volunteers in 1914 when Denis Mc Cullough was the 'centre' in the area. There were a lot of I.R.B. branches in Belfast. They drilled regularly and could buy rifles for £3 and bullets for 4d. He became the I.R.B. organiser for the Cavan region about 1915 and was very active in the area. School teachers and clergy were most helpful to him. He was served with a deportation order but did not comply with it. He was arrested on foot of the Defence of the Realm Act for anti-recruiting activities in relation to World War 1 and sentenced to three months hard labour in Crumlin Road jail in Belfast.

When he was released in January 1916 he was instructed to go to Galway to help Liam Mellows. In the absence of Liam Mellows when he was deported to England in March and April 1916 Monahan continued the training. During his time in Galway he built up links with students and staff in and staff in Galway University.

He was mainly responsible for the area west of Galway City. He was active in the Rising and went on the run with Mellows and Frank Hynes following the disbandment of the forces. All three escaped capture. His brother Charlie was drowned off Ballykissane Pier in Kerry along with Donal Sheehan and Conn Keating on Friday April 21st 1916. They were on their way to take radio equipment from the Cahersiveen radio station to try to make contact with the Aud as it attempted to land arms on Banna Strand. Alf fought in the War of Independence in the Cork area. He was on the Republican side in the Civil War again in the Cork area. He was imprisoned in Cork and Kildare following the war. On his release he was a Gaelic League organiser up to 1926. He then became a teacher of Irish and Art with the Dublin V.E.C. and retired in 1953. In 1929 he married Mary Buckley. He also loved to write and illustrate children's fairy tales. He died in Swords in January 1967.[319]

1901 Census
23 Riley's Place, Belfast, Co. Antrim.
Robert Joseph (57) Mill sawyer, Johanna Monahan (52).
Johanna E (28), Geo Henry (24), Edith (19), James (17) Joseph (15) and **Alfred (12) Scholar**.

Brian Molloy 1889 - 1958

Bernard or Brian was born to John and Margaret Molloy of Coolagh near Brierhill on the outskirts of Galway City near Ballybrit racecourse. He was a leading figure in the I.R.B, since 1907, and the Irish Volunteers in the lead up to the 1916 Rising. Brian was the captain of the Castlegar Volunteer Company and involved in the encounter at Carnmore Cross where Constable Patrick Whelan was killed. His brothers Thomas and John were also involved in the rising. After the rebellion he was arrested and was sentenced to 10 years penal servitude. He was released in June 1917. He was active in the War of Independence organising many ambushes of Black and Tans around the Galway area. His family home was burned by the British forces as a reprisal.[320]

1911 Census
5 Coolagh, Ballintemple, Galway.
John Molloy (60) Farmer, Margaret (52).
Thomas (30), Patrick (24), **Bernard (22) Farmer's son**, John (20) and Celia (16).

319 Ailbhe O Monachain (1889 – 1967- Find a Grave Memorial).

320 Padraic O Laoi, *History of Castlegar Parish* p146. The Connaught Tribune Ltd (1996)

Gilbert Morrissey 1890 – 1971

He was from Rockfield near Craughwell and was in the Irish Volunteers when they started in 1914. He was already in the I.R.B. and was appointed captain of the Volunteers. He played an active role in the 1916 Rising and the War of Independence. The whole family including his brothers John, Martin and Patrick and sister Bridget were involved in the rising.

1911 Census

2 Knockatoor, Greethill, Co. Galway.

John Morrissey (59) Farmer, Bridget Morrissey (58)

Thomas (26), John (23), **Gilbert (21) Farmer's son Labourer**, Norah (17), Michael (16), Martin (14), Bridget (12) and Pat (10).

Matthew 'Mattie' Neilan 1891 – ?[321]

He was born in 1891 to George and Honoria Neilan in Rahaneena, Drumacoo near Kilcolgan in Galway. They were farmers and in the 1911 census had nine children born and seven living. Following school locally he went to train as a teacher in Dublin and returned to teach locally in Coldwood. He joined the I.R.B. and later the Irish Volunteers in 1914. He was involved in the Clarenbridge unit and became one of its leading members. He was actively involved in all areas in the 1916 Rising and was at the meeting in Lime Park when the decision to disband was made. He subsequently went on the run but was captured in May and sent to Frongoch.

Following his release he again became involved in rebel activities and served in both the War of Independence and Civil Wars. He fought on the Republican side in the Civil War and was captured and interned in Gormanstown for up to eighteen months.

On his release he studied Medicine in Skerries and University College Galway.

---

321 Irishvolunteers.org/matthew-mattie-neilan/ By Eamon Murphy.

He made a number of attempts at election before being elected in a by-election for south Galway in 1936 on the death of Patrick Hogan. He was a T.D. for Fianna Fáil but did not seek re-election in 1937. He spent some time as a member of the Agricultural Wages Board, the Galway Board of Health and Galway County Council.

On his retirement from politics he returned to the family farm and also ran the local Post Office.

1901 Census

3 Rahaneena, Drumacoo, Galway.

George Neilan (61) Farmer, Honoria (43).

Lizzie (210, John (19), William (17), Mary (15), George (12), **Martin (10) Scholar,** Delia (6), Kate (4).

William Neilan (63).

1911 Census

4 Rahaneena, Drumacoo, Galway.

George Neilan (71) Farmer, Honoria (60).

Willie (28), George (22), **Martin (20) Farmer's son**, Elizabeth (31), Mary (25), Bridget (16) and Kate (14)

George Nicholls   1887 - 1942

George was a young solicitor working in G. A. Conroy's office. They had a business on Francis Street in Galway City. He was later the county coroner. He was very active in the Volunteer movement and was at the Town Hall in December 1913 when the Irish Volunteers had their inaugural meeting. The Volunteer movement in Galway mainly sided with Redmond after the split and this very much reduced the activity in the city. Many men volunteered for the British army to fight in World War 1 and this also reduced the numbers of Irish Volunteers available to fight in 1916. Nicholls was arrested on the Tuesday of the rebellion and this effectively ended any city activity. He was released after the Rising. He was elected as a T.D. for

Galway on three occasions. In 1921 he served in the Provisional government as Assistant to the Minister of Home Affairs with the task of supervising the courts. He was re-elected in 1922 and again in 1923 this time as a Cumman na nGaedhael T.D. In this Dáil he was parliamentary secretary to the Minister of Defence from 1925 – 1927. George died on May 11th 1942.

1911 Census

45 Kilcorkey, Galway Urban, South, Galway.

Cáitlín Mhic Ruaidhrí (61).

Cáit Nic Ruaidhrí (29), Padraig Mac Ruaidhrí (26) and **Seóirse Mac Niochaill (24)**

William O'Malley 1853 – 1939

William O'Malley was born in Ballyconneely in Connemara and became a prominent M.P. He was educated in Galway and London and was a businessman, politician and journalist. He was elected for the Irish Parliamentary Party originally as an anti-Parnellite candidate in the election of 1895. He was returned unopposed in 1900, 1906, and January and December 1910. However, in the 1918 election he lost to the Sinn Féin candidate Padraic O'Máille when only gaining 23% of the vote.

Involved with the National Volunteers and was a committed supporter of recruitment for the British army during World War 1. One of his sons was killed in France during the war. He was married to Mary O'Connor a sister of T.P. O'Connor's who was a former Irish Nationalist M.P. for Galway City.

During his tenure as M.P. he spent most of his time in London.

Martin 'Matty' Reaney (Reany) 1893 – 1916

He was born in 1893 to Michael and Margaret Reaney. They were from the townland of Rahaneena near Kilcolgan. There were 10 children born to the couple but only six survived to adulthood. Martin was the second youngest. His father was a carpenter, boat builder and a small farmer. Martin was in the Clarenbridge Irish Volunteer Company and involved in the attack on the R.I.C. barracks on Tuesday April 26th. He was badly wounded in an exchange of fire with the R.I.C. either there or during the attack on the Oranmore barracks. He was cared for by Bridie Lane of Cumann na mBan while at Moyode. Too sick to travel to Lime Park with the rest of the rebels he was put up in John Hynes's, the home of a sympathiser, who lived in Creggaturlough two miles from Moyode. She looked after him there for three days. However, he failed to recover and died about a week later. Thus he is the only known Irish Volunteer casualty of the Galway rising.

1901 Census

8 Rahaneena, Drumacoo, Co. Galway

Michael Reaney (60) Boat builder, Maggie (50).

John (20), Thomas (18), Mary Anne (16), Michael (13), **Martia (9)** *(Should read Martin)* **Scholar,** and Bradey (4) Should read Bridget)

1911 Census

5 Rahaneena, Drumacoo, Co. Galway.

Michael Reney (Reaney) (73) Carpenter boat builder, Margaret (60).

Martin (20) Carpenter, Bridget (14).

Tom Ruane 1884 - 1937

He was the captain of the Claregalway Irish Volunteers in 1916. This was a very active company. Tom had been in the I.R.B. since around 1908 and was typical of those who were in both organisations hoping the Irish Volunteers would take part in the rising the I.R.B. sought. He joined with the Claregalway Company under Brian Molloy and they were involved in the battle at Carnmore Cross where Constable Patrick Whelan was shot.

He was an accomplished hurler with Castlegar and team captain at this time.

Following the rising he was arrested and jailed in Frongoch. On his release he was still involved with the I.R.B. He was arrested as part of the German Plot in 1918. When he was released again he took part in the War of Independence. He was a Sinn Féin Justice of the Peace during that time. He served as Chairman of the Galway District Council for seven years. [322]

1901 Census

Carnmore, Co. Galway

Stephen Ruane (51) Farmer, Bridget Ruane (42)

Thomas (18) Farmer, Michael (15), James (13), Maggie (11), Kate (9), John (8), Norah (5).

1911 Census

Carnmore, Co. Galway.

Stephen Ruane (62) Farmer, Bridget Ruane (57).

Thomas (28) Farmer, Norah (15).

Martin Grealish (19) Servant.

The Galway clergy

A number of clergymen were actively involved with the nationalist movements at the time. Many of these were supporters of the Irish Volunteers and were associated with them from the beginning. The older priests were more of a mind that their presence would be a controlling effect on the movement while many of the younger priests, generally curates, had more of a definite nationalist outlook. Priests in Galway took a leading part in supporting the Irish Volunteers after the split in 1914. When the Irish Volunteer review was held in Athenry on November 23rd 1915 there was a large number of priests on the review platform.

'After the review a meeting was held at which O'Rahilly,

---

322 claregalway.info/history/1916-troubles

Fr. O'Loney, (Carmelite, Loughrea), Fr. Connolly,
(The College, Ballinasloe) and Fr. Meehan
were the principal speakers. Others on the
platform were Fr. Tom Burke (Diocesan
Secretary), Fr. Crawley (P.P. Shanaglish),
Fr. Kelly (Galway), Fr. Moran (Claregalway)
and Fr. Feeney.' [323]

Some of these priests were leading members of local Irish Volunteer companies. Among these were Fr. John William O'Meehan in Kinvarra and Fr. Henry Feeney in Clarenbridge.

When the Volunteers rose in rebellion during Easter week a number of priests went both to support and to administer to them. Liam Mellows sent Padraig Fahy to Kinvarra for Fr. O'Meehan to be Quartermaster for the rebels but Fahy was arrested at the Presbytery. O'Meehan took an active part in the rebellion with the Kinvarra Volunteers. Fr Tom Fahy and Fr Henry Feeney were both present with the Volunteers in Moyode and at Lime Park when the decision was taken to disband.

Fr. Connolly

A priest in Garbally Diocesan College in Ballinasloe (for the Diocese of Clonfert) he was a sympathetic supporter of the nationalist movement. He was a good friend of Liam Mellows and Mellows stayed with him on many occasions when he was in the vicinity of Ballinasloe promoting Irish Volunteer activities. Mellows sent dispatches to him and Professor Gaffney on Monday April 24th when the rising began. James Barrett and two others cycled from Athenry via Mullagh with the message. Connolly and Gaffney were to set up lines of communication between Galway and Athlone so that each area would know what was going on.

---

323 W/S 347 Pat Callanan.

Rebellion in Galway

Monsignor Tom Fahy 1888 - 1973

He was born in Gloves, Esker, Athenry on December 5th 1888 to Paddy Fahy and Bridget (nee Creaven). He was the fifth of eight children. He was educated in Esker N.S. and was a student in the Redemptorist Monastery in the 1901 census. In 1911 he was a theology student in Maynooth College. He was ordained in 1912 for Clonfert Dioceses. He spent time in Garbally College in Ballinasloe and was a lecturer in Classics at Maynooth College from 1915 to 1919 when he was appointed Professor.

He was at home on holidays when the rebellion broke out in 1916. He made the short trip from Esker to Moyode to visit the rebels and minister to them. Fr Mc Namara also a Redemptorist went to Esker with him. He met Fr. Feeney there. On Friday morning April 28th he was sent to Galway, by Liam Mellows, to enquire as to what the Bishop of Galway Most Rev. Dr. O'Dea thought of the rebellion. While there he was also to ascertain what he could about the movements of any British forces and R.I.C. The Bishop was at least gratified to hear that there was a religious presence with the Volunteers. On returning from Galway, on Friday night he was able to inform Mellows on the latest regarding troop movements and how likely they were to attack the Galway rebels. He also heard that the rising in Dublin was virtually over. He felt, now that the rising was nearing a conclusion in Dublin, the Galway contingent was very likely to be attacked. His advice was that they had made their point and it was now time to disband and go home before they were attacked and many killed. He was at the meeting of officers to discuss what course of action they would take to give them the information he had picked up on his trip to Galway. Following a vote it was decided to disband the men.

Following the rising he returned to Maynooth. While he was there he was able to secure jobs for John Broderick, Frank Hynes and Alf Monahan who were on the run.

From 1927, for more than 30 years he was Professor of Classics in University College Galway. While there he was on the Governing Body of the College. He wrote many articles on classics, scripture and education. He was president of Maynooth College from 1954 to 1957. Following his retirement he published a book on scripture and was a frequent contributor to the Irish Education Record and the Irish Theological Quarterly. In 1936 he represented the Senate of the National University of Ireland at the centenary celebrations of Athens University.

Monsignor Tom was an excellent horseman and had a lifelong love of greyhounds which he reared and trained.

He died on June 18th 1973 and is buried in the grounds of Kiltullagh Church, Athenry, Co. Galway.

1901 Census.
Redemptorist College, Esker, Kiltullagh, Athenry.
Thomas Fahy (13) Student.

1911 Census.
Collegeland, Maynooth, Co. Kildare.
Thomas Fahy (23) Theological Student.

Fr. Henry 'Harry' Feeney 1889 – 1945

He was from Two-Mile-Ditch in Castlegar and ordained in 1914. He was curate in Clarenbridge when the rising broke out. He wrote to Fr. Tully P.P. and resigned his office to become Chaplain of the Volunteers.

He remained with them through the attacks on the R.I.C. barracks in Clarenbridge and Oranmore and accompanied them to the Agricultural College, Moyode and Lime Park. He was one of those present at the discussions on demobilising and subsequently went on the run. He initially went to the Redemptorists in Esker and then to the Cistercian in Roscrea. Petitions were successfully made on his behalf for a pardon from General Mac Cready. He moved as a priest to Oughterard but he was constantly harassed by the crown forces. He was sent to America where he ministered in Fruitia in Florida for a time. He returned to Moycullen as curate in 1923 and subsequently became Parish Priest of Shrule in Mayo in 1924. While Parish Priest there he spearheaded the building of a new church, school, handball alley and presbytery. He died in 1945.[324]

1901 Census

12 Polikeen, Ballintemple, Galway.

Sarah Feeny (50) Farmer.

Martin (21), Eliza (19), Mary (17), Malachy (14), **Harry (12) Scholar**, James (10), Sarah (7), Mary Feeny (20), Martin Feeny (18) and Margaret Feeny (17).

Fr. Redmond Mc Hugh 1865 - 1947

He was the Parish Priest of Castlegar at the time of the rebellion. He was a very good friend of Padraig Pearse as he knew him well from when he was curate in Rosmuck while Pearse had his cottage there. Originally from Headford he was ordained in Maynooth in 1891. He first served in Ballyvaughan in Clare and afterwards in Beagh and Peterswell. It was while he was curate in Rosmuck from 1900 to 1909 he befriended Pearse. He served in Claregalway from 1909 to 1912 and set up a branch of the Gaelic League while there. He was a conservative man and spoke out against actions in the parish during the troubles in the War of Independence and also against dancing at the crossroads. He later served in Ennistymon and Clarenbridge, where he organised the building of a new church. He died there in 1947. [325]

1901 Census

39 Rosmuck, Turlough, Galway.

Redmond Mc Hugh (36) Catholic clergyman.

---

324 Padraic O Laoi History of Castlegar Parish p193. The Connaught Tribune Ltd. (1996)

325 Padraic O Laoi History of Castlegar Parish. p59 The Connaught Tribune Ltd. (1996)

Bridget Mc Hugh (40) and Margaret Cullinane (40).

Fr. John Moran

He was the curate in the parish of Castlegar from 1912 to 1916. He was a native of Kilconly, Tuam.[326]   He was another supporter of the nationalist cause and was helpful towards the Irish Volunteers throughout the week of the rising. He died in 1923 while he was curate of St. Patrick's Parish.

Fr. John William O'Meehan 1881 - 1923

He was born in Dunkellin in Clarenbridge parish in1881. His father was a police pensioner and farmer. He went to Kilternan N.S., St Ignatius College Galway and Maynooth College. He was ordained a priest in 1906. He became very interested in the Irish language and Irish history and loved to talk to older people about history. As a result of his interest in Irish and Irish history Fr O'Meehan was a good friend of Padraig Pearse and Arthur Griffith. He was appointed as curate to Ennistymon and Ballyvaughan and then spent two years in Australia. When he returned in1912 he spent a number of years teaching in St. Mary's College in Galway City.

His friendship with Pearse led to his advising Pearse to send someone to help organise the west for the likely rebellion. He was then appointed curate in Kinvarra parish in 1915. As curate in Kinvarra he was heavily involved in the Irish Volunteers. He was one of the more dynamic members and recruited many to the organisation. He bought green hats for the members at his own expense.

Leading up to Easter 1916 he had advised all Irish Volunteers to assemble as many arms and much ammunition as possible in anticipation of any action that may take place. As the Volunteers mobilised in Kinvarra he gave a general absolution and heard confessions warning that some may die.

326 Padraic O Laoi History of Castlegar Parish. p68 The Connaught Tribune Ltd. (1996)

Following the firing on the R.I.C. party outside Kinvarra on the Wednesday of the rising (26th April) he discouraged the Volunteers from ransacking the empty R.I.C. barracks in Kinvarra when they returned to the town.

After the rebellion he remained in Kinvarra until 1919 when he was appointed curate in Rahoon in Galway City. Here he met Fr Griffin also a curate in the parish. Both were nationalist sympathisers. Fr Griffin was murdered by British forces on November 14th 1920. After Fr. Griffin's death Fr. O'Meehan went to Scotland. He returned when the War of Independence ended but died on April 12th 1923 aged 42. [327]

Fr. Michael Joseph Tully

He was born in Mayo in 1878 and is returned in the 1901 census as a student in Maynooth College and in the 1911 census in Gweeselia, Rathill, Mayo as a Catholic priest. He was Parish Priest of Clarenbridge at the time of the Rising. When Mellows and his forces attacked the R.I.C. barracks beside the village green on Tuesday morning he pleaded with them to desist so as to spare lives. When the attack continued he continued his pleading and eventually Mellows called off the attack and moved to attack Oranmore. Whether it was in response to Fr Tully's vociferous request or the realisation that the attack was yielding no success is not known.

1901 Census

Collegeland, Maynooth, Co. Kildare.

Michael Tully (23) Student.

1911 Census.

Gweeselia, Rathill, Co. Mayo.

Fr. Michael Joseph Tully (33) Catholic curate.

Mary Carty (40) Servant.

---

327 W/S1,034 Mrs. Mary Leech (nee O'Meehan).

Personalities in the Galway Rising

Bishops

Bishop of Clonfert, Thomas Patrick Gilmartin 1861 - 1939

He was bishop of Clonfert which covers most of east Galway and also takes in the diocesan college in Garbally, Ballinasloe. It includes the parishes of Kiltullagh, Loughrea, Ballinasloe, Portumna and Kilconnell. Born in Castlebar, Mayo in 1861 he was ordained in Maynooth in 1883. He served as Bishop of Clonfert from 1909 to 1918. He was then Archbishop of Tuam from 1918 until his death in 1939.

1911 Census

37 Dunlo St., Ballinasloe Urban, Co. Galway.

Joseph Alfred Pelly (55) Catholic Administrator, Thomas Dunne (33) Catholic Curate, Daniel Mc Hugh (29) Catholic Curate, Michael O'Connor (27) Catholic Curate, **Thomas Gilmartin (47) Lord Bishop of Clonfert, Visitor**, Ellen Lyons (65) Cook, Jane Galvin (28) Housemaid, Ellen Curley (19) General Servant.

Bishop of Galway and Kilmacduagh, Thomas O'Dea 1858 – 1923

He was born in Carron, Kilferora Co. Clare in 1858. He was educated in Ennis and Maynooth. He was ordained in 1882 and then worked on the Maynooth staff including being Vice-President from 1894 until his appointment as Bishop of Clonfert in 1903. He served there until 1909 when he was appointed Bishop of Galway and Kilmacduagh. He died in office in 1923.

During the 1916 Rebellion he was consulted by Fr. Tom Fahy as to what he thought of the rebellion. He was glad that at least there was a religious presence and that the men, as Catholics, were being ministered to and confessions heard.

In her witness statement Bridget Malone, from Craughwell, describes him as one of the Bishops not opposed to the rebellion.

'I do not think it was Dr. O'Dea, who was one of
the two bishops who were not opposed to the
Volunteers, that banished Fr. Feeney to America.'[328]

She felt that he was of a nervous disposition and had a
breakdown following the rising due to the activities, arrests
and executions. [329]

He was a fluent Irish speaker and an avid supporter of the
G.A.A. This is not surprising as he was from the same area of
Clare as Michael Cusack, the founder of the G.A.A. in 1884.

Following his death he was buried in St. Patrick's Pro-
cathedral and later reinterred in a crypt in the new cathedral.

1911 Census

63 Kilcorkey, Galway South Urban, Galway City.

Thomas O'Dea (53) Catholic Bishop.

Maria Watson (64) Servant, Thomas Heanan (30) Servant,
Joanna Keogh (29) Servant.

Athenry priests

Cannon Joseph Canton Parish Priest 1891 – 1919

Joseph Canton was born in Aglish near Castlebar in 1850.
He was educated in St. Jarlath's College Tuam and at the Irish
College in Paris. He was ordained in 1874 and returned to Ireland
He served in Menlough and Cong and was then appointed
Administrator of Tuam dioceses. Next he was Parish Priest
of Letterfrack in 1890 before being appointed Parish Priest of
Athenry in 1891.

Cannon Canton was well liked in the town and he was very
involved in all local activities. He had a history of supporting
the people of the west in their struggles and he spoke at the

---

328 W/S 617 Mrs. Malone (nee Brighid Breathnech)

329 W/S 617 Mrs. Malone (nee Brighid Breathnech)

scene of evictions in 1888 in the Cloondarone and Cloonmore area. By 1893 he was President of the Athenry branch of the Irish National Federation which fought for the rights of tenant farmers. He was interested in educating the local youth and with this in mind he invited the Presentation nuns to the town. They arrived in 1908 and he gave them his house as a convent. They started a National School in 1910 and a second-level school in the early 1920's.

On the tenth anniversary of his death The Connaught Tribune of Sat August 21st 1930 stated that while not directly involved in politics

'.....he followed the country's struggle for freedom
with keen and unflagging interest. The national
cause had in him an unselfish and generous
supporter both morally and financially at all times'. [330]

It also noted he supported his people during the 1870's, 1880's and 1890's and during the Land War. It also remarked Cannon Canton was ever a loyal adherent of the cause supported by the majority of the Irish people.[331]

1901 Census
Cullairbaun, Athenry, Co. Galway.
Joseph Canton (50) Parish Priest.
Mary Canton (47) sister, Mary Jordan (21) Housekeeper (sister of Stephen Jordan's).

1911 Census
Cullairbawn, Athenry, Co. Galway.
Joseph Canton (60) Parish Priest.
Mary (57) sister, Kate (51) sister.

---

330 Canon Canton-Death of Athenry's Venerable Parish Priest – A life of Untiring Zeal and Devotion
331 Canon Canton-Death of Athenry's Venerable Parish Priest – A life of Untiring Zeal and Devotion

Athenry curates.

Fr. Edward Mc Gough 1911 – 1923

1901 Census.

Bishop's Street, Tuam, Co. Galway.

John Tuffy (33) Catholic Priest.

Alexander Eaton (32) Catholic Priest.

Edward Mc Gough (25) Ecclesiastical student.

Fr. Michael Daly 1914 – 1919

1911 Census

Collegelands, Maynooth, Co. Kildare

Michael Daly (24) Theological student.

Cumann na mBan[332]

Following the formation of the Irish Volunteers there was a public interest in founding a similar movement for women. At the time women were not allowed to join the Volunteers. A number of women including Countess Markievicz and Kathleen Clarke felt there was a role for women. There were a number of informal meetings before the inaugural meeting in Wynn's Hotel in Dublin on Thursday April 2nd 1914.[333] There were up to 100 at the meeting. The founders and many of the original members were white-collar workers and professional women. Later and particularly in rural areas more working class women joined. When the Irish Volunteers split in September 1914 following Redmond's speech at Woodenbridge in Wicklow most of the Cumann na mBan members supported Eoin Mc Neill.

There were some in the organisation such as Francis and Hannah Sheehy Skeffington who believed that the movement was subservient to the Irish Volunteers and as such was selling itself short. Indeed its aims were mainly as a support group for the Volunteers. They envisaged themselves raising money for the purchase of arms for the Volunteers which women couldn't join.

However, it did gain good support nationwide and by 1916 it had forty three affiliated branches throughout the country.[334] The organisation was independent of the Irish Volunteers but was to be under its control. There were classes run for first aid, signalling and drilling. These were often run by Irish Volunteer members.

During the 1916 Rising members were active all around the city. Some forty women were fighting in Dublin. Eilis Ni Rian and Emily Elliott were with Edward Daly at the Four

332 Archiver.rootsweb.ancestry.com IRELAND.2007-04 (Caitriona Clear)

333 Cal Mc Carthy *'Cumann na mBan and the Irish Revolution'* p 15 The Collins Press.

334 D. J. Hickey and J. E. Doherty *'A Dictionary of Irish History 1800 – 1980'* p106. Gill and Macmillan.

Courts and Winnie Carney, Elizabeth O'Farrell, Louise Gavin Duffy and Leslie Price were in the G.P.O.[335] They were involved in all activities and not only traditional ones. Many actively fought during the week. One member Margaret Keogh was shot and killed in St. Stephen's Green.[336] Countess Markievicz also fought there. The one garrison where women were not allowed fight was at Boland's Mills commanded by Eamon de Valera. When the rebels surrendered on Friday of Easter Week it was Cumann na mBan's Elizabeth O'Farrell whom Pearse asked to go to the British forces with the message. Others to play a leading role in the Dublin rising were Helena Maloney, Mary Hyland, Lily Kempson, Rose Mc Namara, Nell Ryan and Julia Grenan. Following the Rising up to 70 members were arrested though most were released by early May.

Throughout the remainder of 1916 the women of the organisation were active in writing to prisoners detained in Wales and sending them parcels of food and clothes. They also raised finances to support families of the prisoners. Most involved in the pre Rising activities still maintained their links to Cumann na mBan. In1917 the main issue was anti-conscription and Cumann na mBan were active in promoting rallies against conscription.

By 1918 when World War 1 was ending and there was a general election in the country most of the members were active in canvassing for the election of Sinn Fein members. Some of the candidates were women and Countess Markievicz was elected and appointed Minister for Labour in the First Dail.

During the War of Independence Cumann na mBan were again very active in all activities from fighting to carrying dispatches, giving first aid and helping men on the run.

In the Civil War from 1922 to 1923 most of the members were on the anti-treaty side.

335 Cal Mc Carthy, 'Cumann na mBan and the Irish Revolution.' p 62 – 63.(Revised Edition) The Collins Press.

336 Theirishwar.com/organisations/Cumann-na-mban/

Cumann na mBan in Galway.

Following the foundation of the movement in Dublin it quickly spread to Galway. There were several branches in the county including Athenry in 1914 and Killeeneen by summer of 1915. The branch in Athenry was one of the most active outside of Dublin. A delegate attended the Cumann na mBan Convention in October 1915 when only eight branches from outside the capital attended.

'This convention was held at 2 Dawson Street on
Sunday 31st October 1915. This was the
same day as the Irish Volunteers convention.' [337]

They were of a more traditional kind than the more feminist ideals in Dublin and the members were willing to see their role as a support to the Irish Volunteers. There were first aid, signalling and drill classes often given by Liam Mellows and Padraig Fahy. Large numbers of young girls joined as they couldn't join the Irish Volunteers. Most of those who joined were from republican families who had brothers in the Volunteers. They did intensive drilling in advance of the Rising and there were up to 30 women with the rebels during the week of the rebellion. Most of the duties were collecting food and cooking it for the men. There were also knowledgeable in first aid and were prepared to attend to the wounded. Many of the women were in close attendance when the R.I.C. and the rebels exchanged fire at the Agricultural College near Athenry on Wednesday April 26th and put their lives in danger at that stage.

Following the disbandment at Lime Park they returned home and though some were questioned by the R.I.C. it seems none were detained for any length of time.

Over the next number of years they were active in many

337 Cal McCarthy, 'Cumann na mBan and the Irish Revolution' p 32 (Revised Edition) The Collins Press.

ways helping men on the run in the aftermath of the Rising and then writing to and sending parcels to the prisoners in Frongoch and other jails. As with the national movement they fundraised for families of the prisoners, organised opposition to conscription and helped canvassing for the 1918 election.

During the War of Independence from 1919 to 1921 many were still active and helped in any way possible. Then amid the tragedy of the Civil War between 1922 and 1923 most were supporters of the anti-treaty side.

Members of Cumann na mBan involved in the Easter Week Rising in Galway.

Annie Allum (nee Barrett) 1894 – 1977

She was born in Athenry and was from a staunch republican family. Four of her brothers were active during the Rising. She was involved in Cumann na mBan from the start and took an active role in all activities during the week. She was at the Town Hall packing rations and ammunition and then proceeded to the Agricultural College, Moyode and Lime Park. Annie remained active in the Athenry branch up to the end of the War of Independence. Later she moved to London and married there.

1911 Census

9 Court Lane, Athenry, Galway.

Michael Barrett (50) Painter, Mary (52).

Thomas (21), Christy (18), **Annie (14) Scholar**, Nellie (12), and Margaret (9).

Kate Armstrong (nee Glynn)

She was born in Killeeneen in 1886 one of twelve children to Thomas and Bridget Glynn. She was a founder member of the Killeeneen Branch of Cumman na mBan in 1915 and was elected its President. The branch was one of the most active in Galway at the time. The members did first aid classes and helped with fundraising for the Irish Volunteers.

On Easter Sunday about ten members mobilised and helped to feed the Volunteers after Mass at Rovagh Church. They were disbanded but were re-mobilised on Monday. The Cumann na mBan members fed the Volunteers again before they set out for Clarenbridge to attack the R.I.C. barracks there. On Wednesday she was in Moyode again cooking for the rebels. She remained with them until the disbandment at Lime Park.

She was not very active in the organisation after the 1916 Rising but did allow some men stay in her house in 1920 during the War of Independence. Following her marriage in 1921 she had nothing to do with the branch.

1911 Census
7 Killeeneen More, Killeely, Galway.
Thomas Glynn (73) Farmer, Bridget (71).
Michael (26), **Kate (25)** and Delia Joyce (8).

Ellen Dooley, (nee Kelly) 1887 – 1979
She was originally from Colemanstown, Tiaquin. She joined Cumann na mBan in 1914. Ellen served in Clarenbridge, Oranmore, the Agricultural College, Moyode and Lime Park during Easter week. Her duties included cooking, procuring food and helping with first aid. She later became a National School teacher.

May Higgins 1898 – 1951
May served in the organisation having joined in 1915. She packed food, rations and ammunition in the Athenry Town Hall during the mobilisation. She was active for the week of the rising in the Agricultural College, Moyode and Lime Park. Cooking for the men was another principal duty performed during the

week of the rebellion. Cumann na mBan members were also proficient in First Aid and attended to injured Volunteers.

Following the Rising May was involved with supporting men on the run and sending food parcels to prisoners. During the War of Independence she again helped in any way possible by feeding men, supporting men on the run and delivering dispatches. She was also active on the Republican side during the Civil War.

1911 Census

12 Cross Street, Athenry, Galway.

George Higgins (32) Tailor, Kate (41).

Mary (13) Scholar, Catherine (11), Michael (10), Joseph (8), Bridget (7), James Lardner (73) and Bridget Lardner (81).

Annie Howley (nee Deviney) 1895 – 1969

Annie's parents James and Mary from Ballynacloghy, Maree had twelve children of which she was second. She was a member of the Maree branch of Cumann na mBan and active for the whole of Easter week. She saw service in Oranmore, the Agricultural College and Moyode. She departed Moyode on Thursday evening and made her way home. She had first aid, food collection and cooking duties during that time. Annie continued to be involved in Cumann na mBan up to the end of the War of Independence helping and feeding men who were on the run in the Maree area.

Her brothers Thomas and John were also active in the rising.

1911 Census

Ballynacloghy, Ballynacourty

James Deviney (53) Farmer, Mary (48).

Annie (20) Farmer's daughter, Mary (18), Nora (16), Thomas (15), John (14), Pat (13), Stephen (12), Winnifred (10), Edward (8), Katie (7) and Bridget (5).

Kathleen Kennedy (nee Cleary) 1897 – ?

Kathleen was from the large family of Thomas and Mary Cleary of Abbey Row. Her father was a plasterer. They were a very republican family and heavily involved in all nationalist activities.

Kathleen was a founder member of the Athenry Cumann na mBan and involved in drilling, first aid and signalling. During Easter Week she was at the Town Hall packing rations and ammunition. She accompanied the men to the Agricultural College, Moyode and Lime Park. As a trained nurse she had a very valuable role to play all during the week. She was caught under fire when the R.I.C came to investigate the situation at the Agricultural College and they were driven off by a group of Irish Volunteers.

Following the Rising she was active raising funds for the I.R.A. and involved in supporting roles in 1918 and 1919. She emigrated to England in1919 and returned in October 1921. She was active during the Civil War helping men who were on the run from the Government forces. [338] Her four brothers were also active participants in the rising.

1911 Census

3 Abbey Row.

Thomas Cleary (49) Plasterer, Mary (48).

John (22),Thomas (20), Joseph (15), James(9), Mary (19) and **Kathleen (14) Scholar.**

Bridie Lane 1888 - ?

She was born in Killeelybeg near Kilcolgan about 1888. The family is returned in the 1901 Census as house 5 in Killeely and house 2 in1911. However, there are 12 to 13 years added to each of the children for the 1911 Census and 21 years to the mother Sarah.

338 mspcsearch.militaryarchives.ie/docs/files//PDF_Pensions/R1/MSP34REF3 257KATHLEENKENNEDY/
    WMSP34REF3257KATHLEENKENNEDY.pdf p40

She was in the Kilcolgan branch of Cumann na mBan and was active from 1915 up to 1923. She was involved in all activity during Easter week in Clarenbridge, Oranmore, the Agricultural College, Moyode and Lime Park. She collected food, cooked for the men and was available for first aid when required. She tended to a Volunteer Mattie Reany who was seriously ill during the stay at Lime Park. It is most likely he was injured following an exchange of gun fire with the R.I.C. When the rebels moved to Lime Park he was too ill to travel. He was brought to John Hynes's house in Creggaturlough, two miles south of Moyode, where she minded him for three days. However, he did not recover following his ordeal and died a week later.[339] Bridie continued her association with Cumann na mBan up to the end of the Civil War.

1911 Census

2 Killeeleybeg, Killeely, Galway.

John Lane (40) Farmer.

Sarah (71), Michael (38), James (30), **Bridget (25)** and Patrick (23).

Bridget Lardner (nee Kennedy)1882 - 1966

She was a member of the Athenry branch of Cumann na mBan, joining in 1915. Previously she was a member of the Gaelic League. She was heavily involved in the nationalist activities of the time. In the run up to the Rising she along with other members of the Athenry branch attended first aid, signalling and drilling classes. Married to Larry Lardner the Galway Brigade O/C she saw duty in the Town Hall on the opening days of the Rising. She remained at home on the Tuesday and Wednesday. Along with Dolly Fleming she brought food to the rebels when they were stationed at Moyode.

Following the Rising she was active in Cumann na mBan

339 mspcsearch.militaryarchives.ie/docs/files//PDF_R2MPS34REF20331BRIDIELANE/
WNSP34REF20331BRIDIELANE.pdf p53

all during the War of Independence supplying food, visiting prisoners, raising funds, hiding ammunition, etc.

She had one daughter Kitty.

Bridget Malone (nee Walsh) 1889 – 1955

She was born in 1889 to Hubert and Mary Kate Walsh both of whom were national school teachers in Killeeneen near Craughwell. She became a national school teacher in Drombane in Co. Tipperary where her mother was from.

On the Wednesday before the rising, April 19th, her sister Gretta met her in Limerick and gave her £10 with which to buy bandages. The chemist was suspicious of her buying such a large amount of bandages but she said they were for the Red Cross for a hospital in France. He had not enough for the money she had but he posted them up to her in Killeeneen and they arrived on the following Saturday, April 22nd. Fr. Feeney had written to her in Tipperary to come home during the holidays as there was going to be a rising in Galway. Even though she had intended to stay with her grandmother in Tipperary she did come home with Gretta on the Wednesday. Gretta had told her there was going to be a war and that is what the bandages were for. Fr Feeney wanted her to go to Dublin to deliver messages to the I.R.B leaders there and bring back a parcel to Galway. She was the best person to go as she was not now living in the Galway area and was not known to the police.

She went to Dublin on Holy Thursday on the train and Julia Morrissey joined her at Attymon. She also had a message from Tom Kenny for Tom Clarke. On her return journey she was given a parcel to bring to her home. This was a Volunteer uniform for Liam Mellows who was returning to Galway just in time for the rebellion. She was in her home house when Mellows arrived back from England and when the rising began. She travelled to Moyode with provisions on Wednesday April 26th. She avoided arrest after the rising as she had returned to Tipperary when the R.I.C called to her house in Craughwell to arrest her in relation to supplying bandages to the rebels. After the rising she helped a number of men who were on the run including Eamon Corbett and Pat Callanan and brought them a revolver when they were hiding out in Clare. She found there was great support for the nationalist cause among many priests and religious like the monks in Mount Melleray, the Clonfert Diocesan College in Ballinasloe and the Cistercians in Roscrea.[340]

Following the Rising she married Tipperary man Seamus Malone an Irish teacher. She resigned as a teacher in 1918. She was not involved in the Killeeneen Branch following the Rising as she was married in Tipperary.

1901 Census

23 Killeencenmore, Killeely, Galway.

Hubert Walsh (53) School Teacher, Mary K (37).

Bridget (12) Scholar, Eily (10), Marian (8), Agnes (6), Margaret (4), Patrick J (0), Agnes Mulcahy (21), Michael B. Kearney (3) and Margaret Cloonan (20).

Delia Mc Namara (nee Cummins) 1898 - 1965

Delia Cummins from Coldwood was a member of the Athenry Cumann na mBan branch. Three of her brothers Joe, Willie and Michael were active during Easter Week. She carried despatches and cooked for the rebels during the week. She saw service in Athenry, the Agricultural College, Moyode and Lime Park. Following the rebellion she helped men who were on the run feeding them and getting them clothes. She was not involved in Cumann na mBan following her marriage in 1919.[341]

In the 1911 census she was visiting the Rooney family in nearby Tallowroe where she may have been minding a number of small children. Her own family were recorded in Coldwood.

---

340 W/S 617 Mrs. Malone (nee Brighid Breathnach)

341 mspcseacrh.militaryarchives.ie/docs/files//PDF_Pensions/R2/MPS34REF60139DeliaMcNamara/
    WMSP34REF60139DeliaMcNanara.pdf p32

1911 Census

5 Coldwood, Stradbally, Galway.

James Cummins (59) Farmer, Mary Ann (50).

Thomas (23), Patrick (21), Michael (20), William (19), Maria (16), Ellen (10), Margaret (8) and James (6)

2 Tallowroe, Killeely, Galway.

John Rooney (51) Farmer, Bridget (37).

Thomas (7), Patrick (6), Mary Anne (5), Margaret (4), Hanoria (1).

Martin Rooney (63) **Delia Cummins (13) Scholar, visitor.**

Mary Mc Namara (nee Rooney) 1897 - 1969

Mary was born in Caherroyn, Athenry in 1897 to John and Ann Rooney. Her family were general labourers. She was a member of both Gaelic League and Cumann na mBan in Athenry. For the three weeks leading up to the rebellion she trained intensively in first aid, signalling and drill. During the rising she was in the Town Hall packing rations and then went to the Agricultural College. Mary made several trips between Moyode and Athenry to get food and supplies for the men while they were stationed there. She was also in Lime Park. After the rebellion she was still in the organisation and served through the War of Independence and the Civil War helping with First Aid and supplying food and clothes to men on the run.[342]

1911 Census

4 Caherroyn, Athenry, Galway.

James Rooney (56) General Labourer, Ann (50).

Joseph (26), Patrick (22), John (20), Bridget (19), **Mary (16) Scholar** and Katie (12)

---

342 mspcseacrh.militaryarchives.ie/docs/files//PDF_Pensions/RI/MPS34REF59 605MaryMcNamara/ WMSP34REF59605MaryMcNamara.pdf pp27,28, 41- 43

Rebellion in Galway

Julia Morrissey 1892 - ?

She was from Old Church Street in Athenry and born about 1892. She was a very close friend of Liam Mellows. She was one of the founder members of Cumann na mBan in Athenry[343] and very active in the organisation throughout the troubles. She travelled to Dublin during Easter week with Bridget Malone (nee Walsh) to get a uniform for Liam Mellows for the rebellion. She was one of the main participants during the week of the Rising in the Town Hall, the Agricultural College, Moyode and Lime Park.

1911 Census

40 Old Church Street, Athenry, Galway.
Patrick Morrissey (70) Grocer, Mary (50).
Julia (19) and Martin (17).

Gretta Mullins (nee Walsh) 1897 - ?

She was born in Killeeneen to Hubert and Mary Kate Walsh. They were both National School teachers and Gretta followed them into this profession as did her older sister Bridget. All the family were involved in nationalist activities. Liam Mellows based himself in the Walsh house when he was in the Craughwell area. It was to here he returned on the eve of the Rising. Gretta played a full part in the activities of Easter Week and accompanied the rebels to all areas. Following the rebellion she maintained her links with Cumann na mBan up to the Civil War helping in whatever way she could. She was married with five children.[344]

1911 Census

17 Killeeneen More, Killeely, Galway.
Mary Kate Walsh (37) National School Teacher.
Eily (21), **Gretta (14) Scholar**, Patrick J (10) and Teresa (9).

---

343 C Desmond Greaves 'Liam Mellows and the Irish Revolution' p 77 An Ghlór Gafa.

344 mspcsearch.militaryarchives.ie/detail.aspx?parentpriref= p11

Katie Nelly (nee Fahy/Fahey) 1893 – 1971.

She was from Templemartin, Craughwell and a daughter of Patrick and Norah Fahy. There were 12 children in the family. She joined the Killeeneen branch of Cumann na mBan in 1915. She did the usual training in first aid and drill. During 1916 she was mobilised on Monday and served until Saturday when they demobilised at Lime Park. Following the rebellion she maintained her association with the organisation. She got married in 1918 to John Nelly and moved to Gort. There she joined the local Cumann branch and continued her work. She was active up to and including the Civil War.[345]

1911 Census
1 Templemartin, Craughwell, Galway.
Patrick Fahey (55) Farmer, Norah (45).
John (22), **Katie (18) Scholar**, Maggie (16), Thomas (13), Anthony (12), Francis (9) Norah (6), Michael (3) and Sarah (2).

Mary Josephine O'Beirne (nee Cleary) 1892 – 1966

She was born in Athenry and lived in Abbey Row with her family. Her father Thomas and three brothers were active in the Rising. She had joined Cumann na mBan in Athenry in August 1915. From then on she took part in all the activities of the branch. She was active during Easter Week starting in the Town Hall preparing for the rebellion. She then saw duty at the Agricultural College, Moyode and Lime Park. Following the surrender she was active in the branch up to the end of the Civil War. She married Stephen O'Beirne in 1925.

1911 Census
3 Abbey Row.
Thomas Cleary (49) Plasterer, Mary (48).
John (22), Thomas (20), Joseph (15), James (9), **Mary (19)** and Kathleen (14).

---

345 mspcseacrh.militaryarchives.ie/docs/files//PDF_Pensions/R2/MPS34REF14582KATIENELLY/
    WMSP34REF14582KATIENELLY.pdf p26-28.

Rebellion in Galway

Mary Rabbitt (nee Corbett) 1891 – 1972

She was born in Killeeneen Beg to Thomas and Mary Corbett. There were seven children in the farming family. She joined the Killeeneen branch of Cumann na mBan when it started in 1915 and was active all during Easter Week in Clarenbridge, Oranmore, the Agricultural College, Moyode and Lime Park. During this week she collected and cooked food. She was active during the War of Independence carrying dispatches, looking after men on the run and giving first aid. She continued her work for Cumann na mBan on the Republican side during the Civil War feeding men and carrying dispatches.[346]

1901 Census

1 Killeencenbeg, Killeely, Galway.

Thomas Corbett (58) Farmer, Mary (42).

Thomas (16), Honoria (14), Patrick (12), Edmond (11), **Mary (9) Scholar**, John (7) and Dominick (5).

Bridget Ruane (nee Morrissey) 1898 – 1989

She joined the Athenry branch of Cumann na mBan in 1914. She was sister of Gilbert Morrissey who served as captain of the Rockfield Irish Volunteer Company. Bridget was in all the areas of conflict during the rising. Starting with packing rations and medical supplies in The Town Hall on Easter Monday. She was with the rebels in the Agricultural College, Moyode and Lime Park. She completed first aid courses and was also a fundraiser for the Volunteers to get funds to buy arms in advance of the Rising. Bridget was also active in the War of Independence and served as President and Captain of the Craughwell branch of the organisation. She continued her association with the organisation during the Civil War on the Republican side helping men on the run and delivering dispatches.[347]

346 mspcsearch.militaryarchives.ie/docs/files//PDF_Pensions/R2/MSP34REF9021MaryRabbitt/ WMSP34REF9021MaryRabbitt.PDF p21-28.

347 mspcsearch.militaryarchives.ie/docs/files//PDF_Pensions/R2/MPS34REF/R2/MSP34REF13981 BRIDGETRUANE/WMSP34REF13981BRIDGETRUANE.pdf p29-43.

1901 census

Knockatoor, Greethill, Athenry, Galway.

John Morrissey (45) Farmer, Bridget (44).

Thomas (15), John (12), William (11), Norah (9), Richard (6), Martin (4), **Bridget (3) Scholar** and Patrick (0).

1911 census

Knockatoor, Greethill, Athenry, Galway.

John Morrissey (59) Farmer, Bridget (58)

Thomas (26), John (23), Gilbert (21), Norah (17), Richard (16), Martin (14), **Bridget (12) Scholar** and Pat (10).

Sadie Tierney (nee Burke) 1898 – 1989

She was born in Caherroyn, Athenry in 1898 to James and Julia Burke, one of nine children. She joined the Athenry Cumann na mBan in 1915 and played an active role in the Rising. She packed food and ammunition in the Town Hall following mobilisation and then proceeded to the Agricultural College. She was sent back to Athenry to bring home her young brother who had gone there, likely 13 year old Walter. She was told to get supplies of food and cigarettes and join the rebels at Moyode. Later she lived in Swords and Cabra and was married with 7 children.[348]

1911 Census

3 Caherroyn, Athenry, Galway.

James Burke (45) Agricultural Labourer, Julia (33).

Mary (150, Patrick (14), **Sarah (13) Scholar**, Hanora (9), Walter (8), James Thomas (5), John (4), Joseph (0), Martin Cooley (60) and Terence Grealish (26).

Mary Kate Walsh 1864 - ?

Born about 1864 she was a National School teacher

---

348 mspcseacrh.militaryarchives.ie/docs/files//PDF_Pensions/R1/MSP34REF9029SadieTierney/
WMSP34REF9029SadieTIERNEY.pdf p62

originally from Tipperary. She married Hubert Walsh also a National School teacher. Both taught in Killeeneen school near Craughwell. Liam Mellows used to stay in their house when he was in the Craughwell area. All of their children were involved in the nationalist movement, with the girls in Cumann na mBan and their son in the Irish Volunteers. (Mother of Bridget Malone, (nee Walsh) and Gretta Mullins (nee Walsh) see above).

Areas of Fighting and Activity during Easter Week 1916.

Mellows Agricultural College, Athenry[349]

'The College' or 'The Farmyard' as it was known was an agricultural college set up by the Department of Agriculture and Technical Instruction in 1905. It was situated two miles west of the town on the Galway road.

Sir Horace Plunkett born in Gloucestershire in 1854 was an agriculturalist and Unionist politician. Having spent time in America he returned to manage his family estates in Co. Meath. He felt that much of the Irish agricultural practices were uneconomic and were in dire need of updating. He was instrumental in organising the co-operative movement which he started in Drumcollogher in Co. Limerick in 1890. Thereafter he was successful in getting the government to set up the Department of Agriculture and Technical Instruction in 1900. Plunkett was the first Vice-President and his friend and work colleague Thomas Gill was the first Department Secretary. An agricultural college was set up in each province to help with and promote the development of agriculture in Ireland. Thus, the college for Connaught was set up in Athenry in 1905.

The college was on lands acquired from the recently sold Goodbody estate of 2,000 acres. 640 acres were acquired by the Department for the college and the rest were distributed to local farmers by the Congested Districts Board. The college became a residential college run by the department. Since 1995 it has been run by TEAGASC.

During the 1916 Rising it was taken over by the rebels on Tuesday night, April 25th, and up to 750 men and 25 women assembled there before moving to Moyode Castle. They apprehended livestock for food and horses and carts and cars for transport from 'the College'.

349 Teagasc, Athenry – The Story, - Nuala King. O'Regan's Athenry - Athenry History Archive.

The college is now named after Liam Mellows following it being a centre of activity during the 1916 Rising in Galway.

Carnmore Cross

Located in the countryside east of Galway City, in 1916 it was like any rural area. It is about five miles due east of Galway City on the R339. It is just a few hundred yards from the entrance to where Galway Airport was located.

At the time of the rising it was where two narrow roads crossed. There were a few houses in the area and field divisions were stone walls as they are today. These walls afforded the rebels plenty of cover as they fought the police and British forces on the morning of Wednesday April 26th. The occupants of the houses, at the time, included Cooneys and a number of Grealish families.[350] Six Grealishs from around the area took part in the ambush of the British forces.

It is now a busy junction with a set of traffic lights, a far cry from that fateful day in April 1916 when Constable Whelan was shot.

Clarenbridge

It is now a busy tourist village. There has been a notable development of linear housing along many of the by roads around the village and the population of the area has dramatically grown as it is in the commuter zone of Galway City.

The old R.I.C. barracks was located beside the village green in a terrace of houses. It is now a private house. There is a plaque on the wall of the house in relation to the 1916 activities.

Oranmore

It is now a satellite town of Galway City with a large number of housing estates. The town has long since been bypassed by a relief road going to Galway and also by the new motorway from Dublin.

350 1901/1911 Census, Ireland

Areas of Fighting and Activity

The old R.I.C. barracks is now demolished. The rail station about a mile outside the town near the Dublin –Galway motorway is still there and operational. The bridge over the river which was partially blown up is still in place. There is a memorial statue to Joe Howley who was the leader of the Oranmore Irish Volunteer Company when they attacked the R.I.C barracks. He was later killed, in Dublin, by British intelligence forces in 1920, during the War of Independence.

Lime Park[351]

This house was also part of the Persse family property. It was owned by a different branch though related to the Moyode family. It was situated four miles from Gort off the Gort – Loughrea road. It was about two miles from Ardrahan. The house was deserted at the time the rebels took it over on the Friday night of the rising April 28th. Today the house is in ruins. There is a commemorative plaque on the front of the ruin in relation to its association with the1916 Rising.

The most notable member of the Persse family is Lady Gregory of Coole Park, Gort. She was a leading light of the Literary Revival that saw such notable writers as William Butler Yeats and John Millington Synge at work. She was instrumental in setting up the Abbey Theatre and wrote many plays that were performed there. Lady Gregory was born Isabella Augusta Persse in Roxborough House only three miles from Lime Park near Kilchreest, Loughrea and married Sir William Gregory of Coole Park.

The Census of 1901 returned Henrietta Nolan aged 68 and her daughter Eva (23) both Church of Ireland living in Lime Park. The house was officially in the townland of Bullaunagh North in the parish of Kilthomas. Interestingly both were returned as of 'No Profession'. There were also two servants Ellen Fahy (22) and Martin Reynolds (33). Another family working on the estate

351 landedestates.nuigalway.ie

311

was that of Edward and Mary Maher from Queen's County. They had nine children living with them and Edward's occupation was given as a shepherd. In the 1911 census there was only the Maher family returned for the townland of Bullaunagh North. Edward, now 60, was listed as a 'caretaker' presumably of Lime Park House. Mary and seven of the children were also listed. In total there were 18 children in the family with 14 alive in 1911.[352]

Moyode Castle[353]

Moyode is three miles east of Athenry off the Athenry – Loughrea road at Tallyho crossroads. There is a Norman tower castle there but the Moyode referred to in the 1916 Rising was the mansion house of the Persse family. The Persse family owned up to 1,800 acres in a number of estates in Galway in the1700 and 1800's. The will of Robert Persse of Roxborough between Loughrea and Gort shows him the owner of Moyode. Burton Persse (1746 – 1831) was noted for his love of hunting and was the founder of the Galway Blazers Hunt. The family lost a lot of their credibility during the famine when over 50% of the tenants died compared to 38% locally. The mansion built on the estate was by Burton de Burgh Persse Junior (1782 – 1859). It was a neo gothic style building with a number of pretentious towers. His son Burton Persse born in 1828 was the last of the family to own the estate. He was in residence there in1894 but it was sold to the Land Judges' Court around the turn of the century. In 1906 it was owned by Lord Ardilaun.

In 1901 the census shows five households employed by the demesne down as Moyoda Demensne, Moyode, Galway. Of these, Neil Mc Adams (Church of Ireland) is a servant (a family of eight) from Scotland and James Butler (a family of four) is

---

352 1901/1911 Census, Ireland

353 Hidden Gems and Forgotten People – South East Galway Archaeological and Historical Society. Steve Dolan

a gamekeeper from England and also Church of Ireland. The Heartys, from Louth, (a family of five) were also working on the estate in1901. There were other people living in the area also employed by the estate such as servants and housekeepers.[354]

In the census of 1911 there were four families recorded as living on the estate, Byrnes, Shakletons, Hartys (Heartys) and Brodericks. Their occupations were herdsmen, a gardener and farmers. John Shakleton, the gardener, from Cavan was a Presbyterian as was his wife Ellen who was from Wicklow.[355]

At the time of the 1916 Rising it was closed up and being looked after by a caretaker and was thus easily taken by the rebels who made it their headquarters for Wednesday and Thursday nights of April 26th and 27th.

The house was burned by the I.R.A. during the War of Independence and nothing now remains of it. The stones from the building have long since been taken. There are some remnants of the stables and an old bell tower remaining. However, the Norman tower castle from which it got its name is still standing and occupied to this day.[356]

---

354 1901/1911 Census, Ireland

355 1901/1911 Census, Ireland

356 landedestates.nuigalway.ie

Conclusion

The 1916 Rising in Galway lasted form Sunday April 23rd, with a partial mobilisation, to Saturday April 29th when the rebels disbanded about 3.00 a.m. at Lime Park House near Gort. As they went on the run or back to their homes they no doubt reflected on the various activities of the week. Unfortunately one man, Constable Patrick Whelan, was killed, a badly injured Irish Volunteer, Martin Reaney, died a week later and a number of R.I.C. were wounded. Each were doing what they felt was their duty. The R.I.C. and British sailors and soldiers, be they Irish or British in nationality, were doing the job that they were paid for. The British officials like Leslie Edmunds were endeavouring to maintain law and order as was their duty. Against this background the so-called rebels supported by the wider community, were hoping to do the right thing for their country by revolting against what they saw as a foreign power. Those in Galway who were opposed to the rebels like the Special Constables, the army wives, the businessmen and the business leaders in the city were motivated by their loyalty to the British and their respect for law and order.

With World War 1 at a grave juncture any form of meaningful discussion between dissidents and the British government was unlikely at that time. The British would have stated that Home Rule was on the table for when the war in Europe was over. As to whether it would have been granted in part or in full is now just speculation. This must be seen against the background of the Buckingham Palace Conference, July 21st – 24th 1914. In June 1914 an Amending Bill was passed allowing for between four and six counties not to be included in Home Rule should it ever become law. The conference was an attempt to work out a compromise between all sides and it involved King George V as a mediator. It ended in failure without any compromise.[357] With

357 D.J. Hickey and J.E. Doherty 'A Dictionary of Irish History 1800 – 1980.' p47-48. Gill and Macmillan.

the advent of World War 1 the Home Rule Act was postponed and the nationalists and republicans in the southern counties felt that the chance of a thirty two county Home Rule area let alone a republic were now gone. Thus, many within the I.R.B. felt a rebellion was the only alternative. In the meantime all participants assured themselves they were right.

In the grand scheme of things little was achieved by the rebels during their week's activities. They controlled much of mid and south Galway but only as the R.I.C. and army did not contest it. They attacked two R.I.C. barracks but failed to capture either. They were not able to secure any worthwhile arms. The authorities controlled Galway City, Tuam, Loughrea, Ballinasloe and Athenry and the rebels were cut off from the outside world even if those in the city and towns also were. Only a core group of some 11 companies and other individual members revolted. Following the revolt over 400 were arrested of which 328 were sent to detention centres in Britain.

The lack of arms among the rebels was a serious drawback. Some presented themselves with pikes, a weapon of the 1798 rebellion. Besides a large number of shotguns there were only about 25 rifles and a few home-made bombs. The expected arms from Kerry never arrived and maybe just as well. Should they have arrived the men would have had what might have been described as adequate weapons. It would have insured all those who mobilised would have had arms and indeed more may have risen. Should this have happened it would have been more difficult to have persuaded them to disband on Saturday 29th. Thus, when the British military would have moved in on them the fighting would have been intense and undoubtedly significant numbers of fatalities would have been seen on both sides.

The idea that the I.R.B. carefully and secretly took over the control of the Irish Volunteers and then succeeded in using them as soldiers for their rebellion has some credence in many parts of Ireland. There were undoubtedly some who did not fully know what they were getting into until it was too late. However, in Galway this was different. Constantly the witness statements say that these men had earlier joined the I.R.B. and they were waiting for the opportunity to strike at Britain or her agents in Ireland. They did succeed in taking over control of the Volunteers but it was accepted and supported. When the Volunteers split in Galway the Irish Volunteers went from strength to strength while the National Volunteer units faded away in many areas. The ordinary men may not have been party to when exactly the rebellion was set to take place but there is little to suggest that they were not willing to partake when it did take place. Thus, there is no evidence to suggest that they were duped by the I.R.B. into a rebellion they did not wish to fight. Those who did not wish to fight knew by Monday that the rebellion had begun and that this was a fight against the crown forces and not just a route march. They did not have to mobilise and indeed those who choose not to, did not, and there were many of these. There were also many men whose companies did not mobilise and they joined the fight themselves. In addition, there were times when rebels were free to go home if they wished and those who did were allowed.

The fact that the Rising began on Monday morning in Dublin meant that the authorities in Galway got something of a warning as to what might happen within the county. They rapidly withdrew all constables from vulnerable sub stations and brought them into larger barracks in towns like Athenry, Loughrea and Gort. This meant a fundamental reappraisal of the carefully made plans of the Irish Volunteers/I.R.B. Much of this 'change of plans' had to take place as the rising progressed. Had the Clarenbridge and Oranmore barracks been taken and more guns secured the plans may have taken a different route. As it was, the leaders realised they had not the capabilities to take a well defended barracks no matter how many constables were within. Athenry and Loughrea were off limits as there were large numbers of civilians in the vicinity of the barracks and there were now 30 to 40 R.I.C. in those barracks. Thus, there was very little the rebels could effectively do other remain at large for as long as they could.

While in revolt they were involved in eight engagements with British forces, the attacks on Clarenbridge barracks, Oranmore barracks twice, the skirmish with the Crown forces when leaving Oranmore, the incident at Carnmore Cross, the exchange at the Agricultural College, the engagement with the R.I.C. at Rahard near Moyode and the brief exchange of fire between the Volunteers and the R.I.C. in Kinvarra. These may have boosted morale but had seriously depleted ammunition stocks. Therefore, further attacks looked unlikely and any stocks of ammunition left were likely needed for defence.

Indeed, linking up with rebels in Clare, what seems to have emerged as an alternative, was now out of the question as there was no rebellion in Clare. Operating a guerrilla war from Sliabh Aughta, the hills on the Galway Clare boarder, was also ruled out due to lack of weapons and ammunition. Finally, the stand and fight option was also thankfully ruled out, as to wait in the Lime Park area to be attacked by a force of over 1,000 British military would have been madness.

On the positive side the rebels had some popular support locally during the week. They were well supported and fed. With the help of Cumann na mBan food was sourced, supplied and cooked. Much of this was provided willingly, though no doubt a number of farmers and business people from whom they requisitioned food were not all that happy. The large number of men and women who participated in the rising would suggest that there was good local support for the rebels. These were people that had supported nationalist causes for many years in an area of the county where land issues were fundamental. The Town Tenants' League had secured land for townspeople in

Rebellion in Galway

Athenry and was very popular as a result. The Irish Volunteers paraded openly and had huge support at all their rallies. Many families had sons and daughters in the Irish Volunteers and Cumann na mBan and therefore they received local support outside of Galway City and the main rural towns. Therefore, it can obviously be seen that in the mid and south Galway area that the rising had popular support. This can also be seen due to the fact that when the prisoners were released the following Christmas most of them were back in business working with the I.R.B. against conscription and later as Sinn Fein election workers in 1918. Again these activities had the general support of the community.

There were some elements of success in the Rising. It did show what could be achieved by a group had they better weapons, planning, support and tactics. After all they fought eight engagements without the loss of any men. They did tie down some British military and police for a week and forces were sent from Cork and police from Belfast. They would learn from this experience for the War of Independence. Though Galway was not one of the more active areas in the 1919 – 1921 War of Independence there were a lot more successful attacks on British military and R.I.C. and a number of successful attacks on R.I.C. barracks.

From a rebels point of view the rebellion, though unsuccessful at the time, laid a foundation for the future. There was a sense of camaraderie built up among the participants that would endure through the terms of imprisonment. Rebels and those additional men arrested were imprisoned in various camps in Britain. Most were ultimately sent to Frongoch in Wales but other prisons included Wandsworth, Stafford, Woking, Glasgow and Perth. Many prisoners were originally sentenced to death but this was commuted to various jail terms in light of the outcry over the executions of the main leaders in Dublin.

These places of detention became 'universities' for the

prisoners as they learned so much there. They built up friendships and contacts for when they were released. They were able to discuss the mistakes of the Rising and what they could do differently the next time and they vowed there would be a next time. They looked at the tactics used in the Rising and assessed the successes and failures. It became obvious that a war conducted with a large army in the field to oppose a similar British army would be folly and lead to defeat as would have happened at Lime Park had the rebels not disbanded. They recognised that a tactic, of guerrilla warfare, similar to that of Thomas Ashe in Ashbourne, would be most likely to succeed. The prisoners discussed these ideas and devised strategies in the hope of being more successful when they organised a rebellion again. Prison did not dampen their enthusiasm, it heightened it.

Many men in the Galway area who ended up in jail in Britain were released by Christmas 1916. Others were released later in 1917. They generally got a welcoming reception on their return. The vast majority of them returned directly to anti-British activities and were participants in the War of Independence. Prior to that they were involved in anti-conscription activity and electioneering for the general election of November 1918. Stephen Jordan was arrested for anti conscription activity in 1918. Later, in 1920, as Chairman of the Loughrea Rural District Council, he was jailed for a year for allowing justice to be administered by Sinn Fein courts rather than the British run ones.

They realised that they would need a greater number of weapons to affect a war against the British. To this end it was decided to source these in Ireland by attacking and robbing R.I.C. barracks. It was too precarious to rely on arms from abroad that as in 1916 may not arrive. Instead they would repeat the original plan of 1916 and attack R.I.C. barracks to secure them. They would not take on the British in open battle or get tied down in towns and cities like in Dublin in 1916. The plan of guerrilla warfare was decided on and volunteers could employ hit and run tactics in an effort to wear down the British without putting the men at a greater risk.

Following the Sinn Fein victory in the November 1918 General Election, when they secured 73 of the 105 seats for Ireland, the situation deteriorated rapidly and the War of Independence began in January 1919. The lessons learned from the failures of 1916 were employed and there was far greater success in fighting the enemy.

This war dragged on until July 1921 and was a brutal and bloody affair. Thousands were killed and injured, I.R.A. (formerly the I.R.B.), British soldiers, civilians, R.I.C., British officials, etc. A truce was declared in July 1921 and talks took place between the British government and the Irish representatives. Eventually a treaty, the Anglo – Irish Treaty, was agreed upon and signed on December 6th 1921.

Among the terms of the Treaty were, that six northern counties would remain with Britain and that parliamentary deputies in the twenty six counties would have to take an Oath of Allegiance to the British crown. These became sticking points when the Dial, which now ruled the twenty six county Irish Free State met to ratify the Anglo - Irish Treaty. The Treaty was hotly debated in the Irish parliament between December 1921 and January 1922 with all deputies (T.D.'s) speaking. The vote took place on January 7th and the Treaty was ratified by 64 to 57 votes. However, those who lost the vote left the Dáil. Again the situation in Ireland rapidly deteriorated and by June 1922 the twenty six county Free State was plunged into Civil War over the Treaty. The war lasted until May 1923. Many of those who had fought together against the common enemy from 1916 to 1921 fought and killed each other in what was the most bitter of all the encounters over those troubled eight years.

The Cumann na mBan organisation remained strong and

in place. These women, many of whom were arrested in the wake of 1916 were as equally determined to rally to the cause and were an essential part of the organisation behind the War of Independence. Many also continued to be active during the Civil War.

So how will we look at the 1916 Easter Rising in 2016 on the 100th anniversary?

By all accounts, at the time it occurred, in April 1916 it was unpopular. However, that would seem different in many parts of Galway especially in the mid and south areas both during and immediately after the rising. There seems to have been considerable support for the rising from men and women in the area as over 700 took part in the rebellion. According to accounts many more would have joined had they been notified in time to mobilise or indeed notified at all. Equally there seems to have been little difficulty in procuring food and supplies for the rebels from the locals. When the prisoners returned from jail in Britain there was again considerable support for them and most of them returned to revolutionary activities during the War of Independence and many during the Civil War. Also the various Galway constituencies all returned Sinn Fein candidates in the 1918 and 1920 elections. The Irish Parliamentary Party candidates William Duffy (South Galway) and William O'Malley (Connemara) were heavily defeated.

This support continued and by the 25th and 50th anniversaries they had reached hero status. This was especially seen in the 1966 celebrations. However, talk of 1916 became somewhat muted in the 1980's and 1990's due to the troubles in the North. School children who heretofore could rhyme off all the names of the 1916 leaders now hardly knew the names of any bar Pearse and Connolly.

On the other hand those who had made the decision to fight with the British army in World War 1 were, for generations, rarely spoken of. Indeed, many were unaware of the contribution of their relations to World War 1 as it was often a hidden secret. Thankfully as the various anniversaries of World War 1 approached and also to great work done by many commentators to ignite their cause this changed. They have now been given a rightful place in the history of the country and the county.

So as time passes acknowledgement of the events of the past are given varying profiles and degrees of acceptance. History is being continually revised and many events fall in and out of favour as they are continually reviewed.

One hundred years on from 1916 we can hopefully look at the events without prejudice. Those who fought for what they believed would be a better Ireland for them and their families did so believing to have local support. They also operated at a time when what is today seen as normal political discussion was not as possible as it is today. Their methods may have been questionable but their motivation for what they believed would be a better Ireland cannot be in doubt. It is highly unlikely that Home Rule would have been delivered as promised and they sincerely believed this to be their opportunity and only method to deliver freedom for Ireland. They were certainly foolhardy to revolt with the lack of weapons evident though they may have expected the delivery of promised weapons despite the capture of the Aud. However, their courage could not be questioned.

Those who opposed them saw the revolt as a betrayal at a time of extreme danger with World War 1 at crises point. These found the links to Germany particularly difficult to understand. Many of these were charged with maintaining law and order and it was their duty to ensure that it was restored at all costs.

All sides and points of view deserve respect and consideration for their stance. The rising in Galway was organised by a considerable number of people as was the opposition to it. Thus all can consider reasonable support for their cause. We cannot always judge the events of the past by the standards of today. So let us honour and remember them all, especially Patrick Whelan and Martin Reaney who lost their lives as a result of the rising.

Let us hope that we can learn from history and that we will not experience revolution in Ireland again or experience the conditions in the country that made people feel the only way to right those wrongs was by revolution.

Appendix 1

A List of Special Constables in Galway City Easter Week 1916

J. Allen – Manager Galway Foundry

Henry Anderson – Dentist, Mill Street.

Walter Anderson – Dentist, Mill Street.

Michael Brennan – Blacksmith, Rosemary Lane.

J. J. Burke – Rahoon.

J. Casey – Unemployed.

? Casserly – Railway Clerk.

Charles Cooke – Solicitor's Clerk, Corrib Terrace.

Frederick Coy – Manager Mc Donagh's Sawmill, Kirwan's Lane.

M. T. Donnellan – Shopkeeper, Shop Street.

Jerry Donovan – Fruit Shopkeeper.

Leslie Edmunds – Congested Districts Board, Palmyra Crescent.

J. Fitzgerald

R. Fitzgerald – Commercial Traveller.

W. J. Fogarty – Chief Clerk, Galway County Council.

C. French

? Grant – Headmaster Galway Grammar School

Roger Grealish – Agent, Abbeygate Street Upper.

J. Hession – Unemployed.

P. Hession – Scholar.

Eugene Hickey – Clark Galway County Council.

Elisha Jackson – Manager of Moon's, University Road.

Patrick Joyce – National School teacher.

Christopher Kearns - Farmer, Oranmore.

Jack Kelly.

Peter Kelly – brother of above.

James Kineen – Tobacco and Tea Agent.

J. King

Frank Lenihan – Dentist, Eyre Square.

Jack Liston – Clarke Galway County Council, Mary Street.

M. Long – Clerk.

J. Lydon

P. Lydon – Publican, brother of above.

W. Lydon – Unemployed.

John Miller – Distiller,Mary Street.

J. Mullins – R.I.C. Pensioner.

J. H. O'Connell – Post Office Clerk.

Philip O'Gorman - Stationer. Shop St.

Charles O'Neill – Post Office Clerk.

J. P. O'Neill – Captain of National Volunteers.

Jerry O'Sullivan – Customs Officer.

J. Rycroft – Shop Assistant Moon's.

Robert W. Simmons – Photographer, Devon Place.

Alfred Sowman - Accountant and Mill Manager, Kilcorkey.

A. Syme – Manager of Guinness Company in Galway.

Lewis Tolputt – Self-employed, Roscam.

L. Walsh – Commercial Traveller.

John M. Whelan – Chemist, Foster Street.

Joseph Young – Merchant, Newtownsmith. [358]

(49)

---

358 W/S 447 Thomas Courtney

Rebellion in Galway

If you are aware of a Special Constable that was a participant during the Rising but has been inadvertently omitted of this list please add them in here. You can also email me at kevinjordanlsu@hotmail.com or call me at 087 7989941 with their details so that I can update my records.

Name	Address	Company

Appendix 2

A List of Cuman na mBan Members[359]

The following women accompanied the rebels in Clarenbridge, Oranmore, the Agricultural College, Moyode and Lime Park.

Athenry

Mrs Annie Allum (nee Barrett), Miss Bridget Clasby, Mrs. Mary Kate Connor (nee Shaughnessy), Mrs Ellen Dooley (nee Kelly), Mrs. Dolly Fleming (nee Broderick), Miss May Higgins, Mrs. Kathleen Kennedy (nee Cleary), Mrs. Bridget Lardner (nee Kennedy), Delia Mc Namara (nee Cummins), Josephine Mc Namara, Mary Mc Namara (nee Rooney), Miss Julia Morrissey, Mrs. Mary Josephine O'Beirne (nee Cleary), Mrs. Sadie Tierney (nee Burke) **(14)**[360]

Killeeneen

Mrs. Kate Armstrong, (nee Glynn) Killeeneen, Mrs Bridget Conway, Miss Delia Hynes, Mrs. Bridget Malone, (nee Walsh) Killeeneen, Mrs. Gretta Mullins, (nee Walsh) Killeeneen, Mrs. Katie Nelly, (nee Fahy), Mrs. Teresa O'Shea, (nee Walsh) Killeeneen, Mrs. Mary Rabbitt, (nee Corbett) Killeeneen, Mrs Julia Roche, (nee Forde), and Mrs. Bridget Ruane, (nee Morrissey), Knockatoor. **(10)**

Kilcolgan

Miss Annie Howley (Kilcolgan) and Miss Bridie Lane (Killeely, Kilcolgan) **(2)**.

---

359 mspcsearch.militaryarchives.ie/en/collections/online-collections/military-service-pensions-collection/
    search-the-collection/easter-rising-1916/applicants-at-action-sites p1-14

360 mspcsearch.militaryarchives.ie/docs/files//PDF_Pensions/R2/MSP34REF9351MaryKateConnor/
    WMSP34REF9351MaryKateConnor.pdf p34

Rebellion in Galway

Maree

Miss Margaret Rose Greally **(1).**

Also

Katie Kelly (1).

If there is a member of Cumann na mBan you are aware of that was a participant in the Rising but has been inadvertently omitted of this list please add them in here. You can also email me at kevinjordanlsu@hotmail.com or call me at 087 7989941 with their details so that I can update my records.

Name	Address	Company

Appendix 3[361]

A list of the Rebel Participants in the 1916 Easter Rising.

This list applies to the 1916 Rising only and not to activities thereafter such as the War of Independence or Civil War.

When making a list of those who took part in the rebellion in Galway there are a number of problems in attempting to compile a definitive one.

1. The main areas of action were in Clarenbridge, Oranmore, Carnmore, the Agricultural College, Moyode and Lime Park. However, men also assembled in Belclare, Kinvarra, Ballycahalan, Gort and Ardranhan and others dismantled rail-lines near Derrydonnell and at Attymon. Men were also ready for action in Mullagh. So what constitutes being active during Easter Week in Galway has always been a source of debate.

2. There are excellent lists of those who were arrested and imprisoned after the rebellion but all of these would not have been active during the week.

3. There were also men who were on the run after the disbandment of the rebels and never arrested and these would have been active participants.

4. When applications for Military Service Pensions were being made many more than got them applied. Some of these who would have applied and were not deserving of them while some of those denied them would have deserved them.

5. There were some who were active participants in the rising but for their own personal reasons did not apply for a

---

361 mspcsearch.militaryarchives.ie/brief.aspx

pension and therefore did not get one. As a result these may not be in any list as participants and be only known to relatives.

6. In addition, many had died before the 1934 Service Pensions Act and so may not be recorded as having participated while others would have emigrated and though alive may not have applied for a pension.

7. There were also many who were arrested during the week, as in Galway City and the Tuam area, and did not get a chance to be involved in the action.

8. Finally there were those who helped in various ways, for example supplying food, carrying dispatches, harbouring men on the run, keeping guns in safe keeping, etc. and do these count themselves as among those who were active.

Thus, creating a definitive list is impossible. Therefore, there may be inconsistencies in this list, however, I have decided to compile it in an attempt to list participants and to list as many as possible rather than list none in the hope of leaving no one out. If you are aware of a participant(s) not listed here you may fill them in, in the column provided.

There were acts passed to give pensions to people who had participated in the various military activities from 1916 to 1923 including the 1916 Rising, the War of Independence and the Civil War. These were the Military Service Pensions Acts of 1924, 1934 and 1949. 82,000 applied for pensions and of these 15,700 were successful and 66,300 were rejected. There were varying degrees of pensions given which gave the recipients varying amounts in an annual pension.[362]

The **1924 Pensions Act** gave very few 1916 service pensions. Some Galway men are listed in this regard, they are as

---

362 www.irishexaminer.com/viewpoints/analysis/proud-war-of-independence-revolutionaries-
left-fumbling-in-the- till-319006.1

follows:

John Broderick, John Connor, Patrick Kennedy, Dick Murphy, Michael Murphy, Michael O'Grady, Richard Mulkerns and Michael Mulkerrins (All Athenry), Pat 'The Hare' Callinan (Craughwell)[363] and James Keane (Athenry)[364]

Also Patrick Flanagan (Maree), Daniel Forde (Claregalway), Bernard Grealish (Clarenbridge), John J. 'Jack' Hanniffy (Tallyho)[365] Thomas Hynes (Galway)[366], William Lynskey (Maree)[367] and James Maguire (Oranmore)[368], John O'Rourke and Michael O'Rourke (Maree)[369], Thomas Reidy (Kinvarra), William Thompson (Clarenbridge)[370] Denis Trayers (Oranmore), Michael Treacy (Athenry) and John Waldron.[371]

Later there was the **1934 Military Service Pensions Act**. This was a sworn enquiry in relation to receiving a pension. Note was taken of the areas you were deemed to have been active in and the number of days you were mobilised for. Men and women who were fired at or fired or threw bombs were to

---

363 mspcsearch.militaryarchives.ie/docs/files/PDE_Membership/7/WA21%20(4)_Bpdf.pdf p105

364 mspcsearch.militaryarchives.ie/en/collections/online-collections/military-service-pensions-collection/search-the-collection/easter-rising-1916/applicants-at-action-sites James Keane p9

365 mspcsearch.militaryarchives.ie/en/collections/online-collections/search-the-collection/easter-rising-1916/applicants-at-action

366 mspcsearch.militaryarchives.ie/en/collections/online-collections/military-service-pensions-collection/search-the-collection/easter-rising-1916/applicants-at-action-sites Thomas Hynes p8

367 mspcsearch.militaryarchives.ie/en/collections/online-collections/military-service-pensions-collection/search-the-collection/easter-rising-1916/applicants-at-action-sites WilliamLynskey p10

368 mspcsearch.militaryarchives.ie/en/collections/online-collections/military-service-pensions-collection/search-the-collection/easter-rising-1916/applicants-at-action-sitesJames Maguire p10

369 mspcsearch.militaryarchives.ie/en/collections/online-collections/military-service-pensions-collection/search-the-collection/easter-rising-1916/applicants-at-action-sites p12

370 mspcsearch.militaryarchives.ie/en/collections/online-collections/military-service-pensions-collection/search-the-collection/easter-rising-1916/applicants-at-action-sites p13

371 mspcsearch.militaryarchives.ie/en/collections/online-collections/military-service-pensions-collection/search-the-collection/easter-rising-1916/applicants-at-action-sites p13

get increased pensions. There is a list of names for the Galway area in the Military Service Pensions Collection.[372] Other names come from lists provided in the Witness Statements of participants.

Finally there is no definitive number as to who or how many were involved in the raids on Oranmore and Clarenbridge, the engagement at Carnmore and then on to the Athenry Agricultural College, Moyode and Lime Park. **There are various estimates from 700 to 800 for those involved. Those listed here run to a total of 594 names (men and women) in the main theatre with an additional 124 named who carried out activities in a different area (Attymon, Kinvarra, etc), were mobilised on standby (Mullagh, Kiltullagh, etc) or arrested (Galway, etc).** Thus there are likely to be some 150 names inadvertently missing from the list who were in the main areas of action. There are also a number of others who were mobilised for the week or part of the week around the county whose names I have not been able to confirm.

Thus it is not possible, nor will it be, to create a definitive list.

This list is compiled by cross reference to a number of sources. Interviews, a list of people arrested, Sinn Fein Rebellion Handbook, witness statements relating to Galway and various online Military Archive Records.[373]

(The townlands and streets - shown in brackets - these men and women came from are taken from various witness statements and military records with cross reference to the 1901/1911 census)

---

372 mspcsearch.militaryarchives.ie/en/collections/online-collections/military-service-pensions-collection/ search-thecollection/easter-rising-1916/applicants-at-action-sites pp1-14.

373 www.militaryarchives.ie/collections/online-collections/military-service-pensions-collections

(Note there are often men with the same names in the same companies).

Headquarters

Commandant Liam Mellows, Brigade Commander and Alf Monahan (2nd-in-command). **(2)**[374]

Ardrahan

James Burke, Joseph Burke, W.T. Burke, William Connors, Michael Cummins, Pat Flanagan, Roger Furey, Patrick Howley, Peter Howley, Michael Howley and William Howley (Limepark North), Thomas Kelly, Thomas Mc Inerney (Shanclogh, Kinvarra), Patrick Sylvers (Rathbaun), Patrick Moran (Cloon, Kiltartan), Michael Thompson and William Thompson (Grannagh North) **(17)**.[375]

Athenry

Christy Barrett, James Barrett and Thomas Barrett (Court Lane), Michael Barrett (Caherroyan), Sean Broderick (Church St.), Pat Burke (Caherroyan), James Cannon, Christopher Caulfield (Old Church St.), James Cleary, John Cleary, Joseph Cleary and Tom Cleary (Abbey Row), John Connor, Michael Cunniffe (Swan Gate), Patrick John Daly (Cross St.), Christy Doherty and John Doherty (North Gate St.), Michael Dunleavy (Ballygarraun North), Joseph Egan and Thomas Egan (Abbey Row), Michael Goode (North Gate St.), John Grady and Michael Grady (Church St.), Michael Hansberry and Martin Hansberry (Rahard), Michael Healy (Gloves), Michael Hession (North Gate St.), J.J. Higgins (Clamper Park), Patrick Hughes (Caherroyan), Frank Hynes (Cross St.), Martin Hynes (Cross St.), Martin Hynes (Rahard), Patrick Kane (Church St.), Stephen Jordan (Davis St.), Michael Kelly (Carrowntober East), John Joe

374 W/S 298 Ailbhe O Monacháin (Alf Monahan).

375 W/S 1,379 Peter Howley.

Kennedy, Patrick Kennedy, Patrick Kenny (Caherroyan), Larry Lardner (Church St.), Patrick Lynskey (Kingsland), James Mc Cormack (River St.), Peter Mc Keon (Caherroyn), John Mahon (Laughaunenaghan), Richard 'Dick' Murphy (Cross St.), John Murphy (Old Church St.), Michael Murphy (Church St.), Richard Mulkerns (Caherroyan), Michael Mulkerrins (Caheroyan), James Nolan (North Gate St.), James Plunkett (Davis St.), Michael Quinn (Old Church St.) Francis Reilly (Court View), Joseph Rooney (Caherroyan), John Ryan (Ballydavid North), Martin Ryan (Abbey Row), Michael Treacy (Backpark), John Waldron (Mulpit), John Walsh, Martin Walsh and Michael Walsh (Old Church St.), Patrick Walsh (Old Church St.), James Ward and Charles Whyte (Caherroyan). **(62)**

Ballycahalan
John Coen, Martin Coen and Michael Coen (Ballycahalan) Bryan Connor (Ballycahalan), Michael Cunniffe and Thomas Cunniffe (Knockroe), Peter Deely (Lismoyle)[376], Michael Egan (Ballycahalan), James Kelleher (Hollymount), John Loughry (Knockroe) and Peter Roughan (Knockroe).**(11)**

Belclare
Michael Barrett, John Costello (Cloonmore) and Liam Langley (Tierboy Rd., Tuam).[377] **(3)**

Castlegar
Michael Blake (Clounacauneen), Jim Broderick (Ballintemple), John Broderick (Ballintemple), Patrick Broderick (Ballintemple), Michael Burke (Doughiska), Thomas Burke (Parkmore), 'Sonny' Burke (Doughiska), Martin Carr (Clounacauneen), Tom Carr (Clounacauneen), John Casserly (Two-mile-ditch), Stephen Casserly (Two-mile-ditch), John Conneely, Michael

376 W/S 1,379 Peter Howley.
377 W/S 1,300 John D. Costello

Connell (Castlegar), John Connolly (Kiltulla), Thomas Conner (Cartron), Thomas Courtney (St. Bridget's Tce.), James Coyne (Breanloughaun), Michael Coyne (Breanloughaun) (Breanloughaun), Joe Donnellan (Brierhill), Thomas 'Baby' Duggan (Rosshill), James Fahy (Doughiska), John Fahy (Ballybane), Michael Fahy (Brochagh), Bernard Fallon (Two-mile-ditch), Dan Fallon (Jim) (Two-mile-ditch), Dan Fallon (Two-mile-ditch), John Fallon (Two-mile-ditch), Michael Fallon (Two-mile-ditch), James Feeney (Two-mile-ditch), Martin Feeney (Two-mile-ditch), Michael Flaherty, Michael Flannery (Cahir), Patrick Forde (Two-mile-ditch), Mattie Fox (Clounacauneen), Patrick Giles (Clounacauneen), Thomas Giles (Clounacauneen), Pat Glynn (Kiltulla), Patrick Glynn (Kiltulla), Thomas Glynn (Kiltulla), Thomas Grealish (Kiltulla), Patrick Grealish (Carnmore West), John Hanley (Brucky), Pat Hanley (Ballintemple), Sean Hehir (Ballyloughaun), Johnny Hosty (Casltegar), John King (Kiltulla), Patrick King (Kiltulla), Patrick 'Sonny' King (Kiltulla), Thomas King (Cahir), Peter King (Doughiska), Michael Kyne (Brierhill), Patrick Mahon (Kiltulla), Thomas Mahon (Kiltulla), Brian Molloy (John) (Coolagh), John Molloy (Cahir), John Molloy (John) (Coolagh), John Molloy (Pat) (Coolagh), Thomas Molloy (John) (Coolagh), Bart Mulryan (Kiltulla), John Mulryan (William) (Kiltulla), Michael Mulryan (Kiltulla), William Mulryan (Pat) (Kiltulla), Patrick Mulryan (Kiltulla), Patrick Murphy (Kiloughter), James Newell (Brierhill), Michael Newell (Brierhill) Patrick Newell (Brierhill), Thomas 'Sweeney' Newell (Brierhill), William Newell (Brierhill), Bartley Nolan (Renmore), Patrick Roonan (Castlegar), Gilbert Ryan (Rosshill), John Ryan (Castlegar), Michael Ryan (Castlegar), Thomas Silke (Polkeen), Thomas Summerly (Doughiska), John Wall (Ballintemple), Martin Wall (Ballintemple), Patrick Wall (Kiltulla), Stephen Wall (Kiltulla) and Thomas Weston **(80)**.[378]

378 Padraic O Laoi History of Castlegar Parish (1996) The Connaught Tribune Ltd. p152

Claregalway

Patrick Carr (Cregboy), Martin Casserly, Michael Casserly and Peter Casserly (Cregboy), William Coady (Laragh Mor), John Collins (Carnmore West), John Collins (Waterdale), Edward Commins (Carnmore West), John Concannon, Michael Concannon and Patrick Concannon (Gortadooey), John Connolly, William Corcoran (Lydacan), Thady Corkett (Montiagh South), Michael Coyne, Dan Duggan (Kiltroge West), Henry Duggan and John Duggan (Montiagh South), Thady Duggan (Montiagh South), John Egan and William Egan (Kiltroge East), Patrick Feeney[379] and Tim Feeney (Waterdale), Martin Finnerty (Claregalway), William Flaherty (Cahergowan), Patrick Flynn, Daniel Forde (Corrandulla), George Glynn (Lydacan), Henry Grealish (Castlegar), James Grealish (Carnmore West), James Peter Grealish and Martin Grealish (Carnmore West), Martin Grealish and Patrick Grealish (Carnmore West), James Greally, Patrick J. Hughes (Claregalway), Thomas Keady, Patrick Kelly, John Killalon, Martin Kyne and Nicholas Kyne (Kiltroge East), Martin Lally (Carnmore), Michael Lally (Carnmore West), John Lardner (Lackagh Beg), John Lynskey and William Lynskey (Cahergowan), James Mc Carra, Freddie Mc Dermott, John Moran (Cahergowan), John Moran, Patrick Moran (Cahergowan), Patrick Murphy, Philip Murphy (Gotratleva), Patrick O'Brien, Charles Quinn, Thomas Ruane, Gilbert Ryan, John Ryan (Claregalway), Michael Shaughnessy (Cregboy), John Vaughan and John Walsh. **(61)**

Clarenbridge

John Bindon and Thomas Bindon (Stradbally North), Thomas Brennan (Rahaneena), James Burns, John Burns (Parkroe), William Burns, Patrick Byrnes, Edward Cahill (Creggananta), William Cahill (Brockagh), Michael Callanan (Killeeneen More), Edward Commins, Michael Commins (Shantallow), Thomas Commins (Shantallow), William Commins (Moneymore East),

379 W/S 572 Thomas Newell

John Connell (Clarenbridge), Martin Connolly, John Connors, Patrick Cooley (Tonroe), Domnick Corbett, Eamon Corbett, John Corbett and Peter Corbett (Killeeneen), Thomas Corcoran (Kilcornan), John Egan (Ballynamanagh West), Patrick Egan (Ballynamanagh West), Thomas Fahy, Fr. Henry 'Harry' Feeney (Clarenbridge), George Fleming, John Fleming, Joseph Fleming, Michael Fleming, Patrick Fleming and Thomas Fleming (Clarenbridge), Patrick Forde, Bernard Grealish, John Grealish, Michael Griffin (Garraun Lower), John Halloran, Murty Hanify, M. Hussey, William Hussey, Patrick Hynes (Creggaun), Michael Hynes and Thomas Hynes (Caherbulligin), Tom Hynes (Creggaun), Denis Keane (Clarenbridge), Michael Kelly, Patrick Kelly, William Kelly, John Killalea, Patrick Linnane (Killeely More), Thomas Linnane (Stradbally North), John Mahon (Clarenbridge), William Martin (Ballynabucky), Owen Mullen (Clarenbridge), Thomas Nestor (Stradbally North), Edward Newell and Martin Newell (Caherdine), Martin 'Mattie' Neilan (Rahaneena), Thomas Neilan (Stradbally North), Willie Neilan (Rahaneena), William Neiland (Stradbally North), Michael Owen, John O'Dea, Michael O'Dea, Patrick O'Dea and Thomas O'Dea (Stradbally North), Michael O'Leary (Tarramud), Martin Reaney (Rahaneena), J. Rinden, Michael Ryder (Ballymanagh East) and William Thompson.**(72)**

Coldwood
Michael Commins and Willie Commins (Coldwood), Joseph Commins (Shantallow), Michael Hynes (Caherbulligin), James Kelly, Michael Kelly and William Kelly (Coldwood)[380] **(7)**

Craughwell
Patrick Barrett (Scalp), John Brown (Hollypark), Pat 'The Hare' Callanan and Thomas Callanan (Castlegar), Thomas J. Fahy (Lavally), Michael Forde (Killeeneen Mor), Michael Fuery and Stephen Fuery (Lecarrow) Patrick Kelly, John L Kennedy, Martin

380 W/S 1,562 Martin Newell.

337

Kennedy, John Mannion and Timothy Mannion (Ballynageeragh) and Patrick J. Walsh (Killeeneen) **(14).**

Cussaun

John Bane (Coldwood), Martin Coen and Thomas Coen (Caherateemore South), Patrick Cullinan (Mountbrowne), Philip Fahy (Carnaun), Martin Fahy (Caherateemore South), Thomas Forde, Patrick Hansbury, Martin Joyce, Patrick Kennedy (Carnaun), Thomas Kennedy, Pat Killeen (Carnaun), John Mahon, Martin Moloney (Carnaun), John Moran, Patrick Rabbitt (Caherateemore) and William Walsh (Caherateemore North) **(17)**

Derrydonnell

Patrick Commins (Derrydonnell), John Connolly, Martin Costello (Derrydonnell), Michael Costello (Derrydonnell), James Finn (Moorpark), Martin Freaney (Derrydonnell), Michael A. Freaney (Derrydonnell), Michael M. Freaney (Mountain West, Oranmore), William Freaney, John Girvan, Patrick Grealish (Castlelambert), Patrick Heneghan (Derrydonnell), Peter Heneghan (Derrydonnell), Pat Higgins (Coshla), Michael Higgins (Coshla), Richard Higgins (Coshla), William Higgins (Coshla), John Keane (Derrydonnell North), Martin Keane (Toberroe), Michael Keane (Toberroe) Patrick Keane (Toberroe), John Kelly (Castlelambert), Michael Kelly (Castlelambert), John Moran (Castlelambert), Thomas Mullin (Moorepark), James Murray (Derrydonnell North), Peter Murray[381] and Martin Ruane (Castlelambert) **(28)**[382]

Dunmore

P Dunleavy, Thomas Kilgarriff, William Ewart Mc Gill and Michael Roynayne.**(4)**

---

381 O'Regan's Athenry – Athenry History Archive The 1916 Rising in Athenry and Co. Galway.

382 mspcsearch.militaryarchives.ie/docs/files//PDF_Pensions/R1/MSP34REF37996MARTIN%20COSTELLO/ WMSP34REF37996MARTINCOSTELLO.pdfp p30

Esker

Thomas Corcoran, Joseph Dooley and Michael Dooley (Esker)[383], Fr. Tom Fahy (Esker), Patrick Fitzpatrick (Rathgorgin) and Pat Monaghan (Esker)[384] **(6)**.

Galway
Took part in the rising
J. Corbett, Thomas Hynes, ? Mc Dermott and one other **(4)**.
Arrested on Tuesday April 25th
Seamus Carter, John Conroy, ? Conway, Joe Cummins, Johnny Faller (Williamgate Street), Tom Flanagan, Frank Hardiman (Newtownsmith), Pete Howley, George Nicolls (45 Kilcorkey, South Urban), P.L. O'Madden, Patrick O'Malley (Padraig O Máille) (Maam Cross), Professor Val Steinberger (Abbythomasreeva, South Urban) and Dr. Tommy Walsh. **(13)**[385]
Helped Thomas Courtney the Irish Voluntees' Intellenence Officer.
Paddy Heffernan (Foster Street) and Christy Monahan (St. Patrick's Avenue) **(2)**

Gort

Thomas Burke, Martin Egan, Padraig Fahy and John Fahy (Lurgan), Michael Fahy (Lurgan), Thomas Fahy, Dan Kelleher and Martin Kelleher (Ballycahalan), John Melville (Raheen), J.J. Nelly (Gort), Patrick Piggott (Gort) and Thomas Stephenson (Market Square). **(12)**

Kilconiron

Patrick Coy (Derryhoyle Mor), Patrick Dempsey (Lissalondoon), Michael Donohue (Sliabh Roe), Mortimer 'Murty' Fahy (Sliabh Roe), Michael Fuery (Lecarrow), Patrick Golding (Ballywinna),

383 Mary Joe O'Dea interview.

384 Joe Monaghan Interview.

385 W/S 374 Micheal O Droighneain

John J. 'Jack' Hanniffy (Tallyho), Michael Hanniffy (Tallyho), Daniel Kearns (Caherdangan), Patrick 'Patch' Kennedy (Sliabh Roe), Thomas Kennedy (Sliabh Roe), Tim Manning (Ballywinna) Michael Mahon and Patrick Naughton (Carrowrevagh)[386] **(14)**

Killimordaly
Edward Burke and Frank Burke (Raford Mill), John Carroll, John Craven (Cloonsheecahill), William Duffy (Attymon), Joseph Earls (Lisduff), John Fahey and Peter Fahey (Carnakelly), John Irwin, Joseph Keating and Michael Keating (Attymon), William Kelly (Attymon), John Lawless, Patrick Lawless and Stephen Lawless (Attymon), William Mahon (Cappanasruhaun), Michael Melody (Cloonsheecahill), Patrick Noone (Brackloon), Joseph Whyte (Brackloon) and Pat Whyte (Cloonkeen). **(19)**[387] *(According to William Kelly there were 28 or so on active service.)*[388]

Kiltullagh
Patrick Burke, Patrick Doyle and Thomas Doyle (Kiltullagh North), Tim Fergus (Knockatogher), Patrick Forde (Killarriv), John Gilligan (Knockatogher), Denis Halloran (Clougherevan), James Kelly (Kiltullagh North), Michael Kelly (Kiltullagh North), Michael Mannion (Brusk), Thomas Mullins (Knockatogher), Joseph Ward (Brusk) and Michael Walsh (Knockotogher)**(13).**

Kinvarra
John Burke (Cahermore), Paddy Burke (Kinvarra), Patrick Burke (Loughcurra), Peter Burke (Cahermore), John Callanan (Loughcurra), John Connolly (Gortaboy), James Davenport (Kilvara), John Fahy (Caherawoneen), P. J. Fahy (Kinvarra),

---

386 W/S 1,124 Daniel Kearns.

387 mspcsearch.militaryarchives.ie/docs/files//PDF_Pensions/R1/MSP34REF2957WilliamKelly/
WMSP34REF2957WilliamKelly.pdf p63

388 mspcsearch.nilitaryarchives.ie/docs/files//PDF_Pensions/R1/MPS34REF2957Williamkelly/
WMSP34REF2957WilliamKelly.pdf p26

John Glynn (Dooras), Pat Hanbury (Dungoora), David Hanlon (Loughcurra), Michael Hanlon (Curshoa), Martin Hynes (Dooras), Michael Hynes (Dungoora), Michael Keane (Ballycleary), John Kilkelly (Curshoa), Joseph Kilkelly (Townagh), Michael Kilkelly (Townagh), Patrick Kilkelly (Townagh), Thomas Kilkelly (Curshoa), Stephen Leech (Loughcurra), Thomas Mc Inerney (Cahernamadda), Edward Mc Cormack (Kinvarra), Fr. William O'Meehan (Kinvarra), James Picker (Cahernamadda), Patrick Quinn (Townagh), William Quinn (Caherawoneen), John Reidy (Townagh), Thomas Reidy (Kinvarra), Michael Staunton (Cloonasee), James Whelan (Townagh) and John Whelan (Doorus) **(33).**

Maree
Michael Athy and Joe Athy (Ahapouleen), Michael Branley and Thomas Branley (Ballynacourty), John Burke and Michael Burke (Ballynacourty), Patrick Burke and William Burke (Carrowmore), John Burns, Michael Byrnes, Patrick Byrnes, Patrick Carrick (Prospecthill), P. Connors, William Connors, Edward Cormican (Ballynacourty), Michael Cloonan, Patrick Cloonan, Thomas Cloonan and Timothy Cloonan (Ballynacloghy), Thomas Cunniff (Tawin West), Tom Cunniff (Tawin West), John Deviney and Thomas Deviney (Ballynacloghy), Patrick Egan, Michael Fahy and Thomas Fahy (Tawin West)[389], Patrick Flanagan, John Furey, John Holland (Garraun Lower), Patrick Holland (Carrowmore), Thomas Holland (Tawin West), Joe Howley, Daniel Keane (Garraun Lower), John Keane, Patrick Keane and Thomas Keane (Ballynacourty), Francis Kearney and Timothy Kearney (Carrowmore), James Maguire, James Mc Cormack, John O'Rorke, Michael O'Rorke and Tommy O'Rorke (Garraun Lower), Michael Ruane, Denis Trayers and Michael Trayers (Treanlaur) **(46).**

---

389 W/S Martin Newell.

Monivea

James Glynn, Patrick Healy John Maloney, Martin Maloney, Michael Molloy and Thomas Tully.**(6)**.

Mountbellew

Thomas Haverty (Springlawn) **(1)**.

Moycullen

None out on active duty.

Mullagh

Michael Boland (Killoran), Thomas Connors (Corbally), Martin Daly (Poppyhill), Andrew Finnerty (Eskerboy), Patrick Gannon (Coolagh), Laurence Garvey (Mullagh Beg), Hubert Hanrahan (Ballyvaheen), John Kelly (Abbeycormicane), Malachi Kelly (Balylogue), Thomas Lowry (Coolagh), John Manning (Knockaun), Michael Manning (Knockaun) and Joseph Martin (Mullagh). **(13)**[390]

Newcastle

William Burke (Cormacuagh West), Michael Burns (Cormacuagh West), Patrick Connolly, Robert Connolly (Corrantarramud), Joseph Connor (Derroogh), Joseph Corbett (Shoodaun), John Daly, Thomas Divilly (Laghtonora), Patrick Donnellan (Shoodaun), John Feeney (Corrantarramud), Patrick Feeney, John Gardiner (Knockbrack), Patrick Greally, Daniel Hassett (Lenamore), Pat Healy (Shoodaun), William Heavey (Cloonkeen), John Kelly (Glenagloghan), Michael Kelly (Bingarra), Stephen Larkin, Peter Mahon (Newcastle), John Monahan (Knockbrack), John Murphy, Martin Murphy (Corrantarramud), Bernard Rohan (Bryan Roughan) (Derroogh), Martin Ryan, Peter Sherlock (Lenamore)[391] and Walter Walsh **(27)**.

---

390 W/S 1,062 Laurence Garvey
391 Pat Sherlock Interview.

Oranmore

Joseph Burke (Thornpark), Martin Burke (Glennascaul), William Byrnes, Christopher Carrick (Renville), John Carrick (Renville), Terence Connolly (Moneymore), Michael Commins (Glennascaul), Edward Corcoran (Oranmore Beg), John Corcoran, Pat Corcoran (Oranmore), William Corcoran (Oranmore), Michael Costello (Glennascaul), Martin Costello (Oranmore), Patrick Costello (Glennascaul), Michael Corbett, William Finn (Frenchfort), J. Flanagan, James Fury (Ballynageeha), Roger Fury (Ballynageeha), Tom Fury (Bushfield), Thomas Furey (Oran Beg), Patrick Furey (Oran Beg), Tom Furey (Rhinn), Peter Grealy (Glennascaul), Patrick Harte (Glennascaul), William Harte (Glennascaul), Patrick Hawkins (Rhinn), Thomas Hawkins (Rhinn), Dan Higgins (Moneymore), Michael Higgins (Moneymore), Joe Howley (Oranmore), William Hynes (Oran Beg), James Loughlin (Moneymore), Patrick Martyn (Garraun South), Peter Martyn (Garraun South), John Monaghan (Oranmore), Michael Ruane (Glennascaul) Patrick Ryder (Carrowmonish), Tom Spelman, (Oranmore), Willie Spelman (Oranmore), **Michael Staines (in prison)**, Dan Toole (Oranmore), Martin Toole (Oranmore) and Michael Toole (Oranmore) **(43+1).**

Rockfield

Michael Barrett (Scalp), Thomas Callanan (Mannin), Thomas Callanan (Carheenadiveane), M. Conway, Francis Curran, Jeremiah Deely (Templemartin), Andrew Fahy (Moyveela East), John Fahy, Patrick Fahy (Lavally), Thomas Fahy (Lavally), J. Farrell, M. Farrell, Martin Furey (Illanniard), John Forde (Carheenadiveane), Michael Hession (Parkroe), Michael Higgins, Pat Hynes (Creggaun), M. Kelly, John J. Kennedy, John L. Kennedy, Joseph Kennedy, Martin Kennedy (Lecarrow), Martin Kennedy T. Kenny, Frank Lally (Rathgorgin), James Maguire, John Maloney (Crinnage), Martin Mc Evoy (Roo),

Gilbert Morrissey, John Morrissey, Martin 'Sonny' Morrissey, Patrick Morrissey, Patrick J. Morrissey, Richard Morrissey and Tom Morrissey (Knockatoor), Michael Nestor, John O'Dea (Mountain South), Martin Rooney, John Rooney, Michael Rooney and Patrick Rooney (Knockatoor), Michael Ruane, Michael Shaughnessy and T. Shaughnessy **(45)**.[392]

Spiddal
Micheal O Droighneain (Michael Thornton), (arrested Tuesday April 25th). **(1)**

University College Galway.
J.A. Madden returned to the city on Wednesday **(1)**.

Others of whose companies I am not sure of.
? Daly (Ballyboggan), Michael Hanniffy, John Howley and James Keane (Rockmount) and Colm O'Geary (Rosmuck) **(5)**

Some of the people arrested in the follow up in addition to those who took part in the Rising.
(Listed are 66 who were not known to be participants in the rising itself).

Athenry
Michael Blake, S. Burke, Thomas Connell (Barretspark), Patrick Connolly, Joseph Curreen (Boyhill), Thomas Grealish (Pollacappul), Patrick Joyce (Monroe, Lackaghbeg), James Keane, John Kennedy, Patrick Kennedy and Peter Lawless (Ballyboggan). **(11)**.

---

392 W/S 874 Gilbert Morrissey

Castlegar

Peter King (Kiltulla), James Mahon (Kiltulla), John Wall (Kiltulla) and Michael Ruffley (Ballybrit). **(4)**

Clarenbridge

Michael Fleming, Sen, (Clarenbridge) and P. Kilkelly. **(2)**.

Costello, Connemara.

Cornelius O'Leary **(1)**.

Craughwell

Patrick Fahy (Lavally), James Gardiner, Hugh Graney (Laghtphilip), James Hannify (Glebe), Thomas Mc Namara (Ganty), Martin Moran (Roo) and Martin Quirke.**(7)**.

Gort

M. Trayers. **(1)**.

Kilconiron

Domenick Cooney (Lissalondon), James Coy and Michael Coy (Derryhoyle), Thomas Connolly (Derryhoyle), Lawrence Fahy (Tallyho), Jeremiah Galvin (Moyode), Denis Hynes (Creggaturlough, Moyode), John Hynes (Creggaturlough, Moyode), Martin Mc Glynn (Creggaturlough, Moyode), Michael Mc Glynn (Creggaturlough, Moyode) and Matt Stratford (Derryhoyle) **(11)**.

Kinvarra

George Fleming, Michael Staunton (Cloonnasee) and Michael Quinn (Trellick) **(3)**.

Loughrea

Charles Coughlan (Castle St.), Patrick Coy (Cuscarrick), Patrick Cunniffe (Bride St.), Brendan Donelan, John Fahey (Bride St.),

Rebellion in Galway

Patrick Fahey (Bride St.), Bernard Fallon (Moore St.), James Flynn (Main St.), Joe Gilchrist (9 Mob Hill), Martin Greene (Main St.), Joseph O'Flaherty (Main St.), Ed Roche (Barrack St.), Patrick Sweeney (Moore St.), Peter Sweeney, Patrick Martin (Galway Rd.), Patrick Mc Tigue (Athenry Rd.) and Richard Wilson. **(17)**.

Maree
Michael Hehir **(1)**.

Oranmore
James Burns and Michael Walsh (Glennascaul). **(2)**.

Rockfield
John Quinn (Caherfurvaus) **(1)**.

Turloughmore
Augustus O'Brien. **(1)**.

Others from around Galway
Joseph Connors, John Cullinan, Pat Keane and Michael Rafferty (Ballybritt). **(4)**.

APPENDIX 3

If there is someone you are aware of that was a participant in the Rising but has been inadvertently omitted of this list please add them in here. You can also email me at kevinjordanlsu@ hotmail.com or call me at 087 7989941 with their details so that I can update my records.

Name	Address	Company

Rebellion in Galway

Name	Address	Company

APPENDIX 3

Name	Address	Company

Rebellion in Galway

Name	Address	Company

Appendix 4

A list of some of the R.I.C. members involved in the 1916 Rising in Galway.[393]

Officers:

George Bedel Ruttledge	County Inspector.
Edward Miles Clayton	District Inspector East Riding.
George Bennett Heard	District Inspector West Riding.
Charles Collins	District Inspector Athenry.
Patrick Falvey	District Inspector Gort.
Philip Mc Donagh	District Inspector Loughrea.
Thomas Neylon	District Inspector Oughterard.**(7)**

Head Constables.
John O'Callaghan (Athenry), Hugh Crean (Ballinasloe), John O'Sullivan (Craughwell), John Golden and J Killacky (Galway), Patrick Duffy (Gort), Charles Mc Gowen (Portumna) and Denis Barrett (Turloughmore).**(8)**

Sergeants.
J Oates (Ballygurrane, Athenry), William Elliott (Ardrahan), Matthew Dowd and Michael Gibbons (Athenry), Peter O'Regan (Athenry), James Brennan, John Clarke and Isaac Reid (Galway), Thomas Reilly (Kinvarra), Thomas Redington (Maam Cross), Michael Carmody (Monivea), J Hargaden (Newford, Athenry) and James Healy (Oranmore).**(13)**

Acting Sergeants.
Thomas Walshe (Carraroe), Samuel Mc Carthy (Clonberne) and John Casey (Galway). **(3)**

---

393 Sinn Fein Rebellion handbook. Easter, 1916. Complete and connected narrative of the rising with detailed accounts pp 255 - 257.

Constables.

Patrick Burke, Bernard Gannon, Nicholas Grady, John Lynch, Thomas Murphy, Patrick O'Brien and Michael Reynolds (Athenry), Owen Mc Glade (Ballinasloe), J Brennan, J O'Keeffe and Owen Rooney (Ballygurrane), Jeremiah Hegarty (Castleblakeney), Maurice Walshe (Clonboo), Patrick Coleman (Colemanstown), John Palmer (Corofin), James Shea (Cummer), William O Sullivan (Errismore, Clifden), Martin Callagy, Michael Donegan, Patrick Durkin, James Farrell, Hugh Hamilton, Eugene Igoe, Bernard Mc Breen, Martin Mc Evoy, Patrick Mc Gloin, Patrick Rourke, John Shea and Patrick Whelan (Galway), Florence Mc Carthy (Gort), Denis Doherty and Charles Ginty (Gurteen), Edward Brennan, Martin Crean, Thomas Kirwan and James Maguire (Kilcolgan), James Hanley, D.F. Kelly, Michael Mc Carthy and Richard Noonan (Kinvarra), Michael Levelle (Laraghmore Hut), Joseph Patton (Laurencetown), Patrick Mc Shane (Loughgeorge), David Manning and Michael Reynolds (Loughrea), Florence Sullivan (Mace, Carna), John Conlon (Maam Cross), John Clarke and Joseph Ginty (Moyville), Joseph Mc Caffery and Thomas Mc Govern (Newford Hut, Athenry), Anthony Barrett, Daniel Foley, James Hannon, Peter Heffernan, Edward Reilly and Patrick Smith (Oranmore), Nicholas Collins (Riverville), James Noone (Salthill), George Barrer and W.E. Mc Garry (Tuam) and Thomas Mc Loughlin (Turloughmore).**(62)**

If there is an R.I.C. member that you are aware of that was a participant in the Rising but has been inadvertently left out of this list please add them in here. You can also email me kevinjordanlsu@hotmail.com or call me at 087 7989941 with their details so I can update my records.

APPENDIX 4

Name   Barracks

_____

_____

_____

_____

_____

_____

_____

_____

_____

_____

_____

_____

_____

_____

_____

_____

Appendix 5

British Military and other Officials involved in the rising.

Connaught Rangers

Captain Sir Andrew Harvey Armstrong (1866 - 1922):[394]

Andrew Armstrong was born in London,the son of Rev. Sir Edmund Armstrong and his wife Alice Fisher. The family had a estate at Gallen, Ferbane, King's County. He became the 3rd Baronet of Gallen in 1899 on the death of his father. Andrew joined the military forces and served as a Justice of the Peace for Offaly. He also held the office of High Sheriff for the county in 1914. Sir Andrew served in the Boer War with the Imperial Yeomanry in 1900 and 1901. He also served with the Leinster Regiment as a captain.

On September 28th 1914 he was transferred to the 5th (Service) Battalion of the Connaught Rangers as they trained for deployment to World War 1. He was with them at Richmond Barracks in Dublin and Kilworth Barracks in Fermoy, Cork. On January 7th 1915 he was deployed to Renmore Barracks, the home barracks of the Connaught Rangers, to oversee recruitment duties. It was from here he went to Carnmore Cross on Wednesday April 26th with a number of Connaught Rangers the day Constable Patrick Whelan was shot.

Having retired from the army by 1922 he was on a visit to New Zealand on a fishing trip when he took ill and died. He had let his estate lands in Ferbane to the Sisters of St. Joseph of Cluny in 1912. As he was a single man the estate and title now passed to his brother,Sir Nesbitt Armstrong, who lived in New Zealand and who sold the lands the following year. Sir Andrew's uncle Charles Armstrong was briefly married to Dame Nellie Melba, the renowned opera singer. [395]

394 Landed Families of Britain and Ireland (180) Armstrong of County Offaly and Nancealverne

395 Sir Andrew Armstrong Flicker - Photo Sharing

1901 Census
13 Gallen, King's County
Andrew Armstrong (44) Landowner.
Mary Stevens (22), James Curran (60) and Mary White (50) all servants.
James Armstrong (37) Visitor.

Army
Captain Sir Andrew Harvey Armstrong
Captain J.J. Bodkin

Navy
Commander Francis W. Hannon
Commander W.F. Blunt.
Seaman Stark.

Congested Districts Board Official
Leslie Edmunds.
Thomas Murray **Car Driver**

If you are aware of other British officials or military personnel who were participants in the Rising but have been inadvertently omitted of this list please add them in here. You can also email me kevinjordanlsu@hotmail.com or call me at 087 7989941 with their details so that I can update my records.

Name   Position/Rank
_____

_____

_____

_____

Rebellion in Galway

Name   Position/Rank

_____

_____

_____

_____

_____

_____

_____

_____

_____

_____

_____

_____

_____

_____

_____

_____

Bibliography

Articles

Ailbhe O Monachain (1889 – 1967- Find a Grave Memorial).

Alleged General "Rising": In Ireland; Bloody Work

Athenry History Archive: O'Regan's Athenry Athenry and the Easter Rising 1916 by Ronan Killeen.

familylambert.net Captain Thomas Eyre Lambert 1820-1919 by Ann Healy

Galway Independent/Renmore Barracks Foundation.

Galway Independent Renmore In Irish Hands.

History of Renmore Barracks – Renmore History Society.

Oranmore and Athenry in 1916 Individual Accounts Irish Volunteers 1913- 1923
By Eamon Murphy.

O'Regan's Athenry Athenry History Archive – The 1916 Rising in Athenry and Co. Galway – Finbarr O'Regan.

Galway Advertiser The Crucial Match That Loughrea Lost.

Galway Independent/Renmore in Irish Hands.

Stephen Gwynn (1864 – 1950) – Ricorso.

Teagasc, Athenry – The Story, - Nuala King. O'Regan's Athenry –Athenry History Archive.

The Easter Rising in Galway, by Fergus Campbell History Ireland, 14.2 (March – April 2006)

The Easter Rising on the Bay 1916 an tAlantach.

The Rising of the Moon: Galway 1916. p124 Una Newell. Journal of the Galway Archaeological and Historical Society.

The Royal Navy in Galway/joemulvey

18th -19th Century Social Perspectives, 18th-19th- Century History, Features, Irish Republican Brotherhood/Fenians, Issue 1 (Jan/Feb 2010) Vol 18.

Rebellion in Galway

Books

Burke John, 'Athlone 1900 – 1923, Politics Revolution and Civil War,' The History Press (2015).

Campbell, Fergus 'Land and Revolution Nationalist Politics in the West of Ireland 1891 – 1921,' Oxford University Press (2005)

Colladge, J.J., Warlow, Ben 'Ships of the Royal Navy: The Complete Record of all Fighting Ships of the Royal Navy,' Chatham Publishing. .(1969)

Clare, Anne 'Unlikely Rebels The Gifford Girls and the Fight for Irish Freedom,' Mercier Press (2011).

Collins, M.E. 'Movements for Reform 1870 – 1914,' Edco. (2008)

Collins, M.E. 'Sovereignty and Partition 1912 – 1949,' Edco (2008)

de Courcy Ireland, John 'The Sea and The Easter Rising,' Dun Laoghaire Maritime Institute of Ireland (1966)

Finnegan, Pat 'Pat Finnegan The case of the Craughwell Prisoners,' Four Courts Press Ltd. (2012)

Greaves, C Desmond 'Liam Mellows and the Irish Revolution,' An Ghlór Gafa (1971)

Henry William, 'Galway and The Great War,' Mercier Press. (2006)

Henry, William 'Blood For Blood, The Black and Tan War in Galway,' Mercier Press (2012)

Herlihy, Jim 'A Short History and Genealogical Guide The Royal Irish Constabulary,' Four Courts Press (1997)

Herlihy, Jim 'Royal Irish Constabulary Officers, A Biographical Dictionary and Genealogical Guide 1816 – 1922,' Four Courts Press (2005)

Hickey, D. J. and Doherty, J. E. 'A Dictionary of Irish History 1800 –1980,' Gill and Macmillan (Dublin 1980).

Jordan, Kieran Edited by 'Kiltullagh/Killimordaly As The Centuries Passed,' Kiltillagh/Killimordaly Historical Society (2000)

Kenneally, Ian 'Courage and Conflict, Forgotten Stories of the Irish at War,' The Collins Press (2009)

Lee, J.J. 'Ireland 1912 – 1985 Politics and Society,' Cambridge University Press (1989).

Lyons, F.S.L. 'Ireland Since theFamine,' Fontana Press (1971)

Mc Garry, Fearghal 'The Rising, Ireland: Easter 1916.' Oxford University Press (2010)

Ó Broin, Leon 'Revolutionary Underground, The Story of the Irish Republican Brotherhood, 1858 – 1924 Gill and Macmillan (1976)

O'Comhraí, Cormac 'Revolution in Connacht A Photographic History 1913 – 1923,' Mercier Press (2013)

O Laoi, Padraic 'History of Castlegar Parish,' The Connaught Tribune Ltd. (1996)

O'Malley, Ernie 'The Men Will Talk To Me Galway Interviews,' Edited by Cormac K.H. O'Malley and Cormac ó Comhraí Mercier Press (2013)

Ryan, Anne – Marie '16 Dead Men The Easter Rising Executions,' Mercier Press (2014)

Walker, B.M. Edited by 'Parliamentary Election Results in Ireland 1801 – 1922.' Royal Irish Acadamy (1978).

Power, Dr. Patrick and Duffy, Seán Dr., 'The Timechart History of Ireland,' Worth Press Limited (2001).

Bureau of Military History Witness Statements.

Barrett, James No. 343

Broderick, John No. 344

Callanan, Patrick 'The Hare' No. 347

Conlon, Mrs. Martin No. 419

Conneely, Martin No. 1,611

Costello, John No. 1,330

Courtney, Thomas No. 447

Fahy, John No. 1,331

Fahy, Fr. Tom No. 383

Garvey, Laurence No. 1,062

Hardiman, Frank No. 406

Howley, Peter No. 1,379

Rebellion in Galway

Hynes, Frank No. 446

Hynes, Michael No. 1,173

Hynes, Thomas No. 714

Jordan, Stephen No. 346

Kearns, Daniel No. 1,124

Kelly, Michael No. 1,564

Leech, Mrs. Mary No. 1.034

Malone, Mrs. Bridget No. 617

Molloy, Brian No. 345

Morrissey, Gilbert No. 874

Newell, Martin No. 1,562

Newell, Michael No. 342

Newell, Thomas 'Sweeney' No. 572

O'Drioghneain, Micheal (Miahael Thornton)No. 374

O'Monachain, Ailbhe (Alf Monahan) No. 298

O'Regan, Martin No. 1,202

Interviews

Burke Frank	June 2015.
Cronnelly Gabe	May 2015.
Duggan Sean	Aug. 2015
Killeen Ronan	May 2015.
Larkin Michael	May 2015.
Malpas Paul	May 2015
Mc Walter Patria	May 2015.
Monaghan Joe,	May 2015.
O'Dea Mary Joe,	May 2015.

Quinn Brian,   May 2015.

Scully Anne   May 2015.

Sherlock Pat,   May 2015.

Masters

Jordan, Eoin 'The Problems Encountered Before and During the 1916 Rising in Galway and How These Problems Contributed to the Failure of the Rising.' University of Liverpool (2011). Unpublished.

Newspapers

The Belfast News, Tues. May 2nd 1916.

The Connacht Tribune, Wed. April 26th 1916.

The Connacht Tribune, Sat. May 2nd 1936.

The Daily Express (London), Fri. April 28th 1916.

The Irish Independent, Thurs. May 4th 1916.

The Irish Times, Wed. May 10th 1916.

The New York Times, Wed. April 26th 1916.

The New York Times, Fri. April 28th 1916.

The New York Times, Thur. May 4th 1916.

The Connacht Tribune, 'The Rising County Galway 1916,' Saturday April 9th 1966.

The Sunday Press, December 9th 1951

The Westmeath Independent , February 26th 1966.

The Westmeath Independent, March 12th 1966.

On line

Admiral Sir Lewis Bayly Photo.

All census data on R.I.C. members from the 1901/1911 Census, Ireland.

claregalway.info/history/1916-troubles

Archiver.rootsweb.ancestry.com>IRELAND.2007-04 (Caitriona Clear)

Rebellion in Galway

Brigade Activity Reports Easter Week 1916 County Galway (A/21/4/A) p27.

Canon Canton-Death of Athenry's Venerable Parish Priest – Alife of Untiring Zeal and Devotion

Commandant Larry Lardner, 1916 Rising, War of Independence by Finbar O'Regan. O'Regan's Athenry, Athenry History Archive.

Eircom.net/~celtichistories/constabulary.htm

eprints.maynoothuniversity.ie/5077/1/Tom_Tonge_20140620152731.pdf

Galway County Council Archives, Loughrea Rural District Council Archives Collection GOI/8/2, P421.

Galwayindependent.com/20120229/news/talking-history-52945.html

Hidden Gems and Forgotten People – South East Galway Archaeological and Historical Society. Steve Dolan

http://winters-omline.net/RIC-Barracks-1911/Galway/

http://www.census.nationalarchives.ie/exhibition/galway/main.html

irishconstabulary.com/topic/1577#VRb5b_ysXh4

irishconstabulary.com/topic/786#.VR10xvzF_h5

Irishvolunteers.org/matthew-mattie-neilan/ By Eamon Murphy.

johnny-doyle.blogspot.ie/2014_04_01archive.html

landedestates.nuigalway.ie

'Mr. Galway': Martin 'Máirtin Mór' – WorldPress.com by Dr. Jackie Uí Chionna

mspcsearch.militaryarchives.ie/brief.aspx

mspcsearch.militaryarchives.ie/brief.aspx Stephen Jordan

mspcsearch.militaryarchives.ie/detail.aspx?parentpriref= mspcsearch.militaryarchives.ie/docs/files/PDE_Membership/7/WA21%20(4)_Apdf. Stephen Jordan.

mspcsearch.militaryarchives.ie/docs/files/PDE_Membership/7/WA21%20(4)_Bpdf.pdf

mspcsearch.militaryarchives.ie/docs/files/PDE_Membership/7/WA21%20(4)_Bpdf.pdf John Broderick

mspcsearch.militaryarchives.ie/docs/files/PDE_Membership/7/WA21%20(4)_Bpdf.pdf

Martin Neilan

mspcsearch.militaryarchives.ie/docs/files/PDE_Membership/7/WA21%20(4)_Bpdf.pdf
Martin Newell

mspcsearch.militaryarchives.ie/docs/files/PDE_Membership/7/WA21%20(4)_Bpdf. pdf
Michael Costello

mspcsearch.nilitaryarchives.ie/docs/files//PDF_Pensions/R1/MPS34REF2957William-Kelly/WMSP34REF2957WilliamKelly.pdf

mspcsearch.militaryarchives.ie/docs/files//PDF_Pensions/R1/MSP34REF3257KATH-LEENKENNEDY/WMSP34REF3257KATHLEENKENNEDY.pdf

mspcseacrh.militaryarchives.ie/docs/files//PDF_Pensions/R1/MSP34REF9029SadieTier-ney/WMSP34REF9029SadieTIERNEY.pdf

mspcsearch.militaryarchives.ie/docs/files//PDF_Pensions/R1/MSP34REF14655PATRICK-COOLEY/WMSP34REF14655PATRICKCOOLEY.pdf

mspcsearch.militaryarchives.ie/docs/files//PDF_Pensions/R1/MSP34REF37996MAR-TIN%20COSTELLO/WMSP34REF37996MARTINCOSTELLO.pdfp

mspcseacrh.militaryarchives.ie/docs/files//PDF_Pensions/RI/MPS34REF59605MaryMc-Namara/WMSP34REF59605MaryMcNamara.pdf

mspcseacrh.militaryarchives.ie/docs/files//PDF_Pensions/R2/MSP34REF9021MaryRab-bitt/WMSP34REF9021MaryRabbitt.PDF

mspcsearch.militaryarchives.ie/docs/files//PDF_Pensions/R2/MSP34REF-9351MaryKateConnor/WMSP34REF9351MaryKateConnor.pdf

mspcseacrh.militaryarchives.ie/docs/files//PDF_Pensions/R2/MPS34REF/R2/MSP34REF-13981BRIDGETRUANE/WMSP34REF13981BRIDGETRUANE.pdf

mspcseacrh.militaryarchives.ie/docs/files//PDF_Pensions/R2/MPS34REF14582KATIENEL-LY/WMSP34REF14582KATIENELLY.pdf

mspcseacrh.militaryarchives.ie/docs/files//PDF_Pensions/R2/MPS34REF60139DeliaMc-Namara/WMSP34REF60139DeliaMcNanara.pdf

mspcsearch.militaryarchives.ie/docs/files//PDF_Pensions/RS/MSP35REF13981BRIDGET-RUANE/WMSP34REFBRIDGETRUANE.pdf

mspcsearch.militaryarchives.ie/docs/files//PDF_R2MPS34REF20331BRIDIELANE/

Rebellion in Galway

WNSP34REF20331BRIDIELANE.pdf

mspcsearch.militaryarchives.ie/en/collections/online-collections/military-service-pensions-collection/search-the-collection/easter-rising-1916/applicants-at-action-sites

mspcsearch.militaryarchives.ie/en/collections/online-collections/military-service-pensions-collection/search-the-collection/easter-rising-1916/applicants-at-action-sites James Keane

mspcsearch.militaryarchives.ie/en/collections/online-collections/military-service-pensions-collection/search-the-collection/easter-rising-1916/applicants-at-action-sites James Maguire

mspcsearch.militaryarchives.ie/en/collections/online-collections/military-service-pensions-collection/search-the-collection/easter-rising-1916/applicants-at-action-sites Nicholas Kyne.

mspcsearch.militaryarchives.ie/en/collections/online-collections/military-service-pensions-collection/search-the-collection/easter-rising-1916/applicants-at-action-sites Thomas Hynes

mspcsearch.militaryarchives.ie/en/collections/online-collections/military-service-pensions-collection/search- the-collection/easter-rising-1916/applicants-at-action-sites William Lynskey

mspcsearch.militaryarchives.ie/en/collections/online-collections/search-the-collection/easter-rising-1916/applicants-at-action

N.U.I. Galway Estate Record Landed Estates Database.

Policing in Ireland warwick.ac.uk.../Ireland/constabulary.htm

Theirishwar.com/organisations/Cumann-na-mban/tht.ie/blog/184/Historic-Photograph-Presented-to-Town-Hall-Theatre

www.athenrygaa.ie/en/club-history.html St. Mary's G.A.A. Athenry

www.advertiser.ie/galway/article/25789/woodford-stood-up-to-the-power-of-lord-clanricarde

www.advertiser.ie/galway/article/52516/the-case-of-the-craughwell-prisoners

www.advertiser.ie/galway/article/68870/eamonn-corbett-and-1916

www.bbc.co.uk/history/british/easterrising/aftermath/af01.shtml

Bibliography

www.bbc.co.uk/history/british/easterrising/newspapers/index.shtml

www.census.nationalarchives.ie/exhibition/galway

www.corkcity.ie/services/corporateandexternalaffairs/museum/museumexhibitionsarchives/1916exhibition

www.galwaygaa.ie/index/en/club-hurling-list

www.historyireland.com/20thcentury-contemporary-history/the-most-shoneen-town-in-irelandgalway-in-1916/

www.irishexaminer.com/viewpoints/analysis/proud-war-of- independence-revolutionaries-left-fumbling-in-the-till-319006.1

www.irishmedals.org/civilians-killed-civil-war.html

www.irishmedals.ogr/the-rising-in-other-areas.html

www.historyireland.com/20th-century-contemporary-history/galway-1916/

www.independent.ie/lifestyles/cobhs-forgotten-war-remembered-26546549.html

www.nli.ie/1916/pdf/7.14

www.nli.ie/1916/pdf/7.14.pdf

www.policememorial.org.uk/index.php?page=royal-irish-constabulary

1901/1911 Census, Ireland

Acknowledgements

A big thanks...

.....to my wife Aideen for all her help, guidance, patience and understanding while this book was being written. We met after a History lecture in U.C.G. in 1976 and as they say 'the rest is history'. .... to my children Eimear and Eoin and also Michael Ormonde for all the 'techie' stuff I find confusing ..... to Stephen Shields who told me to go and write the book and stop just talking about it. .....to my sister Una Jordan who did so much to distribute the book. ..... to my brother Paddy for setting up PayPal. ......to my brother Kieran for all the helpful discussions.......to my mother and father for their interest in education, my father was my first History teacher, in National School......to Sean Gohery my History teacher in Presentation College Athenry, Gearoid Ó Tuathaigh, Nicholas Canny, T.P. O'Neill, Steve Ellis among others in the NUIG History Department - all such influential people. .....to all those who provided me with information for the book in any form...... to the internet where I sourced so much information......to those who had the foresight to suggest and record the witness statements...... to all those men and women who gave witness statements......to those who put the 1901/1911 Census on line, I have got such value from it for this book and for my family history...... to those who gave me photographs especially Brian Quinn, Gabe Cronnelly and John Jordan...... to Jerry Drennan don aistriúchán Gaeilge....... to Warren and all in Turner Printing Longford, without whom this project would not have been completed......to all those who bought the book, I hope you enjoy it.

Index

Kevin Jordan

Kevin Jordan is Deputy Principal in Banagher College Coláiste na Sionna in Banagher Co. Offaly. He has taught History and Geography in a number of schools since 1980, Presentation College, Greenhills, Drogheda; Marist College, Athlone; La Sainte Union Secondary School Banagher and Banagher College Coláiste na Sionna, Banagher.

Kevin has an interest in local history and has two previous publications, 'History of Southern Gaels Hurling Club Athlone (Incorporating a History of South Westmeath Hurling since 1885)' and 'La Sainte Union des Sacrés Coeurs, Educating in Banagher 1863 – 2007'. He is also a keen genealogist and researches work on family history.

Originally from Kiltullagh, Athenry, Co. Galway he was educated in Kiltullagh N.S., Presentation College, Athenry and University College, Galway. Kevin has a life-long association with the G.A.A. both in Killimordaly (Galway) and now Athlone, where he currently lives. He is married to Aideen Ward from Renmore, Galway and has two children Eimear and Eoin.